WAR STORIES II

FURTHER ACCOUNTS OF MINNESOTANS WHO DEFENDED THEIR NATION

BY AL ZDON

To Gary
A great sailor
Best wishes
Al Zdon

A PROJECT OF THE MINNESOTA AMERICAN LEGION

MOONLIT EAGLE PRODUCTIONS
2010

War Stories II
Further Accounts of Minnesotans Who Defended Their Nation

Printed in Canada by Friesens Corporation in cooperation with
BookMobile, St. Louis Park, Minnesota

Published by Moonlit Eagle Productions
5064 Irondale Road
Mounds View, Minnesota 55112

ISBN 978-0-9711940-2-1

Moonlit Eagle
Productions

WAR STORIES II

FURTHER ACCOUNTS OF MINNESOTANS WHO DEFENDED THEIR NATION

BY AL ZDON

DEDICATION

For my wife, Mary

And my children, Anna, Corinna, Zachary, Larissa, Nathaniel and Delaney

And to all the veterans who shared their stories with me

ACKNOWLEDGMENTS

I've been writing stories about Minnesota veterans for about 14 years for the *Minnesota Legionnaire* newspaper. This is the second volume of those stories collected into a book. It is important that these stories be preserved in a more permanent form.

All the proceeds from this book will go toward youth programs of the Minnesota American Legion such as Baseball, Boys and Girls State, Oratorical Contest, Legionville, and others. These programs are part of the commitment of the Legion to future generations of Minnesotans.

The ideas for stories have come from many places, but I would like to acknowledge the World War II History Round Table, under the direction of Don Patton, and Minnesota military historian Al Muller for guiding me to so many good stories.

As with the first book, the Minnesota American Legion is taking a huge leap of faith in providing the funds to publish this book. All of the money is provided up front so that the proceeds will go completely toward the programs for which they were intended. Many Legionnaires have been involved in this process including Bill Goede, Dan Ludwig, Jim Copher, Tom Conway, Al Davis, Lyle Foltz and Randy Tesdahl.

Special thanks to Jennifer Kelley on the Legion staff who provides much of the hard work in getting the book to the customer.

The book would not have the quality appearance it does without the artwork and design provided by Louise and Liina Lundin. And the quality of writing would be much diminished without copy readers David Banks and Larissa Zdon. They were valiant about sticking to the project.

Finally, this book also would be nothing without the veterans from Minnesota and elsewhere who went to war to protect their nation, their families, their friends and their way of life. Their service and sacrifice cannot be acknowledged enough.

CONTENTS

BATTLEWAGON AIR FLEET
The USS Massachusetts carried three aircraft on board for artillery spotting and for anti-submarine warfare.

Unless indicated otherwise, all photos are from Tom Dougherty's personal collection.

BATTLESHIP
AVIATOR

Not everyone knows that battleships had airplanes, but Tom Dougherty of Hibbing and Duluth served on the USS Massachusetts in the Atlantic as the pilot of an OS2U Kingfisher, launched off the deck of the ship. Dougherty may have been the first American pilot shot down in Africa during the war.

Tom Dougherty, a young Navy pilot from Duluth, established a number of firsts on November 8, 1942, as Operation Torch, the invasion of North Africa, began.

— He may have been the first American to know that the French Vichy forces were going to fight rather than give in.

— He may have been the first American to be fired upon that morning.

— He may have been the first American pilot shot down in North Africa.

— And, a few days later, he definitely was the first battleship aviator to drink a toast to the victory in Casablanca with Major Gen. George S. Patton.

Flying an airplane off the deck of a battleship was not in Thomas Dougherty's plans when he was growing up in Hibbing. His father was one of the community's funeral directors, and young Tom was in line to take over the family business.

After graduating from Hibbing High School in 1935, a classmate of famous food entrepreneur Jeno

Paulucci, Dougherty attended Hibbing Junior College, then graduated from the University of Minnesota in 1938.

Dougherty had been helping out at the funeral home, making some of the night runs, since he was a freshman in high school. He took over running the funeral home in Hibbing in 1939.

"I knew the draft was coming, and I really didn't feel like doing all that marching, so I started checking into enlisting. I had enough schooling to get into an officers' program."

Dougherty first tried the Army Air Corps and took a physical prior to enlisting in January 1941. "The doctor said, 'Read those letters,' and I said, 'What letters?' He told me I'd better have a physician look at my eyes when I got home."

Back in Hibbing, Dougherty again had his eyes checked, and they proved to be 20-20. "I asked him how it was I couldn't see anything during my Army exam, and he asked me if I'd worn sunglasses on my drive to the examination." It turned

out Dougherty was probably snowblind from driving in the bright snow that day.

"I just took all my Army materials over to the Naval Reserve, and I signed up." He passed the exam, and his recruiter advised him to take his oath right away in case he got drafted. "Sure enough, two weeks later I got my draft notice. I was told to report, but I didn't go.

"The head of the draft board in Hibbing got hold of me, and he was really angry. He told me I could go to

jail. I explained that I'd already enlisted, and he said I should have told him. I said, 'No, I didn't need to tell you.' "

Dougherty headed to Wold-Chamberlain Airport in Minneapolis for what was called elimination training. All the candidates were given seven hours of flight instruction, and then they had to solo. If they didn't, they were out of the program.

Dougherty passed the first hurdle and went on to Corpus Christi, Texas, for additional flight training. From there he was sent to Pensacola, Florida, for advanced flight training.

He was now training in a squadron on the Kingfisher, a scout plane designed to be catapulted off the deck of a battleship or cruiser.

"It was a helluva good plane, but its top speed was only 110 miles an hour. It was no match for any fighters."

On December 7, 1941, Dougherty learned of the surprise attack on Hawaii while he was in Pensacola. That night, he was standing a watch, and when he went down to the watch office to get his flashlight, the officer handed him a .45-caliber pistol.

"I said, 'Where's the ammunition?' and they said I didn't need any. I said, 'Just in case I run into a Japanese, what do I do? Club him to death with the pistol?' They didn't think that was very funny. That was typical Navy to give a guy an empty gun."

As the training wound down, Dougherty was called into the headquarters and ushered into a room with Capt. A.C. Read, a Navy legend who had flown the first seaplane across the Atlantic. Read had him raise his right hand and take the oath. "He said, 'You are now an officer and a naval aviator. Good luck.' And that was that."

Dougherty's orders were to the USS Massachusetts, a battleship just being completed on the East Coast. "This was just three months after Pearl Harbor, but they really needed people. I was the greenest of the green, but I was off to my first assignment."

He took a week's leave to drive his car back to Minnesota and say goodbye to friends and family. On his way, he stopped overnight in Memphis and found himself in a hotel elevator with Bob Hope, Bing Crosby and Hollywood starlet Joan Bennett.

"I was pretty flustered to be with those people, but I had on my green uniform and my wings, and I was feeling pretty good. I said to Joan Bennett, 'Why don't you have dinner with me instead of these two old guys?' Hope and Crosby didn't think

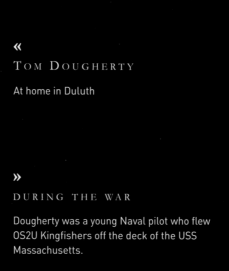

«

TOM DOUGHERTY

At home in Duluth

»

DURING THE WAR

Dougherty was a young Naval pilot who flew OS2U Kingfishers off the deck of the USS Massachusetts.

that was very funny. She said she'd like to, except they were in the middle of a war-bond drive."

His leave over and his car sold, Dougherty reported to Quonset Point, Rhode Island. He was met by the battleship's senior aviator and told to be ready to fly at 0700 the next day.

Dougherty's mission was to fly anti-submarine reconnaissance. "After I flew that first day, I thought we were going to lose the war. You remember the oil spill from the Exxon Valdez? Well, that was a drop in the bucket compared to the oil that was washing up on the East Coast from the submarine attacks.

"There wasn't a white pebble from Maine to Virginia.

"And, everywhere, you could see the hulks and the wreckage of ships the Germans had sunk. At Sandy Hook, I counted the masts of 17 ships that had gone down."

Dougherty said there was an effort to hide from the general population the devastation caused by the submarine attacks along the coast. If a civilian aircraft was found flying where the wrecks were, it was quickly escorted back to land. "They didn't want any pictures."

One of Dougherty's duties on patrol was to check out every fishing trawler. It was suspected that some of the trawlers were spies for the Axis, and that the submarines would raise their periscopes right next to the fishing vessels to provide a cover from the airborne patrols.

On May 12, 1942, the Massachusetts was commissioned, and, on the 15th, she set out on her shakedown cruise. "The Massachusetts was the

OS2U
Kingfisher Statistics

OS2U - 3

Manufacturer
Vought

Engine
One Pratt & Whitney R-985-AN-2 Radial engine. 450 horsepower.

Crew
Two, pilot and observer

Armament
Two .30-caliber Browning machine guns mounted in the wings. The aircraft could carry 650 pounds of bombs.

Maximum Speed (clean)
164 miles per hour

Ceiling
13,000 feet

Range, loaded
805 miles

KINGFISHER

The Kingfisher was limited in its wartime potential because of its small engine and light armament. Still, the plane served a vital function when used as a forward artillery observer for battleships and cruisers and for looking for enemy submarines. It was launched from the stern of the ship and recovered using a net to catch the plane and a crane to haul it onboard.

biggest thing we had in the Atlantic, and it tells you a little bit about how short of ships they were at that time that even on our shakedown cruise we were sent to Iceland to make

well-received. The fact that they drew extra pay and did not stand watches while in port also grated on their peers' nerves.

Dougherty earned further enmity by

spotting for the big guns, and Dougherty was asked to simulate an air attack on the ship and was told to try and sneak by the ship's radar. "I had a bright idea that I could get

---

"When they launched you off one side of the ship, they threw your seabag over the other side to balance the weight. They knew you weren't coming back."

---

sure a couple of German pocket battleships didn't break out from the Norwegian harbors. Thank God they didn't, because we weren't ready in any way to fight a battle."

Aboard ship, the small clutch of aviators enjoyed both a celebrity and a Jonah status among the crew and fellow officers. Their landings and takeoffs were well-attended by crew members who could get away from their daily duties. Their presence in the wardroom with their snazzy leather jackets, however, was not

striking up a friendship with the ship's cooks and often taking a meal with them. Finally he was told by his senior officer, "You can't eat with the crew. You are an officer." Dougherty said he responded, "But the food is better than what we're getting."

"That was the first hoop-de-do I got involved in aboard ship. But I still had a meal now and then with the cooks. And then there was the bakery with those jelly rolls. Oh, they were good."

The Kingfisher crews practiced

to the ship and avoid the radar by coming down the river that emptied out near where the ship was moored. So down the river we came. I'll never forget one guy in a rowboat, fishing. As we came right over his boat, he just got up and jumped in the lake.

"At the end we had to hop over some houses in town to get to the ship, and we nearly took the chimneys off them. Well, the townspeople weren't too happy about that, and I got put on report. In the end, they dismissed it, though. It was legal 'flat hatting.' I'd been ordered to do it."

Part of Dougherty's training was to practice the three different types of recoveries available to the Kingfishers. The scout planes were launched from catapults at the stern of the ship, using explosives to hurtle them down the rails and into the air. "You had to brace yourself pretty good for that."

Getting back on the battleship was a little harder. The Kingfishers' choices were Able Recovery, when the ship was at anchor; Baker Recovery, when the ship was at sea but the sea was calm, or Cast Recovery, when the sea was rough. ("Charlie" hadn't yet replaced "cast" as the naval symbol for the letter C.)

KINGFISHERS ON PARADE

A group of Kingfishers flew in echelon formation in this Navy photograph.

ACCIDENT ON DECK

On the battleship's way to North Africa, a huge wave came over the deck and destroyed one of the USS Massachusetts' planes. Dougherty is the figure standing just under the star of the Kingfisher.

The first two were fairly easy, considering. In the Baker Recovery, the pilot could land anywhere in the sea, then taxi the float plane to the stern of the ship, where a large cargo-net-like apparatus called a "sled" would capture it in the water and where it could be held while it was attached to a hook dangling from a crane off the stern of the ship.

Once the plane was captured, the radioman had to get out of his cockpit, stand on the wing, and guide the hook from the crane to a ring on the plane. The hook itself weighed more than 200 pounds, and the exercise was extremely dangerous. Once that was accomplished, the pilot and the radioman had to attach cables to the wings to stabilize the plane as it was hoisted aboard.

The Cast Recovery was very difficult. The pilot had to time his landing to be close to the end of the ship, which itself was traveling at 25 knots. The theory was that the ship's wake would provide a smooth patch of sea to land on.

In order to be qualified for a Cast Recovery, Navy regulations said a pilot first had to sit in the back seat of the two-seater airplane while an experienced pilot performed the task. Secondly, he had to try it himself while the veteran pilot was in the back seat.

By now, the USS Massachusetts was part of a convoy of 300 ships heading

USS MASSACHUSETTS

The Massachusetts was the second in the South Dakota class of World War II battleships and fought in both the Atlantic and Pacific during the war.

for North Africa.

Dougherty had never done, nor was he qualified to do, a Cast Recovery when he returned from a flight one day. "We flew along the starboard side of the ship, and we could see that they were flying the pennants that indicated they wanted us to do a Cast Recovery. We weren't too happy to see that."

It didn't help Dougherty's confidence when he watched the pilot in the other Kingfisher, who was qualified for a rough-water recovery, hit a wave, bounce 20 feet in the air, then

bounce several more times before he could get his plane onto the sled.

Adding to the complication in the procedure, the battleship also had to turn just before the landing to assure the pilot of the smoothest sea surface to land on. "And you've got to remember that when the battleship turned, all of the 300 other ships in the convoy had to turn also."

With great trepidation, Dougherty lined up his landing. "It wasn't like an aircraft carrier where you had people helping you make the deci-

sion about whether to land. The first time I came around, I decided I was too close to the ship, and I turned away at the last minute."

Dougherty circled the ship and came in for a second try. This time he timed it just right. "That's how I know there are guardian angels. I came in, and just like that, the plane was up on the sled. It was the best Cast Recovery I ever did."

Still, as he descended the ladder from the Kingfisher, he was shaking so badly that he missed a rung and fell the last six feet to the ship's deck. At that point he was informed that he was to see the captain immediately.

Dougherty persuaded the other pilot, who was the senior aviator and a lieutenant, that he had to go with him to face the captain, who he was sure was going to chastise him for taking two approaches for his landing.

"But, when we got there, the captain said, 'Ensign, that was the most beautiful landing I've ever seen. Lieutenant, you can take a lesson from this man.'

"So now, all of a sudden, I was qualified to do Cast Recoveries."

The trip across the Atlantic took about 12 days. "They woke us up about 4 a.m. one morning to tell us we'd arrived." They were just off the African coast at Casablanca, and Operation Torch was about to begin.

The Massachusetts had lost one of its three planes during a violent storm coming over, so only Dougherty and Lt. Carl "Dutch" Doerflinger were scheduled to fly. The aviators had been briefed about their mission on the way over, and Doerflinger was able to use maps and photos to construct a topographical map of the Moroccan Coast using sand and molasses. "It's a good thing he did that, or we wouldn't have known where the hell we were."

Dougherty and his radioman, Bobby Ethridge, had flown many practice and anti-submarine missions by this time. "We had a deal. I taught Bobby how to land the plane. I told him, 'If anything happens to me, you land it. And if anything happens to you, I'll land it. I won't jump.'"

The men were in their planes on the catapults before dawn. Their job was two-fold. The first job was to fly over the end of the long jetty that came out from Casablanca Harbor and see if a white flag was flying from the pole.

There had been much debate and much last-minute diplomacy to persuade the Vichy French not to fight against the Allies. The white flag on the pole would have been a signal that the French were not going to respond to the invasion.

The second job for Dougherty was to spot for the ship's big guns if it was determined the French would fight.

Doerflinger was catapulted, and, a few minutes later, Dougherty also was blasted into the air from the stern of the Massachusetts. "I never saw Doerflinger again that day. We were told we'd have to get back to the ship on our own initiative. They said, 'We're not going to be waiting around for you.' "

Dougherty said the orders reminded him of the standing joke about battleship aviators. "When they launched you off one side, they threw your seabag over the other side to balance the weight. They knew you weren't coming back."

Dougherty took his OS2U Kingfisher to the coast and was able to figure out the landmarks from the molasses and sand map. As he cruised over Casablanca, the sun was just coming up.

At first, Dougherty didn't encounter any opposition, but there also wasn't any flag on the end of the jetty. Cruising at 1,000 feet, he began to notice puffs of smoke in the air. "It was kind of pretty, like the Fourth of July," he said.

The next round of anti-aircraft fire, however, nearly blew Dougherty and his Kingfisher out of the sky. He im-

mediately radioed in the code for encountering hostile enemy action: "Batter up."

The ship's response was to be, "Play Ball," meaning to launch the attack.
Within seconds he heard a radio message from the ship, "salvo," meaning it had launched its 16-inch shells toward the Jean Bart, the French battleship that was tied up in the Casablanca harbor.

The Massachusetts was 10 miles, or about 18,000 yards off the coast, and so it took a while for the shells to arrive. The gunnery people timed the arrival of the shells, though, and indicated to Dougherty when they should arrive by the word, "splash."

Dougherty looked down and saw the splashes of the shells, short and to the left of the target. After making corrections, seconds later, the ship again radioed to the spotter plane, "salvo." Again, some time passed before the message "splash."

This time Dougherty could see no splashes at all. Dodging between the puffs of AA fire, he quickly radioed back, "No observation." Swinging down for a closer look, though, he saw the gantry towers next to the big French battleship were toppling over. He radioed: "Belay that last message. Rapid fire, no change."

The Massachusetts was now dialed in on its adversary and began raining shells toward the beach.

In the air, though, Dougherty suddenly had a new problem. A French fighter came out of the blue and was firing at him.

"On the first pass, he shattered the canopy. We dove for the sea. The only protection we had from fighters was to get down to right over the ocean, and then, when he comes at us, to turn."

Radioman Ethridge was firing at the fighter with his .50-caliber machine gun at the rear of the Kingfisher, and Dougherty tried firing his forward mounted gun. "But it jammed after about the 10th shot. That was normal for that gun."

The fighter made another pass, again raking the Kingfisher with bullets. "We hadn't quite got down over the water, and this time they got Bobby. They also blew out my instrument panel and the windshield. He must have hit something else because my engine stopped."

Fortunately, the Kingfisher was nearly at sea level by that time, and Dougherty was able to bring the plane in for a landing. The French fighter flew over, but did not fire again at the American plane.

The plane drifted into shore and was nearly there when it sank in the shallow water, its pontoons filling up with water from the bullet holes. From over the dunes at the shore, a group of French soldiers came and took the two Americans into custody. "I had a hell of a time getting Bobby out of the back cockpit."

Dougherty and the wounded Ethridge were probably the first two American POWs in the African campaign, and in all the campaigns across the Atlantic.

The soldiers took them to a French military jail. Ethridge was then taken to a Casablanca hospital. "There wasn't much in that jail, just wooden planks to lie on and no blankets." Dougherty was being held with three other pilots from the carrier USS Ranger who had been shot down.

After three days, the four officers

were taken to a soccer stadium in the heart of Casablanca where they joined about 20 GIs who had also been captured in the invasion. After two days at the stadium, the men awoke to find their captors had disappeared.

Dougherty went out to the street, and it was filled with American heavy equipment moving through. He flagged down a Jeep, and the army officer stopped to look over the four naval aviators standing on the street. "What the hell are you doing here?" he asked. One of Dougherty's compatriots answered, "Well, we were here before you were."

The jeep brought the men to a villa at the top of the hill that had been taken over as U.S. headquarters. It had been abandoned only hours before by the German high command.

"We were brought into this beautiful room, and we were greeted by this white haired-general. The villa was really luxurious, with big swastikas carved into the floor. There was a picture of Hermann Goering on one side of the room, and on the other side was an oil painting of Hitler that had been removed from the wall and was lying on this ornate table. The general knew we were Navy pilots, and he came over and shook our hands. He said, 'You know, if it wasn't for you guys, I wouldn't be here right now. Let's drink a toast to this victory.' "

The general had the wine steward bring bottles of fine French champagne. The general wanted to use the crystal glasses in the cabinets, but the G-2 experts wouldn't let him because the furniture had not yet been checked for booby traps. Instead, the staff rounded up five tin cups.

"At one point, someone had poured the wine and was about to put the frosty bottle down on the table. The general immediately grabbed the bottle and said, 'No, don't do that, you'll leave a ring.' And he put the bottle down on Hitler's picture.

"A few days after our toast, I saw this same general in the hospital where Bobby was, and he was going from bed to bed and talking to every man. I had a lot of respect for him."

"I never knew who he was until sometime later when I read about the general who had been removed from duty because he slapped a soldier in a hospital. I looked at his picture and realized that I'd been drinking champagne that day with General Patton."

Patton gave orders to the Navy officers to go to the Anfa Hotel, the best in town, and stay there until a capital ship came in to take them back to the Navy.

About a week later, the USS Augusta, a cruiser, came into port, and Dougherty headed down to check on board. "The officer on deck asked me where my orders were, and I explained that I'd been shot down, been a prisoner, and all the rest. I was a little angry because now I was getting gas from my own people." After a brief and heated exchange, the ship's officer told Dougherty to, "get the hell off the ship."

On his way, though, Dougherty encountered another officer, a captain, who was wearing the aviator's wings. The second officer intervened, and Dougherty was allowed on board.

The ship's officers were restricted to the ship, but Dougherty was able to come and go because he was visiting Ethridge at the hospital daily.

The liberty allowed him to shop for souvenirs for himself and for others in the Augusta's crew. For spending money, he had the $300 in cash that had been sewn into his flight jacket in case he was forced to land in enemy territory. The French had searched him, but never found the money.

Dougherty also got a chance to get back down to the beach and examine his aircraft.

"While we were on our shakedown cruise, one of the officers determined that we could make the plane lighter and extend its range by removing the armor plating behind the pilot and radioman's seats. But when we got to North Africa, the gunnery officer insisted that we put the plating back in.

"When I got to look at the plane, I counted 14 pock marks in the back of my seat from the bullets. One of the bullets also went right through the top of my overseas cap and knocked off the wings I had pinned there. If I'd adjusted my seat one notch differently, I wouldn't be here talking to you."

After a couple of weeks, the Augusta steamed for the United States. "We left on December 5th, and we went at flank speed with no escort. We were going too fast for any submarines." The Massachusetts was already back in the United States.

When Dougherty reached the United States, he called home. What he didn't know was that the Navy had sent a telegram, after he had been shot down, to his family listing him as "missing in action." When he was released from captivity, another message was sent, saying he was okay. Unfortunately, the

second message never arrived.

"My father had received the telegram saying I was missing in action. He didn't tell anyone else in the family. He took it all on himself. In fact, the only person in town he had confided in was a friend, John Nehiba, who had already lost a son in the war.

"And so, when I called home, my aunt answered, and she said to my mother, 'Tom's on the line.' Well, my father just about collapsed."

On his way home on the train, he stopped in Marquette, Michigan, and picked up his fiancee, Jeanne. The two were married during that seven-day leave.

Later, Dougherty served as a chief flight instructor at Corpus Christi, and then he trained on multi-engined planes. He flew PBYs in New York, looking for submarines, and

finished out the war with an assignment in Puerto Rico.

He got out in March 1946 and went back to Hibbing to again run the funeral home. He stayed in the Naval Reserve and continued to fly out of Wold-Chamberlain for some time. "Then one day I was flying, and I lost an engine. I almost ended up at Fort Snelling National Cemetery, literally. I took that as a sign it was time to get out of the Reserves."

In 1949, he moved to Duluth to take over a funeral business there. He and Jeanne were married for 60 years, and they had 10 daughters and two sons. They also lost a son in infancy. The Doughertys have 39 grandchildren and seven great-grandchildren.

At 86, Dougherty still hasn't officially retired. "I still help out when they're busy or when it's a personal friend."

NEW JOB

After his tour on the Massachusetts, Dougherty, left, became a chief flight instructor at Corpus Christi, Texas.

IN TRAINING
Herman Ratelle, with his pipe, posed with his tankmates during training at Camp Campbell, Kentucky.

Unless indicated otherwise, all photos are from Herman Ratelle's personal collection.

HE SAW IT COMING

It was early 1945, and Herman Ratelle was a gunner on a tank attacking a German position near the border with France. He had just fired on a building when he saw a German tank came around the corner and take aim. He could see the shell coming right at him.

Herman Ratelle was one of those few GIs in World War II who actually saw the one that got him.

Looking through his gunner's scope on February 1, 1945, Ratelle had a very clear view of the German .88 shell, the "red onion," coming right at him. There was nowhere to go and nowhere to hide.

That Ratelle was standing on a box of grenades didn't help his situation.

Ratelle was born in International Falls, and, even after his family moved to Minneapolis, he continued to spend time in the border country. A family member owned the Coca-Cola bottling plant in town, and Ratelle worked there.

He also got his first experience with flying from an uncle who on one flight suddenly turned over the controls, saying it was time he learned to be a pilot.

His dad was an engineer and sales representative for one of the large paper-making companies, and Ratelle worked at the paper mill during the summers after he graduated from Minneapolis Washburn High School.

Ratelle began college at the University of Minnesota in fall 1941, and he was there when the war began that December. He had signed up for the ROTC program and trained at the Armory on campus.

By fall 1942, it looked like Ratelle's college days were numbered. "I had almost finished the fall quarter when I realized I was probably going to be drafted because my number wasn't very high." A professor suggested that if Ratelle enlisted, he would give him credit for that quarter.

The U.S. Army didn't call Ratelle for a physical until February 1943, and he took his pre-induction physical at the office of a Dr. Peter Schultz above the Salk Drug Store in south Minneapolis.

From Fort Snelling, Ratelle traveled west to Los Angeles by train, ending up at Camp Callan, about 20 miles north of San Diego. Basic training also taught the young soldiers the operation of anti-aircraft guns, or "ack-ack" as they were known.

Ratelle was selected for the Army Specialized Training Program, which kept promising young GIs in college. He was told he was going to be an engineer.

The group was temporarily housed at the fieldhouse of Pasadena Junior College. "There were 600 of us packed into that building, with just a dirt floor. We played a lot of cards and had a good time."

To his surprise, Ratelle was picked, along with several other soldiers, to go to the Hollywood Canteen to act as escorts for Hollywood starlets during a two-day promotion.

Ratelle's starlet was Jane Russell. At that time, Russell had only made one movie and hadn't achieved the fame she did after the war. It was a splendid two days for the young serviceman. "Jane Russell and I corresponded the whole time I was in the service. In about 1994, I was in a restaurant near Phoenix when a woman came up behind me and gave me a big hug. By gosh, there she was, Jane Russell, and she looked just as good as the first time I saw her."

ASTP brought Ratelle to the University of Indiana and then to the University of Cincinnati, before the Army shut the program down. "We had taken some tests, and I had

qualified for medical school if I wanted to continue. But I didn't want to leave my buddies. We figured that wherever we go, we go together."

Up to this point in the Army, Ratelle knew his duty had been pretty good. Camp Callan was called the "country club" of basic training camps. The rest of the time he was a student. "I don't even know if I had an MOS (Army job classification)."

His next stop was the tank corps. Ratelle was assigned to the 14th Armored Division at Fort Campbell, Kentucky. The division had been in training for some time, and was just about to be sent overseas to join the invasion of France in 1944.

Ratelle's training was mainly in the kitchen early on. "When we got to France, I'd never driven a tank. I'd never fired a gun in a tank. But most of the guys already there were old cadre. They knew what they were

doing. We were just their helpers."

The 14th went to Camp Shanks in New York, then set sail on the Santa Rosa, a converted cruise ship bound for Marseilles, France. "I had been in the Army long enough by then to learn not to volunteer for anything, but the sergeant came down and asked for volunteers for sub watch. It was great. We got to bring our sleeping bags up on deck and enjoy the fresh air. Down in the hold it was awful, a real pest house, a mess. Up on deck, we were even fed by the Navy. But we never saw a sub."

They disembarked in France after 13 days at sea in September 1944, and were soon united with their tanks. "The tanks had been stored in North Africa. We had to get the Cosmoline off them, load them with gas, load them with ammo, the whole nine yards."

The tanks were loaded on a train,

«

HERMAN RATELLE

At home in Edina

»

DURING THE WAR

Ratelle stayed in college through the early years of the war, but ended up as a gunner on a tank in France and Germany.

JANE RUSSELL

While in California, Ratelle was selected to be one of the escorts for a bevy of Hollywood starlets at the Hollywood Canteen. Ratelle's charge was Jane Russell.

and the men headed off to the front. "We lived in the tanks on the flat cars, and we saw what the Army had done to the Germans on our way up." They detrained near Dijon and hid in a forest for a few days.

Ratelle's job was ammo loader for the M4A4 Sherman tank, equipped with a 76-millimeter cannon. "Most of the Shermans had a smaller gun. We were a little gunned up. It made us kind of special, and they sent us into action as quickly as they could. It was kind of exciting."

There were five crew members on that tank: A driver; an assistant driver, called a BOG; a gunner; a loader; and the tank commander. The driver and BOG sat in the front of the tank, and the others were in the turret. The turret was powered and turned 360 degrees.

Each tank had two 30-caliber machine guns in front and a 50-caliber on the top. "It was that 50-caliber

that was just a devastating weapon. The Germans just hated it. As a result, the tank commander took a lot of hits. He usually had his head sticking out of the tank for a better view.

"The tanks were cold. By God, they were cold. Those two big tank engines behind us sucked cold air into the tank. It was not a friendly place to be. But it sure beat walking."

The tanks were gas-powered, and tank crews knew fire was their greatest danger. "The Brits called them 'Ronsons' after the lighter." The slogan for Ronson Lighters at that time was "Lights first time, every time." Ratelle estimates that 85 to 90 percent of Sherman tanks caught fire after being hit by the enemy.

"Plus we had 75 to 90 rounds of shells on board, high-explosive or armor-piercing. You wanted to get out of the tank as quickly as you could after it was hit."

The 14th Armored edged close enough to the front to hear the artillery in the distance, and, in October, took a course over the mountains and into the plains beyond, where tanks would be of more use.

The first combat was at Saint-Dié, "But we just got into it a little bit. The infantry and the French had already done the hard work."

Along the way, the tank column encountered one or two German roadblocks every day. The infantry was on the sides and in front of the tanks, and when a roadblock was found, a tank would be called up to blow it away.

At Obernai, the tanks ran into their first real combat, and the first tank was hit with a German Panzerfaust, similar to an American bazooka. The loader on the tank, Ronald O'Donnell, Ratelle's best friend, was killed.

"The rest of the crew got out. We

SHERMAN TANK

In another photo of training at Camp Campbell, this time Ratelle is standing on the left tread of the tank.

were blocked and couldn't advance anymore, and we had to wait until the infantry cleared out the town."

The Germans in the small villages would usually hide on the second

able to see the huge hole in the floor, so I didn't fall in. When I got over to Fuquay, I saw why he couldn't get out. He had a body on top of him, or part of a body."

like a new man. It was just sort of a delayed reaction, I suppose."

On Christmas Day, Ratelle, who spoke a little French, went with an officer to scout the local villages. In

---

"I saw the big, red onion coming at us. It was an .88 shell, and it was red hot. There was nothing we could do."

---

floor of the buildings, then attack from very close range when the tanks came abreast of the windows.

"It was almost constant at that time. You never dared get out of your tank, even to relieve yourself. If you did, you were taking your life into your hands. And the shelling was also constant. We used to say, 'Those .88s are breaking up that old gang of mine.' "

The tanks went north through Weissenbourg, through the old Maginot Line, and toward Riedseltz. "The column stopped one night, and we pulled into some yards. We were going to be able to get into some buildings and sleep, and it had been a long time since we were able to do that."

Ratelle chose to lay his sleeping bag on the far side of the room. "There was a huge featherbed in there, and it looked inviting, but for some reason none of us got on it. I don't know why."

During the night, a German shell landed right in the middle of the room, hitting an old pot-bellied stove. "It blew the stove to pieces. The room was just full of smoke, dust and noise. I could hear my friend, Jack Fuquay, yelling, 'I can't get out of my sleeping bag.' Luckily, I had a flashlight with me, and I was

It was the torso of a man named Hoffman, who had just come in from guard duty.

"We got out of there as fast as we could. We didn't even take our boots with us. I managed to grab my sleeping bag. When it became daylight, I held up my sleeping bag, and it was absolutely shot full of holes. You could hold it up and see the daylight through it. But I didn't have a scratch on me."

Eventually, the men got new boots, "although they didn't fit," and, after advancing up the road, they came back to Reidseltz, where they again tried to stay the night. "It was a bigger house, with a fire in the stove, and it was nice and warm, which was good because I didn't have my sleeping bag."

Ratelle was sleeping on a table, surrounded by hanging sheets that the French homeowner had been drying inside. He could hear his comrades talking about him. "Someone said, 'I'm worried about Herman. I think he's all shook up. He had to pull Hoffman off of Fuquay, and he had to get blood all over himself.'

"Finally, I fell asleep, but a while later I woke up. I had to throw up so bad that I just barely got to the back steps before I let it go. I threw my guts up, and then I was okay. I felt

the meantime, the kitchen truck delivered the men their hot Christmas dinner. "When we got back, my meal was there waiting for me. It was frozen solid. I made the best of it."

In January 1945, the Americans began to pull back their lines to better defensive positions as the Germans attempted Operation Nordwind, an attempt to push through the Americans in Alsace as all the attention was focused further north at the Battle of the Bulge.

Ratelle recalls how on New Year's Eve he and Fuquay were left in the tank and were ordered to observe a notch in the mountains where the Germans might come through. "It was 20 below outside, and there was two-and-a-half feet of snow on the ground, and Jack and I sat there all night. Luckily we had two Coleman stoves, one to keep our socks warm, and the other to keep the coffee hot. And that's how we got through the night."

The unit pulled back, and, by the middle of January, was fully engaged in the Battle of Hatten-Rittershoffen, called the largest tank battle fought on the Western Front during the war.

"We had our share of scares, but we got through it unscathed. It went on continuously for ten or 11 days. We'd

DAPPER HERMAN

For a while in Europe, Ratelle sported a mustache.

all stay in the line, and one tank at a time would go back for gas, ammo and food. All we had were C and K rations."

It was during that time that his tank took a lucky hit. The German shell came in one side of the sponson and went out the other side. No one was hurt. "We heard it, but we just kept going. We weren't sure what had happened. It wasn't till later that we found the shell hole on both sides of the tank. I guess what you don't know won't hurt you."

After the battle, in which more than 100 tanks were lost on each side, the 14th Armored was able to stand down for a while. An old friend of Ratelle's, Capt. Al Luger of the 45th Division, came by to say hello. It seemed like a good reason to have a party.

"We were in a house that had a basement, and it was full of Alsatian wine. There were also large bags of potatoes. We sent some guys down to find the kitchen truck, and they came back with two gallons of Mazola Oil. We had French fries like

they were going out of style. It was wonderful. A warm house, a couple of bottles of wine."

At the end of January, the unit advanced to the Moder River but had to wait for engineers to construct a Bailey bridge across it. The entire company got across the river and advanced on Oberhoffen.

The tanks lined up and were attempting to destroy the town's buildings in front of them. The Germans were behind the buildings. Ratelle, by this time, was acting as gunner. His tank would aim at one side of a building, take out that wall, then aim at the other side of the building, hoping to take out that wall and collapse the building.

"As the gunner, when I wanted to look out the hatch, I needed to stand on something, and so I was using a steel box that contained tank grenades."

Ratelle's tank had just fired a round, and Ratelle looked through his gunner's scope. He didn't like what he saw. A German tank was coming around the building they were shelling, and it was aiming its gun right at the American tank.

"I saw the big, red onion coming at us. It was an .88 shell, and it was red-hot. There was nothing we could do."

The shell hit the tank head-on, just to the right of the driver. The box of grenades exploded and launched Ratelle right out through the hatch, breaking both of his shoulders as he went through. He landed on the back of the tank and rolled off.

The driver's hatch was jammed, and the driver tried to climb over the transmission to the hatch on the other side, but the tank was hit by another shell that killed him instantly.

The assistant driver found Ratelle at the back of the tank, trying to make a tourniquet out of the shreds of his socks. His left foot was blown off. On his left boot, only the top two laces of his boot remained. Everything else was gone. His right leg was riddled with shrapnel.

"There was machine-gun fire, and burp-gun fire and tank fire all around me. I was just sitting on the ground trying to make that tourniquet. I thought I was going to bleed to death."

One of his crewmates helped him hop about 50 yards to the back of another tank, which took Ratelle to safety over the Bailey bridge. "I couldn't tell where I was bleeding, but I could feel something hot and liquid. It turned out it was recoil oil from the main gun."

"The loader on that tank was Eldon Drake, just a great guy. He had glasses as thick as Coke bottle bottoms. I don't know how they kept him in the service. Anyway, he looked at me, and I was laughing. I'm sure he thought I was off my rocker. He asked why I was laughing. I told him that I'd gotten the million-dollar wound, and I was heading home."

An ambulance took Ratelle to an aid station. From there, he was placed on a stretcher on the front of a Jeep and taken inside. As he was carried into the house, Ratelle saw an old Frenchman by the door with a white beard and white hair. As he looked at Ratelle, he was crying and saying in French, "Poor, poor American soldier."

Ratelle said he was laid out on a table, still on the stretcher. "They had given me some morphine, and

ON CRUTCHES

Recovering from his injuries, Ratelle talked with one of his friends.

that eased some of the pain. A captain asked me how I was feeling, and I told him, 'Not too good.' He asked if I wanted some whiskey. I thought he was kidding.

"He reached over me, to the window, and behind some drapes was a bottle of Four Roses. He had a big water glass, and he filled it up. I think I drank it in two gulps, and he asked if I wanted more. I said I did, and he filled it up again."

Ratelle was again transported, this time to a field hospital where he was laid on the floor. By now, it had been about five hours since his tank was hit.

"There were four lovely nurses there, and they were all dressed up in their starched khakis. They were planning to go to a party. I remember they had a big cake in a box. Instead of leaving, though, they squatted next to me and talked to me. It made my day. That, and the bourbon."

The next thing Ratelle knew he was in Saarbourg, France. He woke up in a full body cast with his arms stretched out to his sides. His right leg was encased in more bandages, and his left leg was gone, replaced by a device that kept the skin stretched out while it healed.

His first acquaintance in the hospital was a fellow Minnesotan, Glenn Strandberg, who asked Ratelle if he wanted something to eat. As they talked, Strandberg said that once

Ratelle was healed and back home, they would have to go hunting together.

"He was a generous, caring man, and we've been dear friends ever since. We go hunting almost every year."

Strandberg told him that the hospital was manned by doctors from the University of Minnesota. Ratelle started naming some doctors he knew, including Dr. Peter Schultz, who had given him his first physical in south Minneapolis.

"Strandberg looked at me and said, 'He's the doctor who took your leg off last night.' "

Ratelle got to see the doctor and eventually took a message home to Schultz's wife, who the doctor hadn't seen in three years of medical duty.

He was taken by train basically back along the route the 14th Armored had taken to the front some months before. He boarded a ship at Marseilles. "It was a glorious trip. They treated me like royalty. If I wanted food, it was there pronto. I got all the ice cream I wanted."

Ratelle was moved to Brigham City, Utah, to a new hospital that had been set up to handle amputees and those who had psychiatric problems. "They kept us separate." He was able to fly home fairly quickly for convalescent leave, but he returned to Brigham City for extensive rehabilitation. He had other operations in June 1945.

He got out of the service in October 1945, and he and his brother, Alex, who had been in the Army Air Force, arrived home in Minneapolis on the same day. Ratelle immediately went back to school at the University.

"I decided I wanted to go to law school, but I was afraid I didn't have enough points to get into the school. The lady at the desk looked at me and said, 'Soldier, you've got more damn points than you'll ever need. You're going to law school.' "

Three years later, Ratelle was in practice with a couple of other lawyers, making the astounding sum of $50 a month. He was also receiving $81 a month from the VA.

He joined Frank Warner in a law firm, and over the years the firm grew. In 1970, the firm merged with another, and the legal corporation of Moss and Barnett was created, with Ratelle as the senior partner. It became one of the largest and most prestigious law firms in the state.

Ratelle eventually put most of his time into investment counseling, and at age 82, he still works about a half-time schedule. He has also

been active as a director of the Kellogg Foundation, the College of St. Benedict, and St. John's School of Theology.

He's had two back operations related to his war injuries, but said he has never felt he was handicapped in any way. He golfs, hunts, and fishes.

He and his wife Therese, were married in 1951, and they have six children and 16 grandchildren. He considers his family his greatest accomplishment and his greatest source of joy.

Looking back to that day he was blown out of a tank on the battlefield, Ratelle feels that he's been extraordinarily lucky in his life. "I always think that day I got hit was the first day of my second life."

HOME AT LAST

Back in Minnesota, still convalescing, Ratelle posed with his sister, Marian, and his mother, Virginia.

ONE STEP FOREWARD

Ken Dahlberg grew up milking cows on a farm in western Wisconsin. As a fighter pilot in World War II, he was a triple ace with 15 kills and was also shot down three times himself. After the war, he developed Miracle Ear into a worldwide business and later, much to his regret, became a central figure in the Watergate scandal.

Ken Dahlberg, whose war record and business accomplishments can only be termed extraordinary, traces one of the great watersheds in his life to boot camp at Fort Leonard Wood, Missouri, in 1941.

The men had been assembled in a squad, and the squad leader, a corporal, asked for a volunteer to step forward.

"We were standing at attention, and we were very uncomfortable in our ill-fitting uniforms. We were making $21 a month," Dahlberg recalled. "Being unsatisfied with where I was at, I took one step forward."

The corporal barked out again, "Men, look at Private Dahlberg. He's a leader, he's one step ahead of all of you." Looking back, Dahlberg said, "I learned a lesson from a $30-a-month professor.

"It was a step into the unknown, a response to curiosity, a response to be more confident. It was one of the great lessons in my life."

Dahlberg has never stopped taking that step into the unknown. It led

him from a farm in Wisconsin to a career in hotel management to being a pilot in World War II (and one of America's top aces) to one of the most successful business careers ever for a Minnesotan.

Kenneth H. Dahlberg was born in St. Paul in 1917, the son of a streetcar motorman. With a twinkle in his eye, Dahlberg tells a fable about how, at age one, he persuaded his father to move to Wisconsin. "He seemingly took my advice, and we settled on a small dairy farm in the little village of Wilson, Wisconsin."

Dahlberg studied in a one-room schoolhouse in Wilson for his first 11 years of schooling, then went to live with an aunt in St. Paul so he could graduate from an accredited high school, St. Paul Harding.

He graduated in 1935 and got a job at the Lowry Hotel washing pots and pans. It was his introduction to the hotel business, but he didn't stay long on the lowest rung. By 1941, he was the food and beverage controller for the 23 Pick Hotels in the

United States.

"I knew one thing from growing up on the farm was that quality is important. The beginning of good food in restaurants was good meat and good produce."

His position meant he was hiring many of the executives in the food and beverage department, including those with master's degrees. Dahlberg's only degree was from Harding.

"I was asked much later about the

difference between the MAs and the ones who came up the other way. I said it was the difference between being force- fed and scratching for a living. It's just like free-range chickens cost more. There's added value in their having had to scratch."

Dahlberg was drafted in 1941 before America entered World War II. It brought an end to his hotel career.

After Fort Leonard Wood, he was sent to Virginia where he was assigned to a coastal battery. Again, he stepped forward and volunteered for cooks and bakers school. "I signed up with the idea that I'd be the first one at the trough."

The process of going through that application exposed him to the headquarters building, and it was there he spotted a posting for two openings for aviation cadets. The candidates had to have two years of college, or pass an equivalency test,

which Dahlberg did.

It also called for two letters of recommendation. "Along the way, I had been an assistant manager at the Oliver Hotel in South Bend, which was the gathering place for the Notre Dame University elite." One of Dahlberg's letters was from the mayor of South Bend and the other was from former Notre Dame football player and coach Elmer Layden.

"You have to have a little luck in life, too. It turns out the interviewing officer on the selection board happened to be a graduate of Notre Dame."

Dahlberg beat out thousands of applicants for one of the two spots and was sent to the West Coast for aviation training. "I had never been in an airplane in my life, but it sounded good. And I got to go to school."

He did six-months' ground training at Santa Ana. One of the in-

structors was a young officer named Barry Goldwater, and he and Dahlberg became good friends when Dahlberg helped out at the firearms course.

Dahlberg did his first solo at primary training in King City, California, did his basic training at Chico, California; and took advanced training and earned his commission and wings in December 1942 at Luke Field in Phoenix.

Like many other graduates early in the war, Dahlberg immediately turned around to become an instructor. He was sent to Yuma, Arizona, where a new base was being built.

"On the train going over, I got to sit next to my friend Barry Goldwater. It turns out that he was going to head the new ground school. For the next six months, we lived in a two-man tent together on the desert. We got

«

KEN DAHLBERG

Now lives in Minnetonka.

»

DURING THE WAR

Dahlberg, shown here, was a cadet in the Army Air Corps program. He later became a fighter pilot.

to know each other well."

While Dahlberg was an instructor, he performed what he calls "the dumbest thing in my military career."

He was showing a new pilot how to do a dive-bombing run, bottoming out just over the treetops. "The cadet was reticent about bringing it down to treetop level. So, I took the stick and decided to demonstrate for him. I rolled over right at the tree-tops, next to the beautiful Colorado River, which I stupidly decided to buzz from my back-seat position.

"Suddenly there was a cluster of huge power lines in front of me. I was too low to get over them, and I tried to get under them. I didn't. There was a blinding flash, and the power lines took off my antenna, my canopy and my vertical tail. The

cadet was limp in the front seat."

Dahlberg managed to get the AT-6 back to base, but he had visions of his flying career coming to a sudden halt.

Working in his favor was his prowess at gambling. "I was a pretty good poker player, and I was reck-less with the dice. I had wound up with a $900 IOU from the command-ing officer in my billfold."

Dahlberg was ushered into the C.O.'s office shortly after his landing in the damaged trainer. "I casually took from my wallet the IOU, and I said, 'I guess I won't need this anymore.' He asked what I wanted, and I said I'd do anything to avoid a court martial."

Dahlberg was grounded and con-fined to base for a month — and he got the job of police and prison offi-

cer. After reporting to the barbed-wire prison on the base, he found out the prison was equipped with two brand-new motorcycles with red lights and sirens.

"I had fun for the next month, riding around the base, harassing my fel-low pilots." The fun came to an end, though, when he responded to an accident on the runway.

"I sped out on the motorcycle with my lights and siren going, but, be-fore I could slow down, I hit some loose sand. I wiped out. I had sand in every opening in my body, and I

A COLD DAY IN FRANCE

Dahlberg makes his way past the parachute rigging tent for the 353rd Fighter Squadron at an air-field in France in 1944.

P-47
Thunderbolt Statistics

P-47 Data

Manufacturer
Republic Aviation Corporation

Engine
Pratt and Whitney R-2800-59 twin row radial engine. Maximum horsepower of 2,535.

Crew
One

Armament
Eight .50-caliber Browning machine guns. Three hard points with a capacity of 2,000 pounds of bombs.

Maximum Speed
426 miles per hour

Ceiling
43,000 feet

Range
1,600 miles

ended up in the hospital.

"The C.O. came to visit me and said he was relieving me of my duties as police and prison officer. He also advised me that he was cutting me or-

war, a lot of things would not have happened. But we didn't have those rules. We had to depend on our common sense rather than the rules to survive. There's only one rule in

"Are you American?" she asked, and he assured her he was. "Then you'd better go hide down by the pond. There are Germans all over the place."

"They said later, all they saw were bits and pieces and no parachute. I must have been either a bit or a piece."

---

ders to send me into combat.

"He said it was better that I go into combat before I killed myself."

Dahlberg was chosen to be a fighter pilot at some point in his training. "There must have been something embedded in the system where they were watching us to determine whether we should be fighter pilots or bomber pilots. Some were shunted one way, and some another. They never told me why I was a fighter pilot."

On his way to Europe, he made a stop back at Luke Field, where he trained Chinese pilots in aerial gunnery and ground-strafing techniques. He also spent time in Florida in an overseas training unit, where he accumulated about 40 hours' flying time in a P-47 Thunderbolt.

In May 1944, Dahlberg arrived in England on a troop ship and was assigned to the 354th Fighter Group. He arrived at his squadron on June 2, and flew his first mission just after D-Day.

The only problem was that he had been practicing in a P-47, and the squadron he was assigned to flew P-51 Mustangs. His total training on the P-51 was a half-hour orientation flight. "If the Federal Aviation Administration had been running the

combat, and that's to survive."

In August, Dahlberg had just returned from a three-day leave when he walked into the ready room of the 353rd Fighter Squadron. He was told the squadron leader was sick, and was asked to take over a flight over right away.

Dahlberg was still wearing his R&R clothes, including low-cut shoes, but he stepped forward and took the mission. "I didn't have my sidearm, my knife, my boots, my escape kit. I didn't have any of this stuff.

"I volunteered because I had become used to volunteering, to taking one step forward, bypassing my own safety. Was it stupid? Yes, but we all do stupid things."

Dahlberg's group of eight P-51s jumped a pack of about 40 ME-109s over Paris. "It was every man for himself. I had shot down four of the 109s, and I was going for my fifth when I got a little careless. My airplane was on fire, and the cockpit was filling with smoke. I ducked into a little cloud and bailed out."

He parachuted to the ground onto a large French estate not far from Paris. It had a large chateau, riding stable and many other buildings. He landed right among them and was soon approached by a French lady.

Dahlberg took her advice and hid among the bulrushes in the water. "I just had my head sticking out, but sure enough, not long after I got there, the German soldiers came looking for me. They must have seen my parachute coming down.

"I snapped off a dry reed, and I was able to get completely submerged and breathe through it like a snorkel. It worked.

"That night, a little Frenchman, who turned out to be the owner, came down. I decided he looked friendly, and so I talked to him. He told me to stay down by the pond because the Germans were all over. He came back later with a trenchcoat to keep me warm. The next morning, he brought me bread and wine."

The Frenchman asked Dahlberg for his sidearm to give to the resistance movement, but the pilot didn't have one because of the last-minute departure. In fact, all he had in his pockets were three prophylactics that had been issued to him before his three-day pass.

"It was kind of a policy in the Army. If you had a three-day leave, they gave you three prophylactics. But, being a good Lutheran from the Midwest, I never used mine."

Later, when the Frenchman and

THE WHOLE NINE YARDS

Dahlberg looks on as machine gun ammunition is loaded into his Mustang. Each bandolier contained nine yards of bullets, and, if the pilot used it all, it was said that he used the "whole nine yards."

Dahlberg were reunited after the liberation of Paris, the French nobleman took great delight in telling the story of how he had asked Dahlberg for his sidearm for the resistance, but had only got the three prophylactics. "I remember he said, "Mr. Dahlberg came to France to make love, not war.' "

On the estate, Dahlberg learned from the French that the American lines were only 40 miles away. He and his French comrades devised a plan to work their way toward the lines.

"I broke the first rule of a downed airman, and I changed into civilian clothes. We were told never to do that because, if you were caught, you could immediately be shot as a spy."

The French tied what looked like a bloody towel around his head, and he and another man set off on bicycles toward the front.

"You have to understand that the countryside was in chaos. There were refugees and ox carts and Jeeps and military vehicles and tanks. The Germans were retreating, but they were still very formidable at that point."

The two encountered several check-points along the way, but in the end Dahlberg crossed back into American lines and made his way back to his squadron.

He was shot down again during the Battle of the Bulge in late December 1944. Dahlberg was leading a squadron of 16 P-47s on a dive bombing mission in the Ardennes forest. The weather had just cleared before Christmas, and the fighters were seeking German tanks.

"As we dove down, I recognized that what we had spotted were not German tanks but American tanks. I called off the run, but in seconds all hell broke loose. I don't know if it was German fire or American fire, but I lost my engine and my electricity."

Too low to bail out, Dahlberg had no choice but to try and land the disabled plane. "I couldn't crash-land just yet because I still had those two 500-pound bombs. So I did an abrupt 180, jettisoned the bombs, and cut through the ground fire. I crash-landed at the edge of a forest, but I cut a swath of about 200 yards through some sapling trees."

Dazed and hurt, Dahlberg crawled out of his cockpit and stood on the wing, holding his .45 pistol in one hand and holding his ribs with the other hand. Within minutes, an American Jeep appeared, even though Dahlberg had crashed behind enemy lines.

"We had been warned about Germans imitating Americans, and so as I stood there, weaving on the wing of the plane, I asked the tank commander in the Jeep what the code word of the day was. He said, 'I don't know any code word; just get your ass in the Jeep.' And so I did."

(Part two of that story comes later.)

Six months into his combat flying career with the Army Air Force, Dahlberg had crashed two planes and escaped enemy capture on both occasions. On his third crash, he wasn't quite so lucky.

He had shot down 15 enemy aircraft at that point, placing him 23rd on the list of all the fighter aces in Europe during the war and making him a triple ace. His fellow pilots often later joked that he should only have 12 kills if you subtracted the number of American planes he lost along the way.

On February 2, 1945, after leading a successful dive-bombing mission near Metz, Germany, Dahlberg was reassembling his 12-plane formation.

"We were at about 10,000 feet when I took a direct hit from a German .88 millimeter cannon. The P-47 has protective armor behind the pilot, and that's what must have saved me because the airplane just blew up.

"I fell about 9,500 feet before I regained consciousness. I pulled the rip cord at about 500 feet and had a very hard landing."

Dahlberg's fellow pilots thought he was a goner and reported him as probably killed in action. That's usually the case with a direct hit from an artillery shell. "They said later,

AFTER THE MISSION

Pilots were often allowed a shot or two of the local liquor after a flight. Dahlberg is in the middle.

all they saw were bits and pieces and no parachute. I must have been either a bit or a piece."

With a bleeding head wound, Dahlberg tried to escape. He headed west toward the American lines, but his progress was impeded by a river. He took off his shoes and crossed the river, but lost his escape kit and compass during the crossing.

"I had no sense of direction. I crawled through the woods all night and ended up back at the river.

"My option was to hide during the day and travel at night, which was the safest. But my head wound was still bleeding, and I didn't know if I'd make it, so I tried to travel during the day. They captured me right away."

Dahlberg wasn't done yet, though. When his guard stopped to take a drink at a fountain, Dahlberg grabbed his gun and hit his captor on the head. He dashed into a French town.

"I found a little French vehicle that had a German medical insignia on it. I stole the car and headed west. I got through all the checkpoints but the last one. Even though I had my red light on, they still stopped me. I tried to go around the extended log, but I crashed the car. They captured me again."

Despite his wound, Dahlberg was marched more than 100 miles to Stalag 7A at Moosburg in the area around Munich. "I always say that was my first experience of suburban living."

Dahlberg said he learned a lot at the German prison camp. "I learned about economics, and I learned about inflation. The first time I traded a cigarette to a German guard, I got a turnip. The sec-

ond time, a few weeks later, it cost me two cigarettes for a turnip. The third time, it took two cigarettes for a half a turnip. That was 100-percent-a-month inflation. Finally, the guard had no turnips at all. My currency was worthless. It was hyper-inflation."

Patton's Third Army liberated the POW camp in May, but instructed the prisoners not to try to find their own way back to their units. "They wanted us to stay together in the camp and wait because after the German Army left, it was chaos. There were literally millions of Eastern Europeans who had been slave laborers, and they were loose, pillaging and raping. They told us it was more dangerous than when the fighting was going on."

"But another guy and I didn't want to wait, so we snuck out of the camp on a garbage truck or something and began hitchhiking back toward France."

As the duo hitchhiked through Munich, a German lady came out and offered them food and a place to stay for the night. Dahlberg and his friend were amazed that a German woman would offer them help, but they learned that she had a 16-year-old daughter and was more afraid of the refugees than the Americans.

"It taught me a basic lesson on the value of freedom. It showed me the intensity of fear that the lack of freedom reveals. It has stayed embedded with me. I've never ever forgotten the look in that lady's eyes. She was helpless."

Dahlberg did manage to work his way back to the coast, and he talked his way onto a troop ship heading for the United States. "The day before the ship pulled into New York,

someone lent me a racy book. I was so engrossed reading it that I didn't realize what the sun was doing to me. My first night back in America I was in a hospital recovering from a severe sunburn."

Dahlberg was put on a 90-day terminal leave, sort of a transition period for soldiers when they are allowed to keep wearing their uniforms. He went back to St. Paul, and he was assured of a good job with his former employer.

He went to a party that night with some of his old friends.
The party merged with another party at the hotel and ended up at the spacious home of a man who owned an electronics firm. A week later, Dahlberg was still a house guest. Eventually, the man hired him as his assistant at his business. Dahlberg knew nothing about electronics and was heading back to the hotel business, but he decided to take that step forward.

The business was Telex, a maker of hearing aids and other communications equipment. Dahlberg joined up shortly thereafter with a National Guard unit in Duluth, and he suggested that Telex try using its hearing-aid expertise in making military helmets. The company became a leader in making headsets.

In 1948, Dahlberg and his brother began their own business, mainly making hearing aids. In 1959, their company became part of Motorola, but in 1964 Motorola divested itself of all consumer projects, and Dahlberg bought back his own company.

Over the years, that company — Miracle Ear — became the largest-selling brand of hearing aids in the United States. In 1994, Dahlberg sold it to Bausch and Lomb and

SHILLELAUGH

Dahlberg climbs aboard Shillelaugh, a Mustang he flew several times during the war. He was flying this ship when he was shot down near Paris in mid-1944. Dahlberg made his way through enemy lines after being protected by a French family.

began a venture capital company called Carefree Capital Inc. He is also the principal owner of Buffalo Wild Wings.

In addition to his business career, Dahlberg also got involved in politics. His wartime friendship with Barry Goldwater led him to be a deputy chairman of fundraising for Goldwater's presidential campaign in 1964.

In 1971, he was Midwest chairman of fundraising for Richard Nixon's campaign, working under Maurice Stans. It was during this time that he became a footnote in the history books during the greatest political scandal of the 20th century.

Dahlberg had received a donation of $25,000 in cash from a Minnesota Democrat, Dwayne Andreas, and

had brought the money to the Committee to Re-Elect the President in Washington D.C. Andreas didn't want his contribution made public knowledge, and, in those days, the law allowed for confidential donations.

Somehow the money, which Dahlberg had converted into a cashier's check with his name on it, ended up in the hands of a Cuban businessman in Miami. The man was later identified as one of the Watergate burglars. The money was the only direct link between the president and the Watergate thieves, and Dahlberg became an object of intense scrutiny as federal investigators tried to pry out of him the source of the donation.

Dahlberg refused, and he was subpoenaed while in Florida to undergo

a grilling by federal agents. "They sent this state's attorney, this goon, down to pick me up at the Doral Hotel. The interview was two hours of first-class intellectual torture, but I told them the law, and I said it was none of their business."

Afterward, the same "goon" drove Dahlberg back to the hotel. As was common among men of their age, the two began talking about their war service. Dahlberg allowed that he was a fighter pilot.

"I was a tank commander during the war," the investigator said. "And in the whole five years I was in, I only saw one fighter pilot, and he was the dumbest son of a bitch I ever met."

Dahlberg asked why.

"It was during the Battle of the Bulge, and my driver saw a fighter plane go down. He told me he thought he knew where it was. I told the driver, 'Let's go for it.'

"When we got there, the pilot was standing on the wreck of his P-47. He was holding his pistol in one hand and holding his side with his other hand, and he was shouting at us for the code of the day."

Dahlberg turned to the investigator and asked, "And how is your driver, Charlie, doing these days?" The investigator was flabbergasted, but the two had made a connection from a wartime incident 26 years earlier. Their strange reunion became a front-page story in the Miami Herald the next day.

Dahlberg and the investigator, Martin Dardis, became friends and communicated at least once a month until Dardis' death many years later. "It turns out there was a lot of mutual respect."

Another incident after the war helped Dahlberg celebrate his wartime experience. In 1967, the Department of Defense notified him that he had earned the Distinguished Service Cross in 1945, but he had never collected it because he was in a prisoner-of-war camp.

The military wanted to know if the medal should be mailed to him or if he'd like it presented. In the end, it was presented in Washington, D.C. by Vice President Hubert Humphrey, a close friend of Dahlberg's, with the Joint Chiefs of Staff and the entire Minnesota congressional delegation present.

In addition to the DSC, Dahlberg also earned two Purple Hearts, the Silver Star, the Distinguished Flying Cross (with cluster), the Bronze Star, and 15 air medals.

In his 90s, he still flies his own jet

> Mrs Mamie J Dahlberg, Wilson, Wis
>
> The chief of staff of the army directs me to inform you that your son capt Dahlberg Kenneth H is being returned to the United States in the near future and will be given an opportunity to communicate with you on arrival.
>
> J A Ulio, the adjutant General

TELEGRAM

Dahlberg's mother, Mamie, received this telegram notifying the family that their son had been freed from the German POW camp.

aircraft as a co-pilot, and he works every day at his venture capital business.

He and his wife, the former Betty Jayne Segerstrom, have three children, seven grandchildren and two great-grandchildren.

Dahlberg, when he takes a moment from a busy day, can look back on a life that has included a political record that earned its way into the history books, a business record that put him in Minnesota's Business Hall of Fame, and a war record that very few can equal for bravery and accomplishment.

And it was all because he was never afraid to take that one step forward.

TRIPLE ACE

Dahlberg shot down German planes in both the P-51 Mustang and the P-47 Thunderbolt during the war.

WOMEN AIRFORCE SERVICE PILOTS

Elizabeth Wall loved to fly, and when the Army Air Corps opened a program for women in 1942, she was first in line. She ended up flying a variety of airplanes at the Army's aerial gunnery school in Las Vegas. She was one of about 1,000 women pilots during World War II, and she was sad to see the program end.

Elizabeth "Betty" Wall Strohfus' second life began at age 71.

An interviewer delving into Strohfus' past in 1991 discovered that the Faribault native had flown airplanes during World War II for the Army Air Corps.

"I say that's when I came out of the closet because I had all my Air Force stuff put away in a closet," Strohfus said. "I found out that people were interested in it."

The digging up of her past meant a new career traveling the state and the nation speaking about her service during the war. Strohfus presents 40 to 50 programs a year to school kids, veterans groups and military reunions.

And at age 90, she's still going strong, still a bundle of happy energy, still enjoying every minute of her life and her military fame. Strohfus was one of about 1,000 female pilots during the war, and she likes nothing better than to tell her story.

Elizabeth Wall grew up in Faribault during the Depression, graduating

from Faribault High School in 1937. "I had such a happy childhood. I didn't even know we were poor."

Incidentally, Wall graduated with Bruce Smith, a good student and football player who went on to be the University of Minnesota's only Heisman Trophy winner. "I was so scared of boys at that time that I didn't know him well. I was too shy. But he was very nice and very humble."

Her father had retired as a farmer, selling his land during the early 1930s. He moved to Faribault and put his nest egg in a bank. The bank folded, and the money was gone. "Obviously, he never trusted banks after that."

Elizabeth was the second-youngest of six kids. "I was a tomboy. I loved to play ball, and I loved to climb things. I was always trying to get up in the air, by shinnying up a telephone pole or sitting on a rooftop.

"I didn't like girly things, and my sister would make me sit still on the couch while she fixed my hair. I

could hardly wait to get out of there and let my hair loose."

After high school, one of her sisters found there was a job opening at the county courthouse in the registrar of deeds office. "In those days, it didn't matter if you liked a job, you were just happy to have one. You didn't get a bonus for good work, you got to keep your job."

Wall worked as a clerk, then advanced to deputy registrar while still in her teens. "I made $50 month, but I didn't need it. I'd come home and

give all my money to my mother except for a few dollars. I had those three older sisters, so I had plenty of clothes."

She found out about a new Sky Club at the little Faribault Airport that had a membership of 15 who each contributed $100 to join. The money was used to maintain a 65-horsepower Piper Cub aircraft. There was also a minimal fee for each hour flown.

For Wall, the Sky Club seemed like a dream. She would go over and clean their office or just hang around, hoping to get a free ride in the airplane. On her first flight, one of the club members decided to give her a little thrill and did a stall and spin.

"He asked if I wanted to do it again. I'm sure he thought I was going to get sick, but I said, 'Sure.' We did it about 10 more times, and when we landed, he was sick."

Wall desperately wanted to join the club, but she didn't have the membership fee. "So I went down to the local bank and asked for a loan. When I told the banker why, he thought I was crazy. But he knew my family, and he knew we were poor but honest. He used my bike as collateral, and he even co-signed the loan."

Wall was in heaven. She quickly mastered the intricacies of the Cub and spent many happy hours flying. "I had always been shy, but being up in the air was where I belonged. And I was treated so well, with 14 guys and only one gal."

In 1942, after World War II had started, Wall learned of a program called Women Airforce Service Pilots, or WASPs. She was eager to join, but there was a little problem: Her boyfriend, who was already in the service, didn't want her to join.

"He said that anybody who goes into the Air Force couldn't be his gal. I told him that whatever I do, I'll still be me." Wall was faced with choosing him or flying. It was no contest.

"You had to have 35 hours of flight time to join the WASPs or a private license." A friend let her get in extra hours on his plane, and Wall qualified for an interview at Fort Snelling.

She was one of more than 25,000 women who volunteered for the new, experimental program. Only 1,800 were accepted. In the end, just over a thousand earned their wings.

Wall was sent to Avenger Field in Sweetwater, Texas, for ground school. As she entered the program, she realized she was beginning a whole new life. Always known as Liz at home and around Faribault, she chose to be called Betty in her new surroundings.

Betty Wall loved the flight training

«

LIZ STROHFUS

At home in Faribault

»

DURING THE WAR

Known as Betty Wall during her WASP days, she trained in Texas and was based at a gunnery school in Las Vegas.

but found much of the academic work very challenging. "What did I know about meteorology? In Faribault, if the sky was clear, we flew. If it wasn't, we didn't." She also had classes on such things as engines and Morse code.

"I thought physics were things you took for a stomach ache."

While she struggled with the ground classes, her flying went well. The students would fly in the morning and do classes in the afternoon, or vice versa. They flew Fairchild PT-19 trainers that had 250-horsepower engines, a big difference from the Cub she was used to.

As training advanced, she flew Vultee BT-13s and later the North American AT-6s, the plane she loved the most. The women did all their training at Avenger Field, unlike the male pilots, who usually changed fields for every stage of their training.

The field became a popular stopping point for male pilots who had – officially — run out of gas or were having engine trouble. The lure of hundreds of female pilots in training was too great. The Army Air Corps, though, finally put the field off-limits, and the friendly visits ended.

As her training came to a close, she again had to choose between her fiancée at the time and her Army Air Force career. For a time, she considered resigning in order to get married. In the end, flying won out again.

"It was between him and the AT-6, and I chose the AT-6. And you know what, we both lived happily ever after."

Wall graduated with the first class of 1944, the ninth class overall to graduate from the program.

Many of the graduates went on to work ferrying aircraft around the country and overseas, freeing up other pilots to do their work in the war zone. Wall and seven others from her class, though, volunteered to fly at a base in Las Vegas, Nevada.

The Las Vegas base was a school for gunnery, and the women got to fly a variety of aircraft, including twin-engined bombers.

On Wall's orientation flight at the new base, a pilot took her in an AT-6 on an adventurous flight that included a dive-bombing maneuver – all with the cockpit open. The pilot then turned the craft over to Wall, who tried to emulate the training flight, including the dive with the canopy open.

"I lost my hat, I lost everything. If I hadn't been strapped in, they would have lost me."

One of her classmates was, in fact, nearly lost. She was with another pilot when they did a roll, and her seatbelt broke. Fortunately, she was wearing her parachute. Back in the ready room, the other pilots were excitedly waiting to hear the woman's story. She simply said, "When I realized I'd left the aircraft, I counted to ten and pulled the cord."

The women and men assigned to the base performed a variety of tasks for the pilots learning gunnery, including towing targets to shoot at and diving into formations to test the gunner's skills. Sometimes live ammunition was used (at the towed targets), and sometimes the guns were cameras that recorded the action.

The live ammo that was used to shoot at the towed targets was color coded. "At least the colored bullets

let us know who was putting the holes in our planes and not in our targets."

"We were only supposed to fly four hours a day, but sometimes the guys would come back from Las Vegas a little under the weather, and they'd ask me to take their shift. Lord, I loved to fly those airplanes. If I could get eight hours a day in, I'd always do it."

At five foot three, Wall was on the bottom end of what the Army Air Force would accept for a pilot's size. The cockpits were designed for larger people. "I'd have to sit on two cushions and have my parachute behind me so I could reach every-

CIVIL AIR PATROL

Before getting in the WASP program, Betty Wall served in the Civil Air Patrol.

thing."

Eventually she did experience some flying fatigue and was sent home to Faribault for a week and then shipped off to Orlando for two weeks

proach.

Below she could see that every piece of fire fighting and ambulance equipment on the base had been called out for her first landing in a

Wall said it wasn't her only miscue in her Air Force career, but she doesn't talk much about the other ones.

It was a glorious year for Wall, but it

"Lord, I loved to fly those airplanes. If I could get eight hours a day in, I'd always do it."

---

to attend Officer Tactical School, where she learned, among other things, how to eat a snake.

Later, she went back to Sweetwater for more training on instruments, was qualified as an instructor, and began teaching instruments to the male pilots going to school at Las Vegas.

On one mission, she was asked to dive into a group of gunners in an emplacement. She thought the orders said 50 feet, and she was happy to oblige. Wall took great delight in watching the gunners hit the ground, flat out. Later, she found out she had misread the orders, and the dive was only supposed to go within 500 feet of the ground.

At one point, she was asked to fly a Bell P-39 airacobra, one of the "hottest" American warplanes. She was confident she could fly it, but she was worried about the landing. The officer in charge told her not to worry because he would talk her down on the radio.

She had a ball in the P-39, finding out what it could do, but when it came time for landing, the radio went dead. Wondering if it was some kind of test, she analyzed her situation. She took the aircraft through a series of stalls to find out the best landing speed, then made her ap-

P-39. Wall touched down right at the tip of the runway, made a very nice landing, but wasn't able to stop the airplane until there were only a few feet left at the rear of the runway.

Happy to have made it, she saw a Jeep scream up to her plane and the officer jumped out. "Hell of a landing, Wall," he said. "But why didn't you use your flaps?"

came to a sad end when the Army decided to disband its WASP program in December 1944. The main reason given for canceling the women's program was that there were plenty of pilots coming home from Europe and the Pacific who had served their tours and could do the work the women were doing.

"They just said, 'Thank you, girls,' and that was it. It broke our hearts."

DIVE BOMBER

Wall's dive to within 50 feet of some gunnery trainees was captured by a cartoonist.

AT LAS VEGAS

Betty Wall and seven of her fellow trainees volunteered for service at the gunnery school in Las Vegas. Wall, at the left, had just arrived back from a mission and was the only one in slacks.

Despite the amazing work the WASPs did in a critical phase of the war, they were never considered an official part of the military. They never were granted commissions, and they never had insurance.

When a female pilot was killed — and 38 died during the war — their families had to pay the cost of shipping the body home. If the family couldn't afford it, the other female pilots chipped in for the burial costs.

Wall found herself back at home in Faribault without a job. "And I'll tell you that after flying a B-17, that 65-horse Cub wasn't much of a challenge anymore."

Wall was now qualified with a commercial license, and she was checked out on many planes, including seaplanes and four-engined planes. She could also do instrument flying.

She tried for a job at Northwest Airlines. "I had all the credentials, but it was too early for female pilots. They offered me a job in the front office, but I told them what they could do with it."

Back home, Wall estimates she had

15 jobs in two years as she tried unsuccessfully to fit back into civilian life. Eventually she married a hometown boy, and they had five children together.

Later, she ran for registrar of deeds in Rice County, but lost the election. Looking back, she says it was a blessing. She eventually moved to New York, where she worked as a researcher for the American Cancer Society.

She traveled to 26 states and did studies for more than nine years. She eventually came back to Farib-

BIG NEWS

Liz Strohfus shared a program with Tom Brokaw during Hormel Spam Days in 2002.

HER FIRST AIRPLANE

Wall leans against the Piper Cub that she learned to fly in the late 1930s.

HER SECOND LIFE

Liz Strohfus loves to tell of her days as a WASP pilot.

ault, where she's lived since 1979.

Elizabeth Wall Strohfus married three times and was widowed three times. She has five children and many grandchildren.

She says she doesn't harbor any hard feelings over the way the Army Air Force ended the program, or treated the WASPs while the program was going.
"I have no regrets. I just feel lucky that I got to fly."

In 1979, with the help of Senator Barry Goldwater, and, after years of work by Gen. Hap Arnold, Eleanor Roosevelt, and Jacqueline Cochran, founder of the WASPs, the women were finally recognized by Congress as veterans.

They were issued DD 214s and given all veterans' benefits. Strohfus, who had been active in the Auxiliary, including as Third District president, then became active in the Faribault American Legion.

Since her "discovery" in 1991, Wall-Strohfus has been in continuous motion, speaking at schools, air shows, and dozens of other places. She's a member of the Eighth Air Force Association and an honorary member of that group's historical society. She's also a member of the Commemorative Air Force.

She loves talking to Air Force veterans. "They're all such darlings, such great people. I like to give them all a hug. I figure there's safety in numbers."

Strohfus has traveled to 22 states with her slide show, and she loves talking to school kids. "I tell them that, unless it's illegal or immoral, they should do everything they can to pursue their dream."

For several years she wore her authentic service uniform to give talks, but it eventually wore out. Now she wears a replica to the sessions.

She said she has had little trouble relating to high school kids who are often considered a tough audience. "I've never found a group that I can't interact with."

She has shared a dais with Tom Brokaw, flown an F-16, and had

Barry Goldwater do a blurb for her autobiography, a book her son helped put together. She has no plans of letting up. "I might have to slow down at some point, just to see how old I really am."

ARMY PILOT

Betty Wall donned her flight jacket and silk scarf for this photo in 1944.

ALL THE WAY
TO THE TOP

John Vessey joined the Minnesota National Guard in 1939 in part because he was promised he'd get to ride on a motorcyle. He had a splendid war record and was an officer by the time the 34th Division came home after World War II. He wasn't done yet, though. He later rose to the highest post in the United States military echelon.

John William Vessey Jr. was born in 1922 and grew up in Lakeville, Minnesota, when it was still a small town of 500 or so.

His dad worked for the Minneapolis, Northfield and Southern Railway, usually called the Dan Patch Line in those days. A World War I veteran, Vessey's father helped establish the Veterans of Foreign Wars Post in Lakeville.

With the Great Depression gripping the nation, Vessey's family moved to Minneapolis when he was in the ninth grade. He attended Roosevelt High School where he was captain of the swim team.

In May 1939, while still in high school and with a little creative math when putting down his age, he enlisted in the Minnesota National Guard.

"It was pretty clear that Europe was getting ready to blow up, but that's really not why I joined the Guard. It was an opportunity for a little adventure, to do something different. Plus, they promised me I'd get to ride a motorcycle if I joined up."

By the following summer, it was clear that Minnesota's 34th "Red Bull" Infantry Division was going to be called up. "They didn't call us until February, 1941, but we knew long in advance that it was going to happen."

Vessey had been working as a package wrapper at the Sears, Roebuck outlet on Lake Street in Minneapolis. "I was making about 25 cents an hour, or some astronomical wage like that. I didn't think there was any use in starting college, knowing that we would be leaving soon."

The men marched from the Minneapolis Armory to the Milwaukee Road Depot. It was 20 degrees below zero.

It was warmer at Camp Claiborne, Louisiana, their destination. "We were organizing the division, and draftees were coming in to fill the ranks. We weren't anywhere near war time strength."

There was no basic training at that point. "All the training was inside the unit. Draftees went directly to the divisions."

Vessey inched his way up the ranks with a promotion to corporal. He also changed jobs from a surveyor to a radio operator. "There was more money in it."

At a training inspection, the sergeant in charge of the radio unit failed the test.

"They asked me if I wanted to be in charge of the unit, and I told them I really didn't know that much about radios. They handed me Field Man-

ual 24-5 and said on Monday morning they were going to give me an exam. They said if you pass, you'll be a sergeant. If you fail, you'll be a private. I spent all weekend with that manual working on those things. On Monday, I managed to pass."

Vessey was serving in the Headquarters unit of the 59th Field Artillery Brigade of the 34th Division. On December 7, 1941, he and his comrades listened to the news about Pearl Harbor on the radio in the day room.

"I think it was a shock for everyone. If you followed the news, you knew something was coming. I had splurged and got a subscription to Time magazine, and I tried to keep up on world events. It was a shock, though, that they bombed Pearl Harbor. It wasn't a shock that we were in the war."

On December 8, the division was

sent to the Gulf Coast near New Orleans to guard the beaches. Knowing an assignment overseas was imminent, the division sent half its men home on leave, and when they came back the other half was sent.

"I had a date for New Year's Eve, but then I got a message that the men at Camp Claiborne had already been loaded on a train." Taking a taxi from the railroad station, Vessey arrived to find the camp deserted. He was told he might still catch the division at Oakdale, Louisiana. He hopped back in the cab and set off for that rendezvous.

"I made it, but that taxi bill exhausted every single dime I had."

The 34th went overseas on the British ship Aquitania as part of a huge convoy. "This was early 1942, and the Germans were sinking Allied shipping in great numbers at that point. We watched ships in our

convoy disappear."

The unit, the first American division brought over to Europe, was sent to Northern Ireland. "Don't ask me why. I guess the idea was to reinforce the European Theater early on."

In September 1942, Vessey was promoted to first sergeant of his company. "At the same time, the Army decided that all first sergeants would be master sergeants, and so I got a double jump in pay and rank on the same day."

At age 20, he may have been the youngest first sergeant in the Army. "I suppose I was tough, you had to be tough. But we really had a good outfit. The company was loaded with guys from Minnesota, Wisconsin, North Dakota and South Dakota. They were hard-working, and they were smart. I only remember one court martial the whole period of

«

JOHN VESSEY

At the dedication of the war memorial at the new University of Minnesota football field

»

DURING THE WAR

Vessey started out as a private, but earned an officer's commission during World War II.

GOING TO WAR

The 34th Division got ready to go to war. The division was mainly made up of National Guardsmen from Minnesota and neighboring states. Vessey is the soldier in the second row, in the middle, behind the shorter soldier with the cocked hat.

World War II in our battery, and that guy was from Texas."

The division eventually took part in the American invasion of North Africa, landing near Oran. The division moved by truck across Algeria into Tunisia.

"We got there in February of 1943, just before Rommel's big attack. We were assigned to the French 19th Corps. The troops were fed into the battle as they arrived, and it was a big mess."

The 34th, like other American divisions, did not fare well in early encounters with the battle-hardened Germans. "We had German tanks running all over the place, plus the Germans had a lot of air support in those days. We were in all kinds of trouble.

"It was a lesson for all of us. We were well-trained, but we were not trained for the war we came to fight. It was a lot harder than our leaders had envisioned.

"Plus, we were miserably equipped

for that war. We had just got rid of our World War I helmets before we got there. We were still using a lot of World War I equipment. Our radios were from the early 1930s. We were really using vintage technology.

"Still we fought well. We fought a lot better than the history books give us credit for."

His job as a first sergeant was demanding. "My main job was to keep the troops alive, make sure they got fed, make sure we were getting replacements, and to get my tail chewed for everything that didn't work."

At Hill 609, a major victory for the division and the Allied forces, Vessey recalled another side of the battle

crossed the Volturno River I don't know how many times."

By Christmas 1943, the Allies had reached Cassino, and early the next year, the 34th Division was the first

"Who knows what happened. I got called back to headquarters with four or five other guys. They told me they wanted to make me a second lieutenant. There didn't seem to be

---

"They told me they wanted to make me a second lieutenant. There didn't seem to be any way to say no."

---

that didn't make the history books. "The night before, they handed out the Atabrine tablets, and they made sure that we all took them. The next day, there were more guys sick from that than there were casualties from the Germans."

The Allies pushed the Germans out of Africa, and the 34th was encamped along the Mediterranean Sea near Bizerte. German air power was still strong at that point, though, and Vessey was wounded during a German bombing attack that summer.

"It didn't take long for me to get over my wound, but I had another medical problem they were taking care of." Vessey had a cyst, and the Army doctors were not at their best in helping it heal.

Word got back to Vessey that if he didn't get back to his outfit soon, he'd lose his job. "I went AWOL from the convalescent camp in order to get back. For a short while, I was listed on the roll as a North Africa Campaign deserter."

In late summer of 1943, the division packed up and headed for Italy, landing at Salerno on D-Day plus five or so. The slow advance of the Americans up the boot of Italy was difficult. "It was just a long series of tough battles. We crossed and re-

to enter the famous monastery town.

Vessey's unit then was pulled back and joined the invasion at Anzio. It was there that he got his next promotion.

any way to say no.

"By this time, we'd been in war a couple of years. I knew that second lieutenants were pretty much cannon fodder. I thought it was okay to be an officer, but it wasn't like I'd just won the lottery. But I could feel

FOUR STARS

Vessey earned his fourth star in 1976, and served as commander of the Eighth Army in Korea.

ADVISING THE PRESIDENT

Part of Vessey's job as Chairman of the Joint Chiefs of Staff was to keep President Ronald Reagan informed on military developments.

some pride that they thought I was a reasonably decent soldier. We had some really good officers in our battery, and it was nice to be counted as one of those officers."

Again, the going was tough as the Americans worked their way north. "That first winter, our clothing was just marginal for the weather. There was snow and mud, wet and cold all the time. And the German shelling

and bombing added to that discomfort."

It was also difficult to move the artillery. "I saw trucks mired up to their beds in mud. We had to use bulldozers to pull things around. The Germans never left a bridge behind, so we had to ford the rivers."

Vessey's new job, with his commission, was to be a forward artillery observer. But that wasn't all. "At one

point, both our battery commander and executive officer were wounded at the same time. For all intents and purposes, I was the battery commander for some time. People just kept the army going, no matter what the table of organization said your duties were.

"I don't want to paint myself as some kind of hero. I wasn't. I just did what had to be done. We all did what had to be done."

As a forward observer, his job was to call in the shelling where it was needed, and for that you needed to read a map and be accurate. "We didn't like to have our artillery landing on ourselves."

Was it dangerous? "The casualty rates for observers were pretty high, but there wasn't any work in Italy that wasn't dangerous."

One of the ways Vessey did his job was to fly in airplanes to figure out where the artillery was needed. "It was probably the best target-acquisition system we had in those days. An eyeball observation from an aircraft gave you a great view of the battle. We did get shot at a lot. The Germans didn't like the idea that you were adjusting fire from up there."

During one flight, Vessey was able to see that an entire German division was coming down a road. The Americans on the ground, not realizing the size of the threat, sent a platoon of armored cavalry roaring down the road at the Germans.

Vessey could see from the air that the little American unit was heading for big trouble, and he tried to warn them. The planes were equipped with message bags that could be dropped to the ground troops.

"We wrote a quick message warning them and dropped it near them. There was a big orange streamer on the message bag, but the guys didn't pick it up. They just kept heading down the road at great speed.

"We dropped a second message bag, and again, they ignored it. Time was running out, and I found a pair of lineman's pliers and tied it to the third message bag. This time we

OFFICIAL PHOTO

General Vessey is the only Minnesotan to rise to the highest post in the military.

flew in really low, and we actually hit the armored car with it. This time they picked it up. The lead armored car just kept going, though, and they were immediately captured by the Germans."

As the war ended in Italy, Vessey's number came up in the lottery to be rotated home. Along the way, he was assigned to escort a trainload of German prisoners to Naples.

In Naples, he found himself one of many trying to get home. "To say there was chaos would be an understatement. There was a long line waiting for an airplane to go home." Vessey was able to get himself designated as a courier and eventually used that precedence to get an airplane seat.

Vessey remained a second lieutenant long after the war was over.

"It was a battlefield commission, and our commanding officer thought they were necessary evils. It was only a wartime emergency that forced the commissions. The 34th Division had an unwritten rule that no second lieutenants with battlefield commissions would be promoted."

In the end, Vessey went from being the youngest first sergeant in the army to perhaps the most senior second lieutenant. The pain was assuaged somewhat when the Army declared that second lieutenants with prior enlisted service would be paid the same as first lieutenants.

"After World War II, I didn't know whether to stay in or get out. I liked what I was doing." In the end, Vessey decided to stay in, and in April 1946, he was finally made a first lieutenant. The rest, as they say, is history.

He attended Army and civilian schools and rose swiftly through the ranks. In 1967, as a lieutenant colonel in Vietnam, he led his 300-man artillery unit against an all-out attack by 2,000 enemy troops. At one point he took up a grenade launcher and, from an exposed position, knocked out three enemy rocket launchers. For that action, he earned the Distinguished Service Cross.

By 1970, he was a brigadier general with assignments in Thailand and Laos. He earned his fourth star in 1976, commanded the forces in Korea, and in 1979 became the Army Vice Chief of Staff.

In 1982, President Ronald Reagan named Vessey Chairman of the Joint Chiefs of Staff, the highest military position ever attained by a Minnesotan. When he retired in 1985, he had served longer than any other person in the Army, 46 years of active duty.

His service was far from over, however, and he later led the U.S. mission to Vietnam that has resulted in the return of the remains of many servicemen who had been listed as missing in action. He still serves on various national commissions, including those looking at the national security of the United States. Vessey was honored in 1992 with the nation's highest civilian honor, the Medal of Freedom, presented by President George H.W. Bush.

Vessey also served on the commission that picked the design of the World War II Memorial in Washington D.C.

He and his wife, Avis, have two sons and a daughter, and they live in a beautiful home overlooking a lake near Garrison, Minnesota. He is planning to begin work on a book about his life.

IN KOREA

Vessey led all U.S. and United Nations forces in Korea during the late 1970s. Earlier in the decade he earned a Distinguished Service Cross for his actions in Vietnam.

September 29th 1944.

Dear Mrs. Polich:-

Tonight at 9.08 P.m.,
E.W.T., Berlin short wave radio
announced the following:

" 1/Lt. Robert Michael Polich, U.S.A.
A.F., service no. O-813418, was captured
when his plane was shot down over
Europe and he is now in a prison
camp in Germany, safe and well."

I sincerely hope the above
information will be a source of
help and encouragement to you.

Very truly yours,
Sanford Lowe

This is the 11,016th notice forwarded by
me from Tokyo and Berlin.

Unless indicated otherwise, all photos are from Bob Polich's personal collection.

AGE 23 AND FLYING
THE FORTRESSES

Bob Polich's B-17 crew needed 30 missions to earn the right to come home. On the 29th mission, however, a voice on the radio on Polich's Flying Fortress told him, "Red Leader, Red Leader, you're on fire." It was the last radio message the young pilot from Crosby, Minnesota, received during the war.

Bob Polich shook his head. "When I look at young people today," he said from his lakeside home near Deerwood, "I think of what we were doing when we were that age."

What Bob Polich was doing, was flying B-17s over Germany.

Polich, now 87, says the war was a long time ago. Still, there are things about the 29 missions he flew that are so fresh that they can bring him to tears or overwhelm him with guilt or make him laugh about the crazy things he used to do.

Polich grew up in Crosby, the largest city on the Cuyuna, the most southern of Minnesota's three iron ranges. Polich's parents had emigrated from Montenegro. His father worked in the iron mines in Michigan before moving to Minnesota.

His father was 32 when he died of pneumonia in 1931. The loss of the family's wage earner, together with the Great Depression, provided a double whammy to the Polich family as they made their way through the 1930s.

"We didn't have two pennies to rub together, but it was wonderful. It was the best time of my life," Polich said. "Everybody was poor."

Polich's mother got a $21-a-month widow's pension, and the rest of the family income came from scrambling. "We picked berries; we did whatever we could to make a nickel or a dime. But we never took welfare, not ever. We were too proud."

Polich graduated from Crosby-Ironton High School in 1939 and worked a year in a Civilian Conservation Corps camp before taking a job building a highway. He later worked in the mines, following in his father's footsteps.

That career was soon interrupted, though, when Polich got his greetings from Uncle Sam in early 1942. A few months later he was working as an anti-aircraft gunner on the California coast. His gun was perched on a cliff that later became the Torrey Pines Golf Course.

It was during this time that Polich married his high school sweetheart, Eunice. "When she was in ninth

grade, and I was in 11th grade, we started dating. She was 19, and I was 21 when we got married. We were married for 60 years, and we had five children."

The gunnery job, however, was not Polich's cup of tea. "I didn't like it. I wanted something better."

On a bulletin board on the base, Polich noticed a poster asking for

volunteers to fly airplanes. "It said you had to have two years of college education, but I lied. I took the test, and I was one of 13 guys in the whole battalion that passed."

Training began at Maxwell Field in Alabama, and the first time he went up in a Stearman trainer with an instructor was the first time Polich had ever been in an airplane.

The training went well, but ended with some disappointment. "I really wanted to be a fighter pilot, but either I wasn't good enough or they just needed more bomber pilots at that time, but I got picked for bombers."

And then there was that little problem with the two years of college. "I dodged it all the way through flight training. Every time they asked to see my paperwork, I'd say that my mother was sending it, but it was wartime you know.

"Finally, three hours before I was supposed to get my wings, the C.O. called me in. I think they realized that I'd never been to college. He used as much foul language as I've ever heard, but in the end he said the government had too much money invested in me to wash me out now."

"I knew a cadet wasn't supposed to lie, but I had. Later that day I got my wings."

B-17 training was in Florida, Georgia and Arkansas. During that time, Polich was given his crew — basically the same crew he would have with him through training and combat missions in Europe.

The B-17, or Flying Fortress, was a huge, four-engined bomber with a crew of 10. In addition to the pilot and copilot, there were two other officers, the navigator and bombardier. The six non-coms included

a radio man, two waist gunners, a tail gunner, a ball turret gunner and a top turret gunner.

The crew was supposed to fly the plane to England, but the Fortress developed an oil problem after the flight to New York. Instead the 10 young men were put aboard the HMS Queen Elizabeth, a luxury liner that had been converted into a troop ship.

For Polich and his officers, it was still pretty swanky. "We shared a stateroom and got to eat in the nice dining room — white tablecloths. It was very luxurious. We were enjoying it a lot while there were 18,000 servicemen down below who didn't have it so nice."

The crew arrived in Chelveston, England, and joined the 305th Bomb Group, part of the 8th Air Force.

Polich's first mission, as might be expected for a rookie, was as tail-

«

BOB POLICH

At home in Deerwood

»

DURING THE WAR

Polich was a 23-year-old B-17 pilot who almost completed his 30 missions in Europe.

FLYING FORTRESS

Boeing's B-17 became the workhorse of the Army Air Corps during World War II, dropping more bombs than any other aircraft. It was able to carry large payloads long distances, and it could defend itself with 13 stratigically placed machine guns.

end Charlie in the massive formation of bombers. The mission went all right until it was over.

"After we landed, the tail gunner jumped out of the plane and ran away. He went berserk. So we had to get a new tail gunner."

The 305th flew three times on D-Day, June 6, 1944. "We arrived just before the troops landed. Our job was to bomb the beach and make foxholes for the guys landing on the beach. I remember looking down and seeing those thousands of ships down there. I felt sorry for those guys landing. They were getting slammed while we were flying overhead with no opposition. Nothing."

Later that day, Polich dropped bombs on the German positions just a few miles inland, and then, on the third mission, the B-17s targeted German positions about a hundred miles inland.

The missions began to pile up, and Polich was promoted to squad leader after his 13th mission, group leader after his 21st mission, and wing leader after his 27th mission.

"You know, I really wasn't a very good officer, but, dammit, I was a good pilot. I knew every rivet on that airplane, and the men trusted me."

Polich said he had great relations with his crew, and sometimes would sneak off to drink at the non-commissioned officers club rather than the officers club, which he found a little bit stuffy.

"I also wanted to know every job on the plane, and so I would let the copilot take the controls, and I'd go back and do every job back there until I knew them."

The ball turret, attached to the bottom of the plane, was perhaps the most difficult, especially for the long-legged Polich. Usually small men were picked for the job because the turret was cramped and claustrophobic.

"Somehow I got in there, with my knees up by my chin. The SOBs in the plane thought it would be a great joke, so they pulled the electric plug. I couldn't move the turret, and I couldn't get out.

"I chewed on them like crazy when they finally let me out, but I have to

admit I was scared shitless. I had a whole new respect for that kid down in that damn bubble."

Polich said the job was so terrifying that the gunner would urinate in his pants on nearly every mission. "And then he'd freeze to the seat; it was so cold down there. He didn't even know he was doing it."

As 1944 went on, Polich said he was lucky to keep his commission. "I should have been court-martialed so many times. I was

B-17
Flying Fortress Statistics

B-17 Data

Manufacturer
Boeing

Engines
Four Wright R-1820-97 "Cyclone" turbosupercharged radial engines, 1,200 horsepower each

Crew
Ten

Armament
Thirteen .50-caliber M-2 Browning machine guns. Weapons bay could carry 8,000 pounds of bombs on a short mission or 4,500 pounds on a long-range mission

Maximum Speed
287 miles per hour. Cruise speed was 182 miles per hour

Ceiling
35,600 feet

Range, loaded
2,000 miles

lucky because the colonel at the base liked me. He thought I was good pilot. But I was a bad boy."

Polich recalled four incidents he said should have ended his Army ca-

knocked him to the ground."

Polich went back to his room and was soon visited by the MPs again, asking him to report to the commanding officer. "I took a shower,

"He chewed me up one side and down the other. He wasn't so mad that I had cut off his tie, but that he was embarrassed because he was escorting a pretty nurse that night.

"What could I do? I hit him. I knocked him to the ground."

---

reer prematurely.

The first was on the Fourth of July, 1944, when he told his men to take the flares out of the plane and use them for fireworks to celebrate Independence Day. "Pretty soon the MPs were there asking that I go see the C.O. He said, 'Polich, what the hell are you doing? Not only did you take the flares out of the airplane, but the whole base is under blackout."

The second incident happened after Polich's bomber was hit on a bombing run. "One engine was out, and I couldn't get the other one to feather. I told the leader that I'd have to drop out and get back the best way I could. We radioed for our little friends to provide some support, but they never showed up. We radioed again for fighters, but nothing.

"Finally, over the channel, they came out of the clouds and were doing barrel rolls all around us. They had been there all the time, but didn't want to give our position away by using the radio.

"When I landed, I went in to be debriefed. The maintenance officer started chewing me out. I was still trembling from the mission, and this guy was bawling me out for using too many RPMs and manifold pressure on the other engines.

"What could I do? I hit him. I

put on my Class As, and went to see the colonel.

"The major I hit was there, and the side of his face was all red and blue. The colonel asked him what he had done, and he said that he was chewing me out for abusing the engines. Then he asked me what I had done.

"I said, 'I brought home that ship and those 10 men on board.' "

"The colonel turned to the maintenance officer and said, "Major, your job is to fix those frigging airplanes. Let my boys fly them."

The third incident in Polich's bad-boy career happened when he got tired of the fighters always buzzing the bombers' field. "So I came across their field about 10 feet off the deck. Well, of course, they got the number of my airplane."

Pretty soon the MPs were at the door requesting Polich's presence at the commanding officer's room. "All I could tell him was that I was tired of the fighter pilots showing off, and that we four-engined guys can do some flying too. He let me off."

Incident four was when one of Polich's buddies, after several libations at the officer's club, dared Polich to cut off the commanding officer's tie. The next morning, the MPs were at Polich's room, and, well, you know the rest.

He punished me by making me buy a $25 war bond."

In the end, Polich's leadership in the cockpit, and not his antics outside it, allowed him to keep his job.

"The other pilots loved to follow me because they knew I could fly. I didn't go by the book. For instance, I'd never make sharp turns because I had flown as tail-end Charlie, and I know how hard it is to keep up with the formation back there. I'd make long, sloping turns that they could follow."

The crew's day began with reveille before daybreak, followed by pre-flight briefings. The planes would take off, assemble in the sky, then head out over the English Channel. Once they got to the Initial Point, they would turn toward the target that day. Polich would steer the plane through the flak and shells until just before the target, then turn it over to the bombardier, who would control the final minute of the flight in.

"I just sat back until the bombs were dropped. You could feel the plane lurch as they went out. I would then take over the ship again and run like hell home."

As the months went by, Polich's B-17 was often hit by flak. On one mission, the plane took a major hit, and several of the crew were

THE CREW

The crew of "Reich's Ruin" posed for a picture before a mission. Standing, left to right, are Sgt. Arthurs, waist gunner; Lt. Sorenstrom, bombardier; Lt. Neufeld, navigator; Polich; Lt. Trathen, copilot; Sgt. Garisam, top turret gunner. Kneeling are Sgt. Coleman, tail gunner; Sgt. Anderson, waist gunner; Sgt. Morrison, ball turret gunner; Sgt. Simpson, radio.

wounded, one severely.

"As I approached the field, we sent out flares. That let them know we had wounded on board, and we had priority to land. They would also send out the ambulances.

"When I got on the ground, I steered the plane over to the ambulances. I quickly got out through the nose hatch and went running around to where they were lowering the wounded crew out of the side of the plane. I was helping to lower one of the men down, and I could see he was trying to say something to me. His lips were moving, but nothing was coming out. I was holding his head in my arms. Finally, he was able to say, 'mama,' and then he died, right in my arms.

"To this day, whenever I think about it, I start to cry."

On another mission a piece of flak came through the plane and hit Polich on his left hand. "I thought something had happened, but I didn't know what. Finally I took my glove off, and it was full of blood. I never reported it, though, because I didn't want to get grounded.

"I remember another time when my navigator got hit in the head by a piece of flak, and he had blood drip-ping down his face. He thought that was really funny, and he was laughing about it. That's one thing about Americans. No matter how bad it gets, they always find some humor in it.

"We were so young. God, we were just kids."

Polich and his crew were required to fly 30 missions to complete their tour. They flew 29.

The final mission was to the Leona Oil Works inside Germany on August 24, 1944. "It was one of the biggest refineries in Germany, and it was well-protected. They were shooting the hell out of us. I was the wing leader, and so I had 105 planes following me in. My regular copilot wasn't there because I had the wing colonel with me to help direct the mission. He was flying copilot.

"When we came over the target, it was obliterated with smoke from a previous bombing run. We couldn't drop our bombs. I told the colonel, 'I didn't come all this way to drop on a secondary target,' so he allowed me to take all 105 of those planes around again in a slow turn over Munich and come over the target again.

"Then we got a message, 'Red Leader, you're on fire.' I looked out, and there was a big hole between the number-one and number-two engines. I could see some mist spraying out, and I knew it must be gasoline.

"The colonel allowed me to keep leading the wing in, but again we got the radio message, 'Red Leader, you are on fire.' I looked out again and there was a huge ball of flame that must have reached out a hundred yards. I radioed for the deputy leader to take over the mission, and I put the ship into a steep dive, trying to extinguish the flame.

"I dove down 3,000 feet, but I looked, and we were still on fire. That's when I gave the order to bail out."

The crew's four officers used the nose hatch on the B-17 to leave the plane. Polich was the last to exit.

"Whenever I flew, I wore my parachute loose because it was more comfortable that way. So, when it came time to bail out, I clipped it up, but the harness was loose. When the shoot opened, it just split me. It pulled my pelvic bones apart.

"That was the first time I was ever frightened — in the air, coming down in that parachute. There was just complete silence. I tried to bring my legs up, but they wouldn't move. That's when I figured out I was hurt.

"When I hit the ground in a pasture, my legs were dead, and so they couldn't absorb any of the shock, and so I fractured my three lower vertebrae. The neighbors around there were so happy to see me come down that they came over and beat the hell out of me. I woke up a couple days later in the city jail."

The German guards interrogated Polich and threatened to take him out in the woods and shoot him. Eventually an air officer came by and offered Polich a cigarette, an American Camel.

"I have to say that the German fliers were the finest of people. They all seemed to know English, and they would talk to us on our missions. They were not at all brutal like those ground troops down there."

After the air officer's visit, Polich was taken by truck to a hospital nearby. He was to spend the next five months there, nursed by another prisoner of war.

"I remember when I first got to that hospital, they cleaned me up. That was wonderful. Then, while I was still naked, they put me through the X-ray machine. There were three technicians running that machine, and they were all female. I recall that they were all giggling."

Polich was flat on his back for three months, then was finally able to get around on crutches. When he was able to walk on his own, he was transferred to Stalag Luft 3, a prisoner camp for airmen located in Poland.

His stay there was fairly short. On January 14, the prisoners could hear the German guns firing at the approaching allies. The men were taken out of the camp and in 30-degree-below-zero weather were marched back into Germany. "All I really can remember is looking at the feet of the man in front of me crunching in the snow."

Eventually the men reached a rail head, where they were transferred to trains for their journey to Stalag 7-A just outside Munich.

Polich's main memory of the stay in the camp was the kohlrabi, or turnip, soup. "It's the only damn soup the Germans knew how to make."

WEAPONS OF WAR

Polich and his squadron co-captain lean on the kind of bombs they carried on missions.

By April, the 14th Armored Division liberated the camp. Polich remembers the appearance of Gen. George Patton. "He had stars all over him. I'll bet he had stars on his underwear. What was strange was that when he spoke, he had a very feminine voice. But could he swear. He had the foulest mouth of any soldier I ever heard."

The men were put on a train heading west. Polich was put in charge of a group of about 22 men and was given the keys to a car on the train that contained the food for the ex-POWs. "But we never had to unlock that car because every time we stopped, the Red Cross or somebody was there to give us hot food."

When the train reached Paris, Polich used his skills in delegation and had one of the non-coms take over the group of men on their way to the ships at Le Havre. Meanwhile, Polich and a couple of officer buddies took some time to visit the City of Light.

Polich eventually did make it back to the United States on a new Liberty ship that docked in New York. "They told us we had to stay overnight on the ship. Some of the guys jumped in the water and swam ashore, but I didn't."

He was processed out at Fort Snelling, and was examined by the Army doctors. He later got treatment through the VA but was not satisfied with the diagnosis. He eventually had surgery on his back at the University of Minnesota at his own expense.

Also, when he got home, he learned of another tragedy. On that last flight, because he was the wing leader, the copilot's seat was taken by the wing's colonel. The copilot had to fly with someone else that day and was killed.

"His son would never speak to me after that. He blamed me for the fact his father didn't fly with me that day."

Polich had thoughts at one time of getting into pre-med at the University of Minnesota, but had to abandon that idea because of the expense. He did pass the test to get into the program.

Back home on the Cuyuna Range, he bought a building in downtown Ironton for $900 and opened a bar. After five years, he sold it. "There were a lot of guys coming home from the war, and there was some brawling going on. My family was getting bigger, and it was not the right kind of business for that."

Polich then built a supper club, "but the people on the Range weren't ready for white tablecloths and candles, and I went broke. He later converted it into a private club, the Sportsman's Club and Restaurant, a business he retired from in the late 1980s.

Polich's wife, Eunice, died a few years ago.

Late in life, Polich had to work his way through some severe delayed-onset Post-Traumatic Stress Disorder. "I saw some pictures of kids killed from a bombing mission, and it just set me off. I just went crazy." After several counseling sessions, Polich is now able to deal with the trauma. "The doctor told me to quit hunting and never kill anything again. And that's what I did. I wouldn't even kill a squirrel now. I gave away all my guns."

Polich lives along Serpent Lake near Deerwood.

During his time in the war, Polich earned a Distinguished Flying Cross, three Bronze Stars, an Air Medal and a Purple Heart. In a strange event, one day Polich received a Distinguished Service Cross, the second-highest award in the military, in the mail from a government office. There was no paperwork with it, and though Polich tried to find out what it was all about, he never was able to learn why it was sent to him. He kept it as a souvenir.

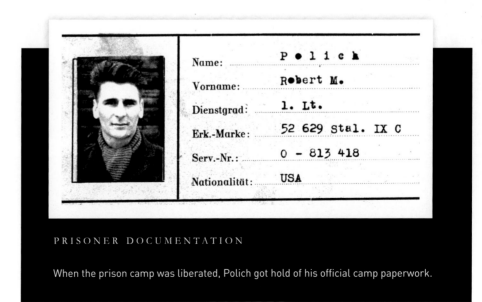

PRISONER DOCUMENTATION

When the prison camp was liberated, Polich got hold of his official camp paperwork.

ARMY BEARDS
On Sicily in 1942, a group of GIs posed with their new beards, gained by bending the rules a little bit. Winfred Polzin is at right.

Unless indicated otherwise, all photos are from Winfred Polzin's personal collection.

EXERCISE TIGER

Winfred Polzin was on the tank deck of a landing ship when it was hit by a German torpedo in the spring of 1944 during a training exercise off the coast of England. When the ship was abandoned, Polzin found himself swimming in 42-degree water. Nearly 750 Americans died in the incident, the worst training loss in U.S. history.

In the dark of a moonless night in late April 1944, nine German E-boats launched a devastating torpedo attack on a convoy of American landing ships which were doing a training run off the coast of England.

Two of the landing ships were sunk, and a third hobbled into port. In all, 749 American soldiers and sailors died in the attack, the worst loss ever in an American training exercise.

In the days following, not one word of the military disaster ever appeared in the press. The invasion at Normandy was slated for just over a month away, and Allied leaders clamped down a wall of secrecy.

And, while there has been no official cover-up, the tragedy off the coast of southern England has never become well known in military or history annals. You'll rarely find an account of it in any World War II history books.

One Minnesotan, though, knows all about the attack and its aftermath. When the Germans hit LST 507 that morning, Sgt. Winfred Polzin of Bra-

ham, Minnesota, was in the hold of the ship. He was one of the few that got out.

Nearly 60 years later, his memory of that night is vivid.

The training operation he remembers was called Exercise Tiger.

Polzin grew up on a farm in South Dakota. He attended the Brookings Agricultural School, and in 1938 he moved with his family to Minnesota. In the midst of the Great Depression, his family had lost their farm near Watertown.

Polzin's father rented a farm near Braham, and young Winfred worked at a variety of farming operations in the next couple of years.

On December 7, 1941, Polzin heard the news about Pearl Harbor on the radio. He knew his days as a civilian were numbered.

"The farmer I was working for said he would try to get me deferred, but I said no. All the other guys were going in, and I decided I might as well go in, too."

It didn't take long for that draft notice to appear. On January 23, 1942, Polzin was sworn into the U.S. Army at Fort Snelling. He was soon on his way to Fort Francis, Wyoming, for training.

"We weren't there very long — they were pushing us out pretty fast." Polzin was sent to Texas for motorcycle maintenance school. "It had been very cold in Wyoming, and we arrived on the train on a Sunday in Texas with our overcoats on. All the

guys there were sitting around wearing T-shirts. They must have wondered where these guys came from."

The young mechanics were not only learning about their two-wheelers, they took them for a spin now and then. "I wrote home that the first thing I'm going to do when the war is over is buy a motorcycle. But I never did."

In August, realizing that with the advent of the Jeep, the need for motorcycle mechanics was probably not great, the Army shipped the outfit overseas on the USS Manhattan for training in Ireland. Polzin was assigned to a supply company.

The company was sent to Africa soon after the invasion in 1942, and the unit was one of the first in the war to take charge of a new vehicle the Army called an amphibious truck or a DUKW — or more infor-

mally a "duck."

The amphibious trucks had to be driven across the Sahara Desert to prepare for the invasion of Sicily. "It was 120 degrees out there. Oh, my goodness it was hot. You couldn't even touch the trucks."

The new trucks had an amazing feature: letting air out of the tires allowed the trucks to be driven right over the desert. "You couldn't even walk in that sand, but we could go 30 or 40 miles an hour through it. In later models, you could control the air pressure from the driver's seat. There was a built-in air compressor. If a tire got hit by a bullet, you could pump enough air pressure into that one tire to keep it inflated until you got where you were going."

The unit practiced with the DUKWs and then took part in the landings at Sicily. "We were hauling everything: ammunition, gasoline, artillery

shells, rations, you name it."

After the capture of the island, the supply company next landed in Italy and Polzin was assigned to be a truck driver bringing supplies to American troops in the treacherous Italian mountains.

"We really had to learn to drive. There was a lot of night driving, and we only had those little black-out lights. When we first started out, when we got to the sharp turns on the mountains, we'd have to do part of the turn, back up, and then do the rest. After a while, though, we'd just make the turn with our tires right on the edge of the road. Sometimes you'd meet a convoy coming the other way, and the roads were so narrow that you'd actually brush the other trucks as they went by. Whooooooosh."

Polzin's unit was pulled out of Italy at the end of 1943 to prepare for the

«

WINFRED POLZIN

At home in Cambridge

»

DURING THE WAR

Polzin drove and later was in charge of amphibious vehicles, known in Army parlance as "ducks."

invasion of France. The Army company ate Thanksgiving dinner aboard a Navy transport en route to southern England.

Polzin was now assigned to the 478th Amphibious Truck Company of the First Engineer Special Brigade based near Devon, England. The unit was not assigned to a division.

"The English people were mostly happy to see us. They knew they needed help to win the war. I talked with one English soldier who had been at Dunkirk. He said that after Dunkirk he walked the beaches of the English Channel on patrol with five rounds in his rifle. He said if the Germans had invaded England, they couldn't have stopped them."

A lot of the practice was getting the DUKWs into and out of the LSTs, which in Navy parlance was "Landing Ship, Tank," but in Army lingo was "Large Stationary Target."

By this time, Polzin had advanced up the Army ladder and was a sergeant in charge of 42 men and 35 amphibious trucks. He didn't have to drive anymore, only tell others how, when and where to do it.

Slapton Sands on the southern coast of England was picked for Exercise Tiger because it resembled Utah Beach, the ultimate destination of the 478th Amphibious Truck Company and a good share of the rest of the invasion force.

There had been several other exercises as the Navy and Army learned to coordinate the massive landings. Exercise Tiger was the largest to that point, and it included real shelling of the beach. There were 300 ships, 30,000 men and 30 LSTs involved in the operation.

"I was unfortunate enough to be in the last ship in the convoy," Polzin recalled. He also was in one of the

last of the 22 DUKWs that was brought aboard LST 507 that day. The trucks were among the last that would be landed in that day's exercise, about 24 hours after the initial landing.

The German E-boats, similar to American PT boats, got wind of the training exercise and sent a group of nine boats to the area outside Slapton Sands. "They knew something was going on, and they came out to see what it was."

They found a group of American LSTs that seemed to be unprotected. There was a British corvette, a small destroyer, assigned as an escort, but it wasn't in position to prevent the attack. Another escort had returned to port because of some damage.

Besides the lack of escorts, the American convoy was also doomed by a mistake in assigning radio fre-

DUKW CREW

DUKWs were used to bring supplies to the beach during invasions. They could leave a landing ship while still at sea, propel themselves to the beach, then drive up on the beach to where their payload was needed.

quencies. When a report was given on the approach of the E-boats, the British commanders didn't pass it along because they thought the American ships were on the same frequency. They weren't.

At 1:30 in the morning of April 28, LST 507's officers were concerned enough about a possible attack that they sounded general quarters.

Polzin at that moment was in the hold, or what is called the "tank deck" of the LST. He wasn't supposed to be there. "Most of the other men were topside where they had been ordered. I was disobeying orders by staying with the trucks."

When the general quarters sounded, Polzin watched a sailor come and batten down the hatch, or doorway, that led to the top levels of the ship. "He used a big pipe to really fasten that door down tight. He wasn't fooling around."

LANDING AT UTAH BEACH

As the DUKWs came ashore at Normandy, they brought their supplies with them.

tighten it with that pipe, and I had to open it with my bare hands. I don't know where I got the strength, but I did it."

Reaching the upper deck, Polzin could see the raging fire at the rear

dered the ship abandoned. Polzin climbed down the cargo net to the water. "There were lifeboats, but I didn't see them. If I had, I'd have been in one."

> "There were lifeboats, but I didn't see one. If I had, I would have been in one."

Another half-hour went by, and nothing happened. At 2:03 a.m., a deafening explosion rocked the ship. A torpedo had hit amidships on the starboard side. "I was in the forward part of the tank deck, and I looked down at the stern, and it was all on fire. I saw guys standing on the DUKWs with the fire all around. I'm sure those guys never got out."

Polzin and one other soldier were the only ones still in the forward section of the deck, and their only exit was through the hatch that had just been closed. "I had watched him

of the LST. The power had been knocked out by the explosion, and there was no way to control the conflagration. It was clear the ship was doomed.

"I could see guys floating all over the place, but I didn't want to go over the side yet. They hadn't yet announced 'abandon ship.' " Polzin had time to talk things over with a small group of men and also to wrap his wristwatch in a waterproof container.

Finally, at about 2:30 a.m., a sailor told the soldiers the captain had or-

"It was very crowded going over the side, and guys were screaming and hollering. It was the only time I've ever seen that kind of panic. Guys were running around the deck, and they'd hit the chains that were used to tie down the Jeeps and down they'd go. It had to hurt, but they'd just get up and start running and screaming again."

As soon as Polzin got in the water, he was grabbed by another soldier. "He had me around the head, and he was dragging us both down. I knew I had to get free from him, and I kicked him away. When we came up, I saw his life belt floating a few feet away. It must have come off him when he jumped in the water. I swam a few feet and got it for him, but when I turned around he was gone.

"I'm sure glad I didn't know that guy. That would have been even worse. But I can still see him just like it was all happening right now. I'll never forget that."

The water was about 42 degrees, and there were no American ships nearby to save the floating survivors. "I'm sure that most of the guys who died were killed by hypothermia."

Polzin estimates he was in the water for an hour, maybe longer. Daylight was just beginning to break when LST 515 approached the

scene. "I was told later that the skipper of that LST had been ordered to head back to port, but he disobeyed orders to come and get us. I heard later that he was court-martialed."

The men in the water were helped up the cargo nets to the deck of the LST. "I was so cold, I couldn't even close my hands anymore."

The men were told to take off their clothes and wrap themselves with blankets. There were 244 survivors out of about one thousand men on the two LSTs that were sunk.

LST 531, a sister ship of the one Polzin was on, sank so fast after it was torpedoed that only 40 of the 600 men aboard survived.

"When we were leaving the ship, we had to find whatever clothes we could. I grabbed a sailor's pants and

shoes, but a lot of guys only had their blankets. When we got to the beach, there we were, marching along, some guys only wearing a blanket and no underwear."

They were taken to a nearby hospital.

"They had instructed the hospital people not to talk to us. They wanted to keep the whole thing a secret. They didn't want the Germans to know what kind of damage they did to us.

"But by noon, we were pretty hungry. We hadn't eaten in a long time, and many of the guys had thrown up what they had eaten. I approached one of the nurses and asked her what we could eat. She looked at me and said, 'Lunch is over.' And that was that. She didn't dare say another word."

OPEN WIDE

When the LST opened its big bow doors, the amphibious vehicles could launch, or, later on, be taken back on board.

SUPPLY DUMP

The Army stockpiled goods at Utah Beach as the invasion moved inland.

The army transported the 244 survivors to a house. "But there was
nothing there, only an empty house.
The Red Cross heard about us,
though, and came and got us. They
brought us to one of their R&R facilities and gave us shoes and socks
and shaving gear and toothpaste —
everything we needed. We finally got
some food. They had big tables laid
out with all kinds of food."

The 244 men were now under the
protection of the Red Cross and not
the Army. As good soldiers will do
when given the chance, they spent
the weekend heading into town for
some recreation.

"For three days we could go anywhere we wanted, but then the Army
heard about us. They came and got
us and brought us back to a camp
barracks and told us we couldn't
talk to anybody. If we went to the
store, we had to have an armed
guard go with us. When we went to
eat, we had guards with us."

The men were finally sent back to
their units. The 478th Amphibious

BOOT CAMP INSTRUCTOR

Polzin, second from right in front, completed his duty stateside as a basic training instructor.

Truck Company had lost 28 men and many of its trucks in the attack. Replacements and trucks had to be ready for D-Day on June 6.

The irony of the series of events was that the company took no casualties in the landing on Utah Beach. In fact, more Americans were lost in Exercise Tiger than were lost on D-Day at Utah Beach.

Polzin's company spent the following weeks ferrying supplies from the ships to the supply dumps at Utah Beach. When larger ports were finally opened, the company was given the job of cleaning up the beach. "We were even assigned German prisoners to help fix the trucks and to do other work. I was in great demand because I could speak German."

In January 1945, the company was sent home. "They just didn't have much use for amphibious trucks any more. There were no more invasions planned."

Polzin ended up at Fort Lewis, Washington, as a boot camp instructor. "It was good duty. The young guys who were in camp had a lot of respect for those of us who had been overseas."

On September 4, 1945, Polzin was mustered out at Camp Randall in Wisconsin. In later years, he farmed, worked at a creamery, sold cows, and worked as an arc welder, a job he retired from in 1984.

He married his hometown sweetheart, Dallas, in 1945 while en route to his posting in Washington, and they had three daughters. Polzin has nine grandchildren and three great-grandchildren. His wife passed away some time ago.

At his home in Cambridge, Polzin creates intricately carved, wooden art objects. He is a member of the American Legion post at Pine City, and he's a three-time post commander of the VFW at Rush City. Looking back at Exercise Tiger, Polzin said there was never any doubt in his mind, even when he was in the water, that he was going to survive. "I guess I had the reputation of being pretty calm. When word got back to our company that I had been trapped on the tank deck, and I was probably dead, one of the guys said, 'No way. If Polzin's dead, I've got to see his body.' They never thought I'd get killed."

OFF TO WAR

Polzin was drafted soon after the war began.

HOMECOMING

Polzin married his sweetheart, Dallas, en route to his posting in Washington state.

OVER THE SEAS, UNDER THE SEAS

Bud Quam was on board the USS Yorktown aircraft carrier when it was sunk by a Japanese submarine at the battle of Midway. Shortly thereafter, he volunteered for the submarine service in the U.S. Navy. He served on two submarines for the rest of the war, and found out what life was like on the other side of the water's surface.

Ellsworth R. "Bud" Quam saw action in World War II from both sides of the Pacific Ocean – above the water line and below it.

Quam was aboard the carrier USS Yorktown when it was sunk by a Japanese submarine at the Battle of Midway. Switching to submarine service, he was aboard an American submarine that sunk six Japanese merchant ships and a host of smaller vessels.

Born in 1922 and a native of Willmar, Quam almost didn't survive long enough to serve in the military because of a couple of dangerous hunting episodes.

When he was 15 and out plinking with a buddy, an errant shot hit Quam in the elbow. The wound wasn't life-threatening, but the healing was a long process. In the end, Quam had to walk around with a bucket of sand in order to straighten the arm out.

Then, in 1940, Quam and his friends were out hunting when they were caught in the famous Armistice Day Blizzard, one of the major snow-

storms in the history of Minnesota. The young hunters were trapped in a whiteout but managed to find a farmer's fence and follow the fence line to a barn.

Recuperating from the first hunting incident had put Quam behind his class, and when they all graduated in 1941, Quam instead joined the Navy – signing a six-year enlistment.

After graduating from the Great Lakes Naval Training Center, Quam was sent to the East Coast, where he was assigned to the USS Yorktown, an aircraft carrier. America was not yet in the war, but U.S. ships were providing escort duty for the British convoys across the Atlantic.

Carriers, making such big targets, were not ideal for this type of duty. Adding to the difficulty were high seas in the North Atlantic that prevented the carriers from using their aircraft. "We had 100-knot winds in one storm. The water was coming over the flight deck."

Yorktown came back to Norfolk, Vir-

ginia, for a much-needed overhaul at the beginning of December 1941, but, on December 7, the Japanese bombed Pearl Harbor.

"I was out roller skating, and we heard about Pearl Harbor over the loudspeaker at the roller rink," Quam said. "They told us, all service personnel were to return to base immediately. We stopped at a bar for a quick beer on the way back, but the shore patrol were there to make sure it was really quick."

Instead of an overhaul, the Yorktown got a quick paint job and headed through the Panama Canal to become active in the Pacific theater. By February 1942, it was escorting a convoy of Marines to Samoa. Not long after, the carrier's air wing was the first to attack the Marshall and Gilbert islands.

Quam had reported aboard the carrier as a deckhand, the lowest rung on the Navy's organization ladder. He was immediately sent to the ship's kitchen, where he scrubbed pots and pans for three months.

Quam applied to be an electrician's mate and was accepted, but his new division was obliged to send somebody to the mess decks, and Quam found himself back in the scullery. "When it got wavy, it got a little slippery in the scullery. It could be an exciting place to work."

Quam spent the first six months of his shipboard experience in the scullery.

By the time of the Battle of Coral Sea in early May, Quam's battle station was as an ammunition handler for a five-inch gun. He was stationed below decks, taking the shells out of the magazine and putting them on an elevator that took them up to the gun.

"There's more terror being below decks and not knowing what's going on," Quam said. "You can hear the attack and feel the attack, but you don't know what's happening.

"First the ship goes to flank speed, and the whole thing vibrates. Then the five-inch guns start firing; that must mean the planes are in sight. Then the smaller guns start firing, and you know they're close. But you never know when you're going to get hit.

"You're scared as hell. You're really shook up over the ones that miss as well as the ones that hit you."

In the Coral Sea, the Japanese and Americans fought the first sea battle in history in which the ships never saw one another.

The USS Lexington, a sister carrier, was sunk in the battle. Yorktown took a direct hit by a bomb but was able to keep operating, although severely damaged.

« ELLSWORTH R. "BUD" QUAM

At home in West St. Paul

» DURING THE WAR

Quam was a six-footer in this official Navy photograph.

"We knew we'd been hit, but it didn't stop us. We heard the bomb had hit Repair 5 and all the guys were killed. Later on, they let us go up, a few at a time, to get some food. For me, that was a mistake. I walked into the mess decks, and they had all these guys laid out, mangled. Needless to say, my stomach wouldn't take food after that."

Yorktown limped back to Pearl Harbor, where it was expected that temporary repairs would be made in order to get the ship back to the United States for a complete overhaul. The ship had been to sea for 101 days, with only a brief stop for provisions during that time.

Admiral Chester Nimitz, commander of the Pacific Fleet, had other plans. After Navy code breakers told Nimitz that the Japanese were coming to Midway, he ordered his three remaining carriers, Hornet, Enterprise and Yorktown, to a position off the northeast coast of the island. Nimitz gave the dock workers 72 hours to get the Yorktown operational, and they did.

During those 72 hours, the ship's officers allowed the crew some liberty. "I suppose a lot of the guys got boozed up, if they could."

Heading out to sea again was not a happy thought for Yorktown's crew. "They told us that the Japanese were coming to Midway — that we were just going to repel them and then head back to the states. We were pretty disheartened."

On June 4, the Japanese fleet arrived and immediately attacked the American forces on Midway. A Navy flying boat found the enemy carriers, and the three American carriers launched their aircraft. By the end of the day, the Japanese had lost four major carriers and a cruiser — and their ability to control the high seas.

During the battle, though, the Japanese carrier Hiryu sent 18 dive bombers that found the Yorktown. Seven made it through the U.S. defenses, and three scored hits on the American carrier.

For Quam, with his station below decks, it was a repeat of the Coral Sea battle, except worse. The three bomb hits left the ship dead in the water, and when the Yorktown did get up steam and begin to move, it was hit by torpedoes from Japanese submarines.

"There was an immediate 25-degree list, and all the guys knew we were in a multi-million dollar coffin. They ordered abandon ship, and we were more than happy to open the hatches and go up on deck."

One difference for Quam in this battle was that he was wearing anti-flash coveralls. Several ammunition loaders during the Battle of the Coral Sea had been burned, and the Navy now required its ammo handlers to wear the coveralls.

Quam, whose nickname was "Whitey" because of his blonde hair, scrambled to the deck and began

USS YORKTOWN (CV-5)

After the Battle of the Coral Sea, the Yorktown returned to Hawaii for major repairs. This photo, in May 1942, shows the Yorktown in drydock just before the Battle of Midway. *U.S. Navy photo.*

climbing down a rope. "I had suffered a really bad sunburn some months before, and I knew we'd probably be in the water for a time, and so I left the anti-flash coveralls

The odds of finding Quam in the confusion of the oily water were remote, but Quam's white hair stood out from the spreading oil slick, and Wilger and Newberg spotted him.

him remove the sodden coveralls that had been dragging him down.

After some time in the water, Quam and the others were picked up by a destroyer, the USS Benham. The "tin

---

"The coveralls were dragging me down. I was having a hell of a time staying afloat."

---

on. It was a big mistake."

Quam hit the water, and the sailor entering the water above him pushed him under. "There was a thick coating of oil on the water, and I got it in my mouth and throat. The coveralls were dragging me down. I was having a hell of a time staying afloat."

On top of everything, it was Quam's 19th birthday. It was starting to look like his last. He was in the water with 2,300 other sailors, and he was barely keeping his head above the surface.

Then a miracle happened. Or maybe it was just a high school reunion. There were three Willmar men aboard Yorktown. They knew each other fairly well, but with their different jobs, they didn't see each other all that often. All three entered the water from different parts of the ship.

Harold Wilger was a bomber pilot aboard the Yorktown. After the order was given to jump in the water, he went and got a two-man life raft from his plane. Wilger was floating on his raft when he saw Pete Newberg from Willmar swimming. Wilger got Newberg aboard, and they started to keep an eye out for Quam.

The two were able to get Quam into the life raft. Quam said they may have saved his life.

Quam had made it about 10 yards from the sinking ship when he was rescued by his friends. They helped

can" had a crew of 200 and took more than 700 sailors on board.

"I spent a lot of time just trying to scrape the oil off myself. There wasn't any room to even lie down, but I finally found a spot in a passageway

WOUNDED CARRIER

Smoke pours from the stern of the Yorktown after three bombs crashed through her decks. *U.S. Navy photo.*

USS SEGUNDO (SS-398)

The USS Segundo served the nation for 26 years. It was commissioned in 1944 and decommissioned in 1970.

where the deck was warm. It felt really good to lie down."

The rescued sailors were high-lined over to the USS Portland, a cruiser, the next day, then transferred to the USS Fulton, a submarine tender, two days later. "I was nauseous for a few days. That oil just isn't very tasty."

Quam finally worked his way back to Hawaii where, after a rest period, he was put on board the battleship USS California, a victim of the Pearl Harbor attack. The ship was headed for a drydock and repairs in Bremerton, Washington.

"While I was there, they had a call for volunteers for submarines. I volunteered — don't ask me why. Maybe it was because a sub sank my carrier and got away with it, and I thought I could be aboard a submarine and get away with it."

He took three days of exams and got into sub school, "although one of the doctors looked at me and said I wouldn't last six months."

The school was tough, with a 60-percent washout rate, but Quam hung in there. One of the tests was to swim upwards through 100 feet of water while wearing a Momsen lung, a primitive aqualung. "We had to stop every eight feet to depressurize. They told us if we went straight up, we'd die. It was a relief to get up there."

The submariners were also expected to know every piece of machinery aboard their boat and to be able to use it. Those who couldn't master the whole package were sent packing.

After the basic school, because he was an electrician, Quam was sent to battery and gyro school. In

late 1943, he was assigned to the crew of the USS Pilotfish. Part of his job was to tend and water the sub's batteries. The submarine had 252 batteries, each weighing 1,700 pounds.

Quam made one patrol on the Pilotfish. It was his introduction to life below the seas. "For one thing, you

SS 398
Segundo Statistics

SS 398 Data

Builder
Portsmouth Navy Yard, Kittery, Maine. Launched February 1944.

Class
SS Balao 285

Dimensions
311 feet long, 27 feet wide, 16 feet deep, displacing 2,400 tons when submerged.

Engines
Two Fairbanks/Morse 10-cylinder diesel engines. Four Elliott electric motors. Two propellers.

Crew
10 officers, 70 enlisted.

Armament
24 torpedoes, 10 torpedo tubes. One five-inch gun, one 25 caliber gun, four machine guns.

Maximum Speed
20 knots, surfaced, and 8.75 knots submerged.

Endurance
75 days on patrol, 48 hours submerged.

Range
11,000 miles

Maximum Depth
400 feet.

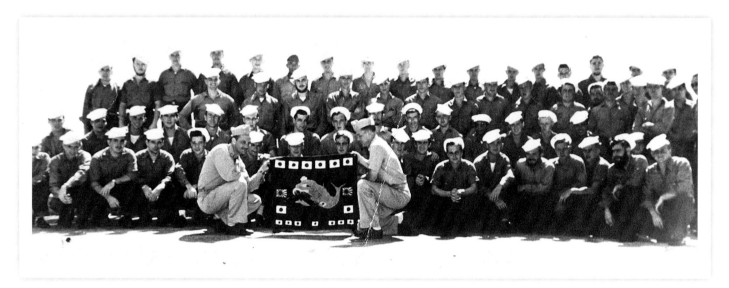

BATTLE FLAG

The men of the Segundo gathered for a photo with their battle flag, showing the damage the sub had done to Japanese Navy and merchant shipping.

only get a little basin of water to wash in every day. No showers. After a long cruise it didn't smell very good anymore."

Actually, there were two showers on board, Quam said. "But the captain filled them with beer. He'd let us have a beer now and then."

The Pilotfish's sister subs had good luck on the patrol. "Later, they told us that we had a noisy reduction gear, and that may have scared away any ships. They were able to evade us, and then come back and depth-charge us."

Quam's experience with depth charges is not quite what the movies have portrayed through the years. "We had some close ones, but we never had the ones where the lights pop out or anything like that. Once we had to stay down for 14 hours."

Staying submerged for long periods was difficult because the sailors had to keep breathing the same air. By 14 hours, the air is pretty rancid. The sailors laid special devices out

on their bunks to soak up the carbon dioxide.

Back in port, Quam had an opportunity to rotate to another sub called the Seawolf. The orders were all set to go through when another electrician with more seniority filed a complaint. Quam was bumped.

Several weeks later, the Seawolf went down with all hands. "In fact, it was sunk by one of our own destroyers. I guess I was pretty lucky."

In all, during the war, the United States lost 52 submarines and more than 3,500 sailors. It was the highest casualty rate of any area of the military service. American subs took out 60 percent of Japanese commercial shipping and 30 percent of Japan's warships during the war. The sub crews also rescued over more than 500 U.S. pilots.

Quam's next boat was the USS Segundo (SS-398). On the Segundo's second patrol — accompanied by two other subs in a wolfpack attack — seven Japanese merchant ships

were surprised, and all were sunk. The Segundo got two.

"One of the ships was an ammunition ship, and it blew up just like a firecracker. One second it was a radar contact, and the next second it was gone. Just like that."

Segundo sank six merchant ships and a host of other smaller Japanese sailing vessels during the war.

In a nighttime surface action, Segundo engaged two Japanese patrol boats that were firing at the submarine. "I was the pointer on the five-inch deck gun. The pointer aims and fires the gun. I had difficulty seeing the targets until one of our 20-millimeter gunners hit and lit up the bridge of one of the patrol boats. I was able to blow the bridge away. We then methodically destroyed both the patrol boats."

Another time, the Segundo got caught in a typhoon. Submarines can usually weather storms by staying submerged, but at some point the batteries must be recharged, meaning the sub must run its engines on the surface.

"We had two lookouts who were up on the conning tower. It was everything we could do to keep the submarine afloat, and they were getting tossed around pretty good. The other guys told me they heard one of the lookouts scream and then hit the deck. He was gone in seconds."

Quam's bunk on the Segundo was near where a spare torpedo was stored. When it came time for bed, he would pull his bunk out next to the torpedo — 600 pounds of explosive. "I could feel it gently nudging me throughout the night."

The breaking of the Japanese merchant marine code during the war enabled American submarines to find their prey with extraordinary accuracy. By the end of the war, more than 90 percent of the Japanese merchant fleet had been sunk, and that nation's ability to wage war was greatly diminished.

"They never told us about the code-breaking, but we always thought it was more than mere coincidence that we were able to intercept these convoys the way we did."

Sometimes the Segundo would stay out for two months at a time. "If you didn't have a job topside, there was no reason for you to be up there. Some guys went two months without seeing the sky. Sometimes they would let guys go up at night, one at a time, to get some fresh air. When the sub would surface, and they would pump fresh air in, it was one of the most exhilarating feelings in the world."

The crew worked four hours on, eight hours off for the most part. Food was good and fresh for the first few weeks of a patrol, and then pow-

dered eggs, powdered milk and other storable provisions took over. "We missed fresh fruit a lot. And we missed ice cream and veggies."

During the war, the SS Segundo had to surface four times to take on enemy ships. Those were difficult times.

The last time, when Quam came on deck to man his gun during combat, his heart began racing, and he couldn't make it stop. He told his chief about the problem, and the chief must have told somebody else. When the patrol ended, Quam was reassigned to the Remora, a submarine under construction in Portsmouth, New Hampshire.

"I was in Pearl Harbor, standing on the deck of a small carrier that was transporting me back to the U.S. when the war ended. All of the ships in Pearl Harbor were blowing their

whistles. It was a wonderful feeling."

His one regret was the Segundo was one of the ships chosen to be in Tokyo Bay when the surrender was signed.

Quam had been awarded a degree by his high school in Willmar, but when he enrolled at the University of Minnesota, he was short some classes in math and English, so he attended Marshall High School in Minneapolis for a short time. He earned his degree in chemical engineering in 1952 and enjoyed a 28-year career at Univac in Eagan. He supervised the main chemistry and spectral chemistry labs.

In 1986, he retired. He and his wife, Rose, have three children, 10 grandchildren and eight great-grandchildren. The couple lives in a townhome in West St. Paul.

YOUNG LOVE
Quam proposed to his wife, Rose, while he was still in the Navy.

TANK CREW

On their way across France with the Second Armored Division; Smilanich, far right, and his crew posed for the camera. The hat had been liberated from a local farmhouse.

Unless indicated otherwise, all photos are from George Smilanich's personal collection.

'HELL ON WHEELS'
TANK DRIVER

George 'Pecky' Smilanich was a starting guard for the Minnesota high school basket-ball state championship team in 1941-42. A year later, he was driving a tank as the Second Armored Division fought in Africa, Sicily, France, Belgium and Germany. He was in three tanks that were destroyed by enemy fire.

If you go to Martin Hughes High School in Buhl, you'll find two very large team pictures mounted in the entrance hallway.

Those pictures show the 1941 and 1942 boys' basketball teams. Both included a starting guard named George Smilanich. Both teams won the Minnesota State Boys' Basketball Tournament.

The state titles were the crowning athletic glory for Smilanich. Less than a year later, he was driving a tank in North Africa. Over the next couple of years, Smilanich, as part of the famous "Hell on Wheels" Second Armored Division, participated in the landing at Omaha Beach, the hedgerow fighting in France, the Battle of the Bulge, and the final victory in Germany.

George "Pecky" Smilanich grew up near Buhl, the son of Mane "Mike" and Yelena Smilanich. Mike worked in the Wanless Mine, and the family lived in the Wanless Location, a mining community about a mile from Buhl.

"It was during the Depression, and things were a little rough. Nearly all the mines were shut down. My dad was a pump man at the Wanless, but he took whatever work he could find."

Smilanich did the same. In fact, he interrupted high school for two years to work in a Civilian Conservation Corps camp, sending his pay-checks home to help support his family. When he did get back into school, he worked in the summers on the track gangs on the railroad.

He inherited the name Pecky from his brother. "Everybody had a nickname. They called my brother Pecky, and then they called me Little Pecky because I did everything he did."

In those days, it wasn't unusual for small towns to produce tremendous basketball teams. Led by all-state guard John Klarich, the Buhl team went 26-3 in 1941 with a team made up of juniors. It was coached by Melvin "Muxie" Anderson.

After a battle with Chisholm to win the District Seven title, Buhl ad-

vanced to the state tourney and beat Red Wing 31-29 in the title game.

The next year, Coach Anderson asked for a $50 pay raise to support his family. "The school board said he could have the raise if he won the state championship the next year. He couldn't take that chance."

The school board hired a young coach, Mario Retica. "The new coach told us, 'I'm not going to do any changes, just play the same way you

did last year. If you have any questions, ask me.' "

The team roared through the season with a 28-0 record and defeated Marshall 30-29 for its second consecutive state championship. The player who scored the winning free throw, George Klasna, had been knocked unconscious earlier in the game.

Both Smilanich and Klarich hoped to further their careers in basketball and football at La Crosse State Teachers College in Wisconsin. In fact, Smilanich had a job in La Crosse cleaning up the Elks Lodge when he got his greetings from the federal government.

"I had an opportunity at La Crosse to get into the V-12 program for Naval Air and avoid the draft, but my brother, who was already in the service, told my parents I should keep my feet on the ground. I didn't want to disappoint my parents, so I went in the Army."

His group of draftees left on a bus from Hibbing to Fort Snelling, and, like good Iron Range lads, they celebrated their last taste of freedom. "They drove the bus right into the stockade and just waited until everybody sobered up."

Smilanich took his basic training at Fort Knox, and, after taking tests that revealed his background in operating heavy equipment, he was assigned to train in the tank corps.

Four months later, he was in Gen. George Patton's Second Armored Division. He served in Easy Company of the 67th Armored Regiment. Smilanich joined the division in Oran, North Africa. "All we did there was train. The First Armored Division got all beat up at Kasserine Pass, and guys from the Second replaced them. We replaced the guys from the Second that went to the First." After about four months in Africa, in July 1943, the division was landed at Sicily. "We landed at Gela and drove up to Palermo, but it was pretty easy going. The Italians were surrendering faster than we could capture them."

The next stop was England to get ready for the Normandy invasion. "The U-boats were all over at that time, and so our ship swung way over about 200 miles from Florida and then headed to Scotland." The Second Armored eventually made it to its base at Tidworth Barracks in England.

The training intensified as D-Day drew nearer. One day, after a long road march, the tank crews were busy taking care of their machinery – changing the oil, greasing the treads, changing the plugs.

"I was under the tank by the back

«

GEORGE 'PECKY' SMILANICH

as a coach for Hibbing High School

»

AS A TANK DRIVER

Smilanich was part of the Second Armored Division, known as 'Hell on Wheels.'

hatch, and I was as greasy as everything else. Pretty soon, I hear a guy talking to me. He says, 'How's that tank, soldier?' I told him, 'Not too damn hot.' He said, 'What's the problem?' And I said, 'It's just got too damn many miles on it.'

"So, he said, 'Burn the son of a bitch.' "

By this time, Smilanich noticed the shiny shoes of the stranger, and he crawled out from under the tank. As he stood up, he found he was talking to General Patton himself.

"I said, 'I'm sorry, sir, I didn't know who it was...' But he just looked at me and said, 'Carry on, soldier,' and he walked away."

A shaken Smilanich was quickly approached by his company officer who wanted to know what Patton had said. "I told him that Patton told me to burn the tank. He looked at me and said, 'Don't do that or you'll be in the Army the rest of your life.'"

The Second Armored practiced getting tanks into and out of the landing ships, and even did some dry runs toward the French coast when the clouds were low and the planes couldn't fly.

The unit landed on Omaha Beach on D-Day plus three when the tanks were needed to continue the assault into France. The men were sealed in their tanks with a layer of thick grease all over the tank to protect it in case it was dropped into deeper water. There was also a shroud over the top.

As the Landing Ship, Tank ap-

proached the beach, the LST next to them took a direct artillery hit and was destroyed. Some of the men survived and swam over to the LST Smilanich was on.

"When we finally got to the beach, the LST dropped the hatch and we drove out, right onto dry land. The tide had gone out."

By evening, the tanks had made it to the top of the ridge overlooking the beach. A German plane attacked as the men slept, but the only near-miss was a chunk of dirt that was kicked up by a shell that hit the pup tent a major was sleeping in. "He

NEW SHELLS

Smilanich, on left, holds a 76-millimeter shell, which he says was a marked improvement over the 75-millimeter shell the U.S. used early in World War II. In the background is the Sherman M4 medium tank that was the workhorse of the Army in the war. The driver's hatch is in the front of the tank.

Sherman M4
Tank Statistics

Sherman M4 Medium Tank

Designer
Unites States Army Ordnance Department

Engine
Continental R975 C1 gasoline engine with 400 horsepower.

Crew
Five including commander, gunner, loader, driver and co-driver.

Armament
75-millimeter gun, a .50-caliber machine gun and two .30-caliber machine guns.

Maximum Speed
25 to 30 miles per hour

Weight
67,000 pounds

Range
120 miles on 175 gallons of gas.

got up and yelled at the plane, 'Come back, you SOB, you haven't got me yet.' "

The tanks headed inland and took part in the St. Lo Breakthrough, then headed out into the hedgerow country. A tank would have to climb to the top of the hedgerow and balance for a time before heading down the other side. With its belly exposed, a tank was most vulnerable to being hit by a German anti-tank weapon.

"At that point, it was easy for them to hit us from below with a bazooka. The thinnest piece of metal on a tank is on the bottom. I always kept the front of my tank covered in sandbags, so it was protected from the front."

Once, as Smilanich's tank exposed its bottom on a hedgerow, it was hit by a shell and started burning. All of the crew was able to get out. It was the first of three tanks Smilanich was in that were destroyed during the war.

the orders were given to capture a crossroads. Two light tanks and the medium tank that Smilanich was driving were ordered in.

"They let the two light tanks go by, then they hit us. It must have been an .88 shell because it went right through the tank and right through the commander's leg."

The tank was engulfed in flames, but all of the crew except the commander were able to get out. Smilanich was free of the tank when he heard a voice screaming, "Smiley, help. Smiley, help." It was Stan Novak, the tank commander.

"I grabbed a bed roll off the back of the tank and wrapped it around me. I got back into the tank and tried to get him out. But he was a big guy, about 215 to 220 pounds. Finally, I got him on the back of the tank. The amazing thing was the Germans stopped firing while all this was going on."

Smilanich signaled for another tank

that leg?" the doctor demanded. "I did, sir," Smilanich answered.

"Well, you just saved that man's life."

Smilanich was awarded the Bronze Star for his actions. Strangely enough, the officer who recommended Smilanich for the medal received a Silver Star, even though he had nothing to do with the rescue.

Life in the tank corps was not easy. Smilanich said there was great stress, and some men couldn't handle it. "You had to be alert all the time or get shot. I just tried to keep everybody happy."

Inside, the tank was full of jostling and close quarters, but it was bearable, at least until the tank was under attack, and it had to be buttoned up for an extended time. "Then you had to eat in there, sleep in there, and take care of your other needs in there."

At one point, a Belgian family attached themselves to Smilanich's

---

"Then you had to eat in there, sleep in there, and take care of your other needs in there."

The second loss was the worst. "It was a bazooka that got us. The tank exploded immediately, and four guys couldn't make it out. Have you ever seen metal burn? You saw it when those tanks caught fire."

Each time Smilanich lost a tank, he had to make his way back to a depot to get a new one. "And, every time I did that, I got a new tank crew."

As the tanks drove into Germany,

to come up, and at this point the firing began again. They managed to get the wounded tank commander to safety. "He was in so much pain, he was biting on my collar. So, I got his pain killer out and jabbed him with it. That didn't seem to work, so I jabbed him with mine."

At the hospital tent, Smilanich hung around to see how his friend was doing. After a time a doctor came out. "Who put that tourniquet on

tank for a time because they were starving. Smilanich would share his rations and cook for the family. After the war, on a visit to Belgium, Smilanich located the family and found out they were one of the wealthiest families in that part of Belgium. "And they remembered the name of every kid in that tank."

The Second Armored Division had driven into Germany by October, but had to change directions in Decem-

ELVA MAE

The Tank crew of the Elva Mae gathered for a photo in front of their Sherman.

ber and race into the Ardennes to help stem the German attack into Belgium – the Battle of the Bulge.

One of Smilanich's most vivid memories is of a German shell ricocheting off the road and shaving off the top of the head of one of the American officers.
The division cut off a German advance on Christmas Day, and the encircled Germans fought to get free.

"It was a night battle, you couldn't believe it. Nobody was taking any prisoners. It was kill or be killed, and that was it. There were no lights. The Germans would try to move their column by going bumper-to-bumper down the road in the dark. And so we'd shoot the first tank and the last tank, and the others would be trapped. They'd have to get out of their tanks, and that's when the shooting would

begin. I don't like to talk about this stuff."

The weather turned bitterly cold in early January. "As long as the tank was running, the transmission was right next to me, and that kept me warm. But you couldn't run the tank all the time — especially at night, you didn't want to give away your position."

The tankers would call in a bull-

THAT CHAMPIONSHIP SEASON

Pecky Smilanich, at right, was a member of the 1941 and 1942 teams at Buhl High School that won the state tournament both years.

dozer to dig a wide trench the tank could hide in with only the turret and 76-millimeter gun sticking up. When the tanks ran out of gas, eventually a supply truck would catch up with them. "We'd have to fill it with five-gallon jerrycans, and it took 179 gallons to fill the tank. It also used twelve gallons of oil."

Even when the tank could run, the cold was intense. Smilanich couldn't wear his boots to use the pedals and could only wear his felt liners. On January 10, he finally had to go to the rear with frozen feet. He was sent all the way back to England where he spent three weeks in a hospital before his feet healed up enough for him to return to his unit.

In March, the division drove across the Rhine, and in early April it was

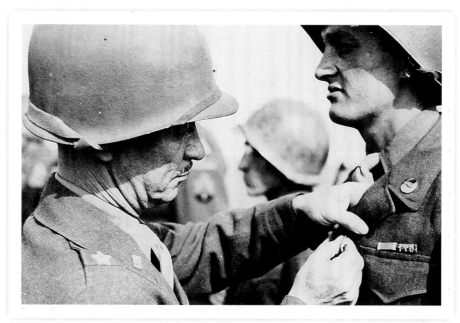

BRONZE STAR

Smilanich recieved the Bronze Star from Brigadier General John H. Collier for his heroic action in saving his wounded tank commander from a burning tank.

the first American division to reach the River Elbe. "We were just about to enter Berlin, but they stopped us. We had to stay on the outskirts for two weeks, waiting for the Russians to take it before we were allowed to go in." Still, the division was the first U.S. unit to enter the German capital.

Smilanich and his companions were billeted in a barracks that had been used for the athletes in the 1936 Olympics.

With the war over, the men thought of little but going home, but it wasn't meant to be for the Second Armored. "We were the honor guard at the Potsdam Conference. I got to see Truman, Churchill, Zhukov. We were Patton's wonderful outfit. We headed up every parade that came along. I had enough points to go home, but they wouldn't let me leave."

Finally, in November, Smilanich got his orders home. He made his way to Camp Lucky Strike at Reims, but there were no ships available because of a longshoremen's strike. The men were sent to Marseilles on "cattle cars" to find another ship, but had to wait two weeks again while an army unit that was also going on the ship received two shots of penicillin each day for 14 days. The young men had contracted venereal disease.

Smilanich was released at Camp McCoy, Wisconsin, and started college at St. Cloud State Teachers College in January. He immediately joined the basketball team and was part of the team that went to the National Association of Intercollegiate Athletics national championship game that year. That fall, he was the kicker on the football team and earned the nickname "the golden toe."

He married his wife, Mary Jane, in 1946, and, after that football season, gave up playing sports to settle down to work and schoolwork. He got a teaching and coaching job in Erie, Illinois, and worked there for four years before he got a similar job in his hometown of Buhl in 1954.

He taught and coached there 13 years, then moved on to Hibbing in 1967. He retired in 1984. He and Mary Jane have three children, two boys and a girl.

He has been back for two major reunions in Belgium, the first to commemorate the 60th anniversary of the Battle of the Bulge. On his second trip, he was the only American visitor as the people of Celles, Belgium, celebrated the anniversary of their liberation on Christmas Day 1944.

"You can't understand how grateful those people were and are to be liberated. Even the people who weren't born then are part of it." Once Smilanich walked into a room of several hundred people and everyone stood up and applauded. The Smilaniches had a similar experience at a restaurant.

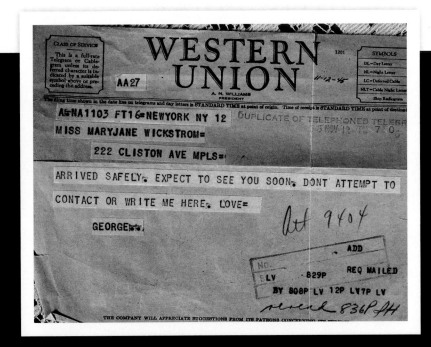

COMING HOME

Smilanich sent his future wife a telegram to let her know that he had arrived back in the United States in November 1945.

WHERE NO MOTORIZED VEHICLES COULD GO
The 613th Field Artillery crosses a river with mule power while driving deeper into Burma in pursuit of Japanese forces.

Unless indicated otherwise, all photos are from Alton Knutson's personal collection.

MULE SKINNER
BLUES

Alton Knutson combined his Norwegian heritage, his farm skills and his Christian faith to survive stubborn mules, dense jungle, heat, disease and enemy shells as part of the Mars Task Force and its 280-mile hike through the mountains of Burma.

Alton Knutson's worst fears were realized when he looked on the floor of the Jeep and saw it was covered with oats.

Knutson had arrived at Fort Sill, Oklahoma, in 1943 for basic training, and he had been warned by the "people who knew" on the base that he should avoid mule-pack training like the plague.

"They told me it was one tough outfit," Knutson recalled. "They said I should stay away from mules, no matter what."

Four or five days after he arrived, Knutson's name was called and he was told to get his duffle bag and wait in the front of the barracks. He obeyed his orders, and soon a Jeep pulled up.

"I threw my duffle bag in the back and I looked down at the floor. It was covered with oats. I knew where I was going."

Knutson was not unfamiliar with domesticated animals. He grew up on a farm near Ashby, Minnesota, during the Depression. His Norwegian family worked hard to survive. "We had plenty of food on the table, and that was about it."

He left school after the eighth grade to work full time on the farm, but then became part of a special high school program at the University of Minnesota's School of Agriculture at Crookston.

The students crammed nine months of schooling into the span between October and March so they would be free to work on the farm during the growing season. Knutson stayed at the school until 1942, tacking on an additional year at the school's college prep program.

Knutson knew, though, he wasn't going to be a farmer. "I got the call to the ministry when I was 15 years old. It said in my high school yearbook, 'He will be a pastor.' "

At the Crookston school, Knutson remembers that he entered a speech contest in which he orated on the assertion that the Japanese shouldn't be harshly criticized for their ongoing war with China. "Of course I didn't know anything about the atrocities or what was really going on, but I did win the speech contest."

He was 20 when he finished up at Crookston and became eligible for the draft. He signed up with the Navy's V-12 program, which allowed students to stay in college.

He started at Augsburg College in Minneapolis in 1942, but contracted what doctors thought was rheumatic fever and had to drop out. He informed the Navy of his illness and was discharged.

Feeling better that summer, he went to work for a farmer near his hometown and was given a farm deferment. "But I wasn't comfortable with it. It was part of my upbringing that I should do my duty no matter how difficult. I let the Selective Service know I was giving up my defer-

ment." In September 1943, he was drafted.

Earlier in the year, Knutson had met a pretty nurse, Margretta Ramaley, at Fairview Hospital, where he worked part time as a janitor and elevator operator. They were both interested in becoming missionaries, and their first date was a missionary conference at Augsburg.

"It was almost love at first sight. Things blossomed pretty fast."

When Knutson was ordered to report to Fort Snelling, he told Margretta, known as Toodie, and they decided to get married. The families agreed, and after the proposal on Monday, the couple was married in a church wedding on Friday. They had two weeks to honeymoon before Alton had to report.

After two weeks of odd jobs at Fort Snelling, he was ordered to report to Fort Sill, the home of the Army's artillery training.

The Army has had a long history of using mules to move supplies and equipment, and it had been proven that the four-legged transports could move artillery pieces where motorized vehicles could not go. Pack-mule battalions had already been sent to Italy to fight in the mountains there.

Knutson was assigned to a group of soldiers who were put in charge of seven mules and one 75 mm howitzer. The gun could be broken down into pieces and put on the backs of five mules. Other equipment was put on the remaining two mules.

Toodie came down to Fort Sill and worked as a maid for an officer's family. Knutson was able to see her on weekends, and whenever else he got the chance.

The training group was moved to another camp at Colorado Springs to train with the mules at altitude. Again Toodie followed along, and the two rented a basement apartment.

It was in Colorado that the 613th Field Artillery Battalion (Pack) was formed and began training as a unit. One day after a hike of about 14 miles, the artillerymen settled in for the night in their tents.

"We woke up in the morning and our pup tent was squeezed down tight. About 14 inches of snow had fallen during the night. All we could do was pack up our 200 mules and march through that snow back to the base. It was one of those times I was really tired.

"But I think growing up on the farm always helped me. You learn to endure, to keep on plugging no matter what."

A mule is the offspring of a male donkey and a female horse. The result is an animal with good size and

《

ALTON KNUTSON

At home in Forest Lake

》

DURING THE WAR

Knutson was sent to Fort Sill, where he learned that he would be in charge of some old-school transportation devices.

THE CREW

Knutson, at left on his knees, was a loader for this 75-millimeter howitzer team. The photo was taken shortly before the 613th Field Artillery Battalion left Burma at the end of the war.

the ability to carry heavy loads. "I had always worked with horses on the farm, but never mules. I would say that the mule has a different temperament, much more solid and not as excitable."

Knutson was a gun loader on the howitzer crew. Someone would hand him the shell, and he would slam it home before someone else pulled the lanyard. "I don't think it did anything good for my hearing."

On September 20th, 1944, the unit was put on a train and sent to Fort Ord in California. On October 22, the 613th boarded the USS General Butler en route for the Far East.

"There were 4,000 U.S. troops on board, and 2,000 Chinese troops that had been training in the United States. With the Chinese on board, we figured we were probably going to India."

The ship was not part of a convoy, but zigzagged by itself across the Pacific, stopping in Australia and then arriving in Bombay on Thanksgiving Day in 1944. Immediately, the battalion was put on a train and shipped across India to Calcutta. There, at Dum Dum Airport, the men were loaded in transport planes and taken to Myitkyina in central Burma. The city and airport had been freed from the Japanese by Merrill's Marauders earlier in the year.

When the Marauders were disbanded, many of them joined a new composite unit that included the 475th Infantry and the 124th Cavalry (dismounted), a National Guard unit from Texas. The new group, along with the 612th and 613th field artillery battalions, was called the Mars Task Force and took up where the Marauders had left off.

The Japanese were retreating south and west, with Chinese troops in pursuit. The Mars Task Force was making an end run to the east, and was traveling over some of the roughest terrain in the world without the benefit of a highway.

"We left with 60-pound packs, and it was hot and it was dusty. Plus we were not in condition anymore to march after being on the ship for 31 days. It was a very, very long first day."

When the troops set off, it was a long line with 430 men and about 300 mules. The task force marched every day, the mules carrying the howitzers. It skirted around the city of Bhamo, and the men could hear the fighting going on in the distance, their first intimation of combat.

"Some of the more ingenious men rigged up carts for the mules to pull, and much of the gear was hauled that way. And some of the officers had commandeered Jeeps. But south of Bhamo, we struck off into the jungle and all the carts and Jeeps had to be abandoned or sent back."

Knutson said that none of the men of the Mars Task Force wore any type of uniform markings of rank or unit. "We had learned that the Japanese snipers looked for anyone with rank."

As the mule train headed onto the narrow trails, Knutson said, the discarding began. "Anything you didn't think you needed, you tossed. The natives along that trail must have had a field day."

The discarded items included tennis shoes, an extra blanket, any extra clothing, and half of the mess kits, including the knife and fork. The men kept their machetes, knives, ponchos, canteens, and first-aid kits, plus the other half of the mess kit with the spoon. A spoon was all you needed to eat K-rations.

The traveling group was supplied by air drop every three days, but it wasn't a perfect system. If the rains came, it could get pretty hungry along the trail. The K-rations consisted of a tin of tuna, scrambled eggs, beef stew or pork, plus a

dian and a great guy. But that night he just disappeared. He must have used his instincts, but somehow he found some native liquor. He came back to the tent singing. It's the only time in my life I slept with a drunk."

Knutson had spent his Christmas Eve reading the Christmas story out of the New Testament to the other GIs. He said it was somewhat diffi-

"The one thing I would not do was to use the crude language. In fact the other guys would say, 'Knutson wouldn't say horse____ if his mouth was full of it.' But it was my way of witnessing, letting them know what my Christian faith meant to me."

Every morning the men would pack up and get ready to go. They would grab a quick bath at a nearby stream

"I just told Him that if I survived, I was going to go wherever He wanted me to go. I wasn't bargaining with God, I was just telling him my intentions."

hardtack biscuit, a square of chocolate, powdered coffee and powdered lemon juice.

While the K-ration boxes were covered with wax, the hot and humid climate made its mark on the GIs' food. "The biscuits were stale, the chocolate had turned white, and the coffee was one hard glob."

The feeding of the mules was accomplished with double-thick burlap bags full of oats that were simply pushed out of airplanes without the benefit of a parachute. "You didn't want to be standing under one of those. We killed several mules that way, and had some close calls with the men."

Knutson had teamed up with another GI to share blankets and ponchos. The two matched each other in working hard at the end of the day's journey, so had extra time to pick out the best camping spot. On Christmas Eve, the 10th day of the march, Knutson's roommate wandered off into the jungle.

"He was a full-blooded Cherokee In-

cult to maintain his Christian demeanor in the rough-and-tumble of a combat army.

if they had a chance. The pieces of the howitzer were so heavy that it took four men to put them on the mule's back.

JUST MARRIED
Alton and Toodie Knutson were married in 1943 in Forest Lake, just two weeks before he was to be inducted into the United States Army.

The Mule
Various Statistics

What is a mule?

A mule is the offspring of a male horse and a female donkey, resulting in a sure-footed animal that can carry a fairly large load.

Can they reproduce?

Nearly all mules are sterile.

Size

A mule generally weighs from 800 to 1,200 pounds.

Load

A mule can carry about one-third of its weight. An Army pack saddle weighed about 100 pounds, so the Army tried to keep the loads to 200 pounds or so.

Food

A mule was fed about 10 pounds of grain a day while on a mission.

Nowadays

Mules are still sometimes used in unusual circumstances. The Army used mules in Afghanistan in recent years to bring supplies over the mountains.

UP THE MOUNTAIN, DOWN THE MOUNTAIN

The terrain in Burma did not allow for motorized transportation. Artillery moved on mule back.

Knutson's mule was a reddish color and so naturally was called "Red." All the mules were tied to picket lines strung between trees during the night.

The cooks prepared the water for the day by boiling it, then storing it in 30- or 40-gallon "Lister" bags.

By January 7, they had reached the Schweli River, and they were now getting closer to the fighting. "It was about a mile and a half down to the river, and it was raining. It was just mud, mud, mud. To keep the mule from tumbling over, I took his halter and we would step together, step together, sometimes slide together. We made it somehow."

The 613th crossed the river one at a time on a makeshift bamboo bridge, and was told that once they got across there would be an air drop waiting. The unit was completely out of food.

"When we got there, we found that the infantry had gotten to the air drop first and all that was left was what they considered inedible — like the biscuits. We were pretty sad. It was the only time we were seriously starving. But the next morning we lined up for mess, and they served us hot oatmeal.

"We don't know how they did it, but they must have pulverized the mule feed somehow and made oatmeal out of it. It saved us."

On the 16th and 17th of January, the battalion made a forced march down a valley, found that it was trapped, and marched back for the high ground. "There was a stream in the middle of the valley, and I kept count. That day we crossed that stream 49 times."

By the 19th, the 280-mile, 34-day march began to pay off as the 613th dug emplacements in a mountainside and finally began firing its weapons in support of the infantry advance in front of it. "Ours was the first gun to zero in on the enemy."

Telephone wire was laid from the forward observers back to the firing position, and the battery fired several hundred rounds over the next two days as the spotters phoned back the coordinates. The only problem was that the firing tipped off the 613th's own position, and the Japanese began firing back.

"There were two kinds of shelling. One was a big cannon that just went 'woof, woof, woof.' The other went 'whisssshhh-bang, whisssshhh-bang.' That was by far the most dreadful."

The GIs had dug deep foxholes and bunkers, but the shelling was still lethal, with gunners being killed and wounded. It was during this time, Knutson said, that he offered his life to the Lord.

"I just told Him that if I survived, I was going to go wherever He wanted me to go. I wasn't bargaining with God, I was just telling him my intentions."

After some days, the emplacements were moved to a location on the other side of a ridge that was more protected from the Japanese shelling. Knutson said the men were not too happy with the officers for picking the original exposed position.

How did Knutson justify his deadly work with his Christian values? "I would pray as I loaded the shells that the enemy wouldn't be killed by our shelling, that they

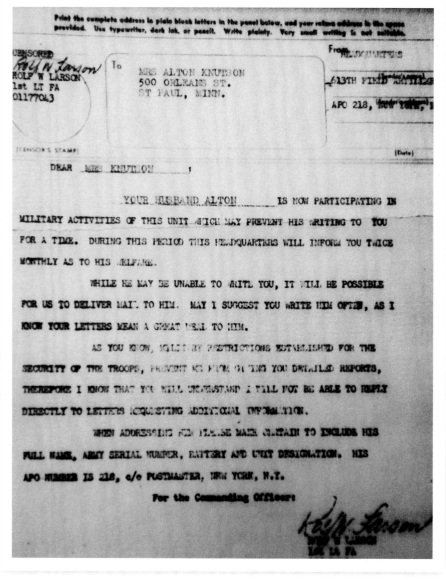

LETTER HOME

Knutson's wife, Toodie, received this message from the Army noting that her husband wouldn't be writing home for a while.

would only get gangrene."

The daily shelling went on until February 4. The next couple of days there were no calls for artillery support, and the men assumed the battle was over. In fact, it was. The remaining Japanese again took up their retreat to the south. This latest action, though, had freed up the Burma Road and allowed an over-

land supply route to China.

The 613th packed up its guns and headed down the Burma Road, where the scenes of the battle were all around. Many dead Japanese soldiers were alongside the road.

"I saw the body of one Japanese soldier. The GIs had already rifled his personal effects, and there were pictures scattered around. One was of a little girl. It really struck me. They were men with families just like us. I knew he'd never see that child again. It's the awfulness of war."

The further south the men marched, the worse the heat became. "It was just miserable. They made us wear our steel helmets. It was more than hot. The flies were just terrible, trying to crawl into your eyes, your ears and your nose."

As he led his mule down the road, Knutson noticed a building that was different than the usual shacks. It was made of corrugated metal, and it had a cross on top. It was a makeshift church.

"Right there in that godforsaken place was the cross of Christ. I wasn't so miserable after that."

The 613th finally made it to a rest camp, and the mail caught up with it. "I got a letter from my dad, and I was apprehensive because he rarely wrote. He told me that my older brother had died. That was a hard one for me."

After some time in the rest camp, the unit was told to turn in its mules. Knutson said despite their long journey together, there was little sentimentality about it. The men were happy to be free of their constant companions. "We didn't feel too bad about it at all."

The next journey for Knutson was on May 10 on a C-47 to Kunming, China, a major army base for the Chinese. On September 8, after the war was over, the 613th was officially disbanded.

Knutson had no job. "They hauled us to China, but they didn't know what to do with us. So I volunteered at the dispensary."

One day Knutson was one of the ar-

tillerymen, and the next day he was giving them shots. "And they didn't even let me practice on an orange."

Knutson later was moved to Shanghai, where he was assigned to take care of vehicle needs for officers. He also made contact with British missionaries there, and he learned how to drink English tea, "with plenty of milk and sugar — what a treat."

Back in the United States, Knutson was discharged on February 4, 1946. He used his GI bill to finish up at Augsburg and then do three years of seminary school.

In 1951, he fulfilled his pledge to the Lord and his longtime dream and

became a missionary — in Japan. He and Toodie spent the next 33 years of their lives in Japan. They had four children, two born in the United States and two in Japan.

The Knutsons came back to the United States in 1984. He has served three stints as pastor of Faith Lutheran Church in Forest Lake where he and Toodie still live. In fact they live at the same place where they spent their honeymoon 65 years ago.

Alton Knutson goes to national reunions of his artillery battalion, and he serves his comrades as their chaplain.

WARTIME BEAST OF BURDEN

The old gray mule, she ain't what she used to be.

A WARM DAY IN ITALY

Norb McCrady posed for this picture, shirtless on a Jeep. The photo was taken at Castelfiorentino in Tuscany.

Unless indicated otherwise, all photos are from Norbert McCrady's personal collection.

ONCE A PFC, ALWAYS A PFC

Norbert McCrady joined the Minnesota National Guard in 1939 and then went to war with the 34th Division in 1940. After six years in the military and over 600 days in combat, McCrady came back home to Minnesota as a Private First Class, a rank he was proud to wear on his sleeve.

Norb McCrady actually did make corporal once in his six-year Army career, but it was short-lived, thanks to the lingering effects of a strenuous game of craps.

Otherwise, he was happy to weather his World War II tour of duty in Minnesota's 34th Division as a Private First Class.

Twice, the Army offered him a career path that could have resulted in his being an officer, but neither time was the temptation strong enough.

"I got along fine with most people — as long as they respected me as an individual. But those who thought their rank made them intelligent, I had problems with."

Norbert A. McCrady was born in 1923 and grew up in Owatonna, Minnesota, on the outskirts of town. "It was one of those places that had an outdoor biffy. We were on a clay and dirt road, and we had chickens, sheep, a barn and a hay mow. As you look back, it wasn't a palace, but we were happy with it."

McCrady's dad worked at the post office until he contracted tuberculosis in 1934. With Dad unable to work, the family soon lost its house. For young Norbert, it meant quite a bit of moving around in the next few years, living with relatives and in board-and-room arrangements. "It sounds terrible, but it wasn't so bad. I never felt the world was against me. People were good to me."

When not in school, he helped his milkman, who had gout, deliver his route. For that service he got a quart of milk and a pint of chocolate milk every day, and a pound of butter every week.

He also sustained himself by setting pins at the bowling alley, racking balls at the billiard hall, washing bottles for the bootleggers, and "doing whatever anybody asked me to do." McCrady would also hustle a little pool action on the weekends.

He learned to drive at a tender age when he and his mother would travel to the sanitarium at Aw-Gwah-Ching, near Walker, Minnesota, to visit his father. "My mom would be too tired after a full shift of nursing, and so she'd prop a couple of pillows under me, and I'd help her drive."

McCrady fibbed on his age and joined the Minnesota National Guard in May 1939. "I was not suited to be a soldier. I was strictly in it for the money. They paid $2 for a drill night, and, so, every three months I got a check for $12. That was a lot of money to me."

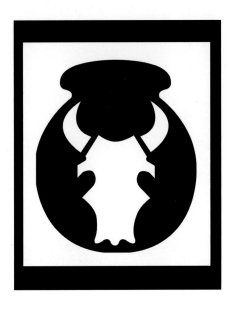

In 1940, word came down that his unit was being federalized into the regular Army. "We were so unsophisticated, we really didn't see it coming. I know that's hard to understand now, but we thought Owatonna was the center of the world. We couldn't see how Hitler could possibly affect us."

Several of McCrady's contemporaries dropped out of the Guard before being called up, but McCrady decided to see it through. "You've got to remember there were no jobs back then. I was lucky to get seasonal work at the canning factory. I decided to stay with the outfit."

Before leaving school, though, a special plan was worked out for the five seniors who were being called up to get their high school diplomas. "My trouble was with math. I still don't know if it's 'plane' geometry or 'plain' geometry."

In the end, though, McCrady approached the teacher and convinced him it was a good idea if he passed. "Sometimes, you just have to assert yourself. I've used that technique many times since then when I found myself on shaky ground."

McCrady was assigned to F Company, Second Battalion, 131st Infantry Regiment. On their day of departure, the Owatonna men gathered in the armory before heading to the railroad station. "We were all joking around up to that point. We thought it was a lark. But, when we started marching over to the station, it was a dead silence. All you could hear were the boots crunching in the snow. The stark reality suddenly hit us."

Camp Claiborne in Louisiana was a huge change in lifestyle for the Midwesterners. "The snakes weren't garter snakes. There were wild boar running around. And there were chiggers. Plus, there was a truly hostile civilian populace. They were anti-Yankee, plus they had contempt for soldiers."

McCrady recalls that one soldier was walking past the local municipal swimming pool, where a sign proclaimed, "No Negroes, No Dogs and No Soldiers," when he spied a fair young damsel in the pool area. Forgetting his place, he softly called out "yoo-hoo" to the young lady. A general, overhearing the young soldier's call, had him put in the stockade.

"There was recognition of the fact that this general had been elevated beyond his talents. Once word got around about his putting this soldier in the stockade, he became known as General Yoo-Hoo. It followed him the rest of his career."

The attack on Pearl Harbor in late

«

NORB MCCRADY

At home in Eden Prairie

»

DURING THE WAR

McCrady fought in Africa and from one end of Italy to the other. This photo was taken late in the war in the Apennine Mountains south of Bologna.

National Guard Training

McCrady, second from left, stood at attention during a training session at Camp Ripley in 1939.
From left are: Walt Wagner, McCrady, Jim Manthey, Les Whiteis.

1941 was, again, something of a mystery to the rustic lads from Minnesota. "We didn't know where Pearl Harbor was. We had to look on a map just to find out where Hawaii was. It was more confusing than anything else. We didn't know this would lead to war. We still had delusions that we were going home after a year."

The unit was quickly assigned to Lake Pontchartrain near New Orleans to stand guard duty. The assignment had some of the soldiers taking their job very seriously.

"One of our guys, who was not the brightest guy in the unit, had been told that if anyone comes near, he was to ask for the password. Well, after a while our commanding officer went out to inspect the guards. When he approached this guard, he was challenged for the password. He said, 'I don't need to know the password, I'm the colonel of the regiment.' The guard shouted back, 'Screw you, colonel. What's the

password?' "

The next move was to Fort Dix, New Jersey, to get aboard a ship. "We left so fast that my buddy and I had to leave our car behind. We used that care for a little business we had selling half pints to the guys."

The men boarded the British ship RMS Aquitania in April of 1942 to travel to the British Isles as part of a massive convoy. In Northern Ireland, part of their duty was to guard the border with the Republic of Ireland.

In early December 1942, the men left for Northern Africa. They landed near Oran and made their way across to Tunisia to help the British pursue the retreating Germans. It was the Americans' first taste of real combat.

"It was there that we found out how ill-prepared we were. We thought our training had been pretty intensive, but we were like a spitball champion getting in the ring with Joe Louis."

McCrady was a battalion scout, and one of his duties was to walk in front of the unit to give early warning of of enemy presence. "But the Germans were clever enough to just let the scouts go through and then attack the main body."

McCrady said the early fighting was a tough but lasting lesson about being in war. "You learn how to protect yourself. The first time you saw someone dead who you had known, or even badly wounded, you came close to going into a state of shock. After that, you get kind of a cocoon that wraps itself around your psyche. It only allows a certain amount of information into your brain. It kind of dehumanizes you. You don't become brave, but at least you don't panic anymore when something bad happens."

The example of the British Army provided a great learning experience for the Americans. "I remember one time early on we were trying to dig foxholes in the solid ground when the British came up to our position. They didn't bother with foxholes, they just threw a camouflage sheet over their truck. They sat down and started these fires, so they could make tea, and the smoke was billowing out. Here we were, hunched down in our foxholes, and they were lounging around drinking tea. We felt pretty silly.

"But you had to understand that they had seen their homes bombed and their families killed. For them, war was just like going to work. For us, it was a trauma."

At one point, with their position in danger of being outflanked on both sides, the commanding officer ordered a retreat through a mountain pass. "They told me to go back and find the rear-guard platoon and show them where the pass was. They said they'd leave the command car waiting for me when I got back. I went back, and it was a bright, moonlit night. I was sneaking along

wouldn't let me go. Geez, he was a stubborn guy. About 12 hours later, we were starving to death, and he said he'd go. He left, and he never came back."

and he was not liked or respected by the men. "He was stealing cigarettes by the case and selling them on the black market. Plus, he was a tyrant."

"We thought our training had been pretty intensive, but we were like a spitball champion going up against Joe Louis."

---

the banks of the river, keeping out of sight, when I heard voices.

"I decided I'd better get a little closer, and, when I did, I found out they were speaking German. I just about turned green. I raced back to the pass and found out that the rear guard had already gone through. And the command car was gone, too.

"I had to walk 40 miles to get back to our defensive position. There are still marks on my feet from the blisters I got that day. They've healed over, but they still hurt at times."

As the Germans retreated to the coast, McCrady was given another assignment. "They told me and this other guy to take our walkie-talkies and go up to this knob on a hill and report back what we saw. They told us, in no uncertain terms, not to leave until we got orders to leave. So we stayed up there, and there were just thousands of Germans marching past.

"Well, a couple of days went by, and now we're out of food and water. The batteries are dead on our walkie-talkies. And by now, there aren't Germans marching by; they're all Americans.

"I said to the other guy, 'Why don't you go down and get some food and water?' But he wouldn't do it, and he

McCrady waited as long as he could on the hill, but hunger drove him from his post. He found an American unit and begged a can of already opened sardines from a soldier. "He warned me that it might be spoiled, but I was so hungry, I just gobbled it down. It wasn't long before I knew I had the worst case of stomach poisoning possible. I spent the next three days in the hospital."

Oddly enough, the next time McCrady saw his partner from the knob on the hill was several years later at the Tomb of the Unknown Soldier in Washington, D.C., where his former comrade was on guard duty.

Still in the hospital and still weak from being unable to eat, McCrady found out his division was going to march in a victory parade in Tunis. He talked his way out of the hospital and found his comrades.

"We were marching 40 abreast, and, as we got near the reviewing stand, I was smoking a cigarette. I figured no one could see me in the middle of the pack, so when they did 'eyes right,' I was still smoking. I bet I was the only soldier that day to march past Eisenhower and Churchill and Montgomery and Patton and de Galle while smoking a cigarette."

At one point in North Africa, the company got a new commander,

McCrady was a friend of Harold Nelson, a fellow Owatonnan who had been an officer in the 34th Division but had been forced to retire because of age.

Nelson now held the position of charge d'affaires for the Port of Oran. McCrady was asked by his fellow soldiers to see if Nelson could use his pull to get rid of the crooked company commander. McCrady was welcomed warmly by his hometown friend. In the end, though, Nelson told McCrady there was nothing he could do. "I went back, and the guys accepted it grimly. A week later, though, orders came through, and the officer was demoted from captain to second lieutenant and sent away. He was later discharged from the Army."

The 34th Division landed at Salerno on the Italian coast, and McCrady was sent back to his old company where he went through truck-driver training. He eventually became the driver for the company commander.

"I was probably a better driver than I was a soldier."

After some unfortunate incidents with bomb craters, McCrady was told to practice his driving skills, and, on one of his excursions, he encountered two Navy men by the side of the road. Neither wore any in-

YOUNG BUCKS

The young soldiers had plenty to smile about at Camp Ripley in 1939. War was still a distant possibility. From left: Emil Skalicky, Bob Klemmer, Les Whiteis, Jim Manthey, Norb McCrady, Jake Ellerman.

signia to show his rank.

"I asked them if they wanted a ride, and they said, 'Sure.' I asked them where their boat was, and they told me it was tied up at the pier." Mc-Crady drove them down to the waterfront. "All of a sudden there were whistles blowing and people shouting. It was the most attention I'd ever gotten as a driver. Everybody was jumping all over themselves."

The two riders invited McCrady to come aboard. "I said, 'No, I can't leave my Jeep.' The next thing I knew there were two sailors guarding it at either end with rifles." The riders then brought him up the gangway, onto the ship, and then down to the ship's store. They told the storekeeper to give McCrady anything he wanted.

"They were loading up boxes of cigarettes and boxes of candy. I said,

'Hold on, I don't want all that. Just give me a carton of smokes and some candy.' And the sailor says, 'Well, when the fleet commander tells me to give you what you want, I do it.'

"So it was the fleet commander. I was just calling them, 'you guys.' "

After landing at Anzio, McCrady found out he might be suffering battle fatigue. "The shells started coming in from Anzio Annie, and I ducked into a bunker. All of a sudden I just had to get out of there. I couldn't stand being shut up in there anymore. I dove into a crater filled with water and sat there during the shelling, all wet and cold. I slept in that crater that night rather than go back into that bunker."

At one point, the company's commanding officer was wounded and was sent to a hospital in Naples. He

contacted McCrady and asked him to bring down his personal gear. Mc-Crady received permission to make the trip but was told he'd be accompanied by two other men.

"We found out that, as part of our trip, we were to pick up our dead at Anzio from F and G companies. They had been there a few days, and they were bloated. We put them in bread sacks with one dog tag attached to the outside of the bag. Then we just threw them on the truck like cordwood. The smell was awful.

"The worst part was that we knew these guys. We left them at a cemetery and drove into Naples. The CO thought we'd be happy to be there, but we just had this faraway look in our eyes. We were stunned by what we had just done."

The unit marched through Rome, and McCrady took advantage of a

TAKING A BREAK

McCrady sits next to a large tub in the mess area of a camp in Italy.

chance to get some R&R in the Eternal City. By then he'd been transferred again, this time to an artillery company.

"It was time to head back, and I asked the guy if this truck was going to the cannon company, and he said it was. I didn't recognize anybody on the truck, but I was new in the company, so I didn't think twice. I was sleeping away in the back of the truck when it arrived. I found out they had taken me to the cannon company in another division."

McCrady had to retrace his route to Rome, then scramble back to his unit, several hours after his pass expired. "But it worked out. They treated me like an elder statesman. After all, I was 22 years old."

Many months later, McCrady was asked to report to headquarters. He

IN MONTE CATINA, ITALY

McCrady enjoys a pass into a local town.

VESSEY AND McCRADY

Jack Vessey and Norb McCrady both joined the Minnesota National Guard in 1939. Six years later, Vessey was an officer and McCrady was still a PFC. Vessey later became the Chairman of the Joint Chiefs of Staff. In later years, McCrady and Vessey became good friends, and McCrady served as Vessey's agent in booking speaking engagements.

was told he was being considered, under a special Army program for enlisted men, to be sent to West Point for training as an officer. Mc-Crady and the commander discussed the discipline needed to survive the hazing at the military academy.

"They asked me what I'd do if some senior classman kept sending me, a war veteran, out to pick up cigarette butts. I said that at some point I'd knock him on his ass. We all agreed that West Point wasn't for me."

The division fought its way north until the war ended. Again, the chance to enter the officer ranks was presented to McCrady. He was told he was being sent home for 30-days' leave, then would report back to his unit as an officer with a field commission to serve in the occupation army.

"They said I had no choice, but I told them I wouldn't raise my arm to take the oath. There was a time when I'd have accepted a field commission, but not now."

Instead, he was given orders to go home. His first stop was at a replacement depot in Naples. Every day, while the homeward-bound troops were waiting for transportation home, they were told to fall out to police the grounds and do other menial work.

"I just told them I wasn't going to fall out. They called the sergeant of the guard, and he called the officer of the day who was a first lieutenant. He brought me into his office and told me I was facing a serious charge.

"I said, 'Lieutenant, let me put it to you this way. I've been overseas for four years without ever getting leave. I've spent over 600 days in combat. I've got enough points to get out of the Army two-and-one-half times. I'm not going to fall out to pick up cigarette butts. You'll just have to court-martial me.'"

The officer looked at him and said, "Let's have a drink." He gave Mc-Crady two nickels and sent him to the Coke machine. They poured whiskey into their Cokes and relaxed. Finally, the officer said to him, "Listen, every time you are ordered to fall out, you come here to my office. You get a nickel and get a Coke. You put whiskey in it. And then you wait until the other men come back."

McCrady remembers with wistful eyes. "Sometimes, they would fall out two or three times a day. But I figured I had earned it."

In the end, he did get out. Times were still tough in Owatonna, but he eventually became Steele County treasurer. In 1962, he was asked by the Republican Party to run for secretary of state against DFLer Joe Donovan. He lost the election, but the statewide exposure opened many doors for him.

He became the executive vice president of the Independent Bankers of Minnesota and spent many years lobbying at the State Capitol and in Washington, D.C. The pictures in his collection show him with U.S. Sen. Dave Durenberger, Gov. Wendell Anderson and a host of other Minnesota and national leaders. He retired but continued to work, both as a writer and in running a speakers bureau.

He and his wife, Natalie, married in 1946. They have five children, 12 grandchildren, and 14 great-grandchildren.

LATER LIFE

McCrady's lack of advancement in the Army never bothered him in his post-war career. Here he graces the cover of Commercial West in 1985 as the executive vice president of the Independent Bankers of Minnesota.

Jim Mildenberger drove a DUKW ashore on the Easy Red section of Omaha Beach on June 6, 1944.

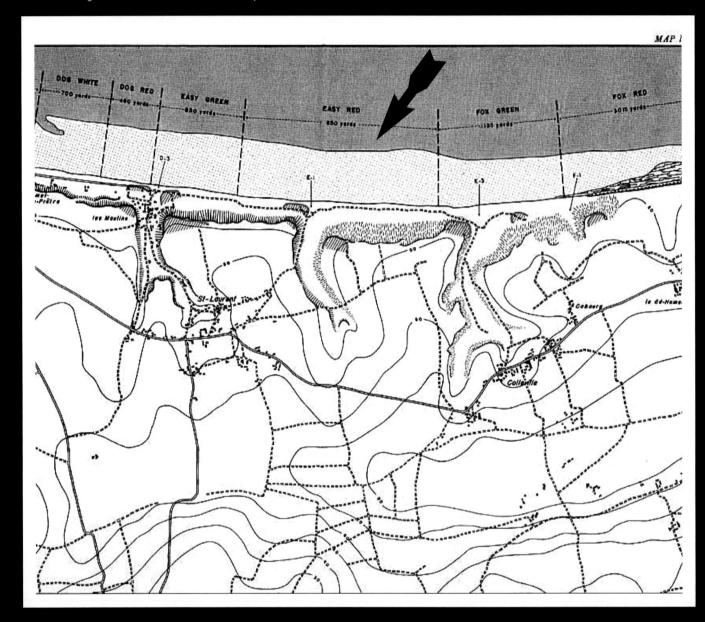

Unless indicated otherwise, all photos are from Jim Mildenburger's personal collection.

MESSAGES FROM OMAHA BEACH

In other landings, the U.S. Army had difficulty maintaining good communication between the beach and the officers on the ships at sea. One solution was the creation of a DUKW, an amphibious vehicle usually called a "duck" that would carry a radio transmitting station. Jim Mildenberger had the privilege of driving that DUKW.

Jim Mildenberger of Hackensack was at Omaha Beach on D-Day only because he had done his duty as a military policeman. Otherwise, he would have been with his National Guard comrades in the 34th Infantry Division fighting in Italy.

A native of the north side of Minneapolis, Mildenberger went to Hamilton Grade School, Jordan Junior High and North High School. His dad had been a World War I veteran, serving overseas.

In June 1940, he signed up with the Minnesota National Guard. "I don't know why for sure. Some of my friends were in the National Guard, and they talked me into it."

In January 1941, the Guard unit was federalized and became the 135th Infantry Regiment of the 34th Division. It was sent to Camp Claiborne in Louisiana. After the bombing of Pearl Harbor on December 7, 1941, Mildenberger and the rest of his unit were sent to New Orleans briefly to protect the harbor from invasion.

The next move was to Fort Dix, New Jersey, where Mildenberger was put on military police duty. It was the job of the MPs to check the ammo dump, power plant, water plant and other places regularly.

By chance, he and his partner arrived at a regular stop at a bowling alley just as a near-riot was being quelled by another MP. One of the intoxicated antagonists took off running, but as the three MPs were talking the event over, the assailant returned with a rifle he had forcibly taken from a camp guard.

The soldier shot all eight rounds at the MP stationed at the bowling alley. Mildenberger and his partner drew their sidearms and killed the attacker.

"We had been issued three rounds each, and five of the six hit this guy."

Though there was no evidence of guilt on the part of the two MPs, it was standard operating procedure for the Army to submit them to a court-martial in order to protect them from ever being tried again for the incident. It took more than a month before the court was convened, and by the time Mildenberger

was found innocent, the 34th Division had sailed across the ocean.

Mildenberger was transferred into the Army's V Corps headquarters company. His training had been as a radio operator.

The V Corps was soon sent overseas on the Queen Mary, and in May 1943 it was stationed at Clifton College in Bristol, England. In March 1944,

Mildenberger was transferred, this time to the headquarters company of the 56th Signal Battalion. The unit's duty, as the invasion of France came closer, was to supply real-time information from Omaha Beach back to V Corps commander, Major General James Gerow, who was aboard the USS Ancon off Omaha Beach.

Col. Benjamin B. Talley, who had recently participated in the Aleutians invasion, and who also participated in the D-Day planning, was transferred into Mildenberger's unit. "He told the top brass that the biggest problem with invasions up to that point was maintaining communications from the troops on the beach to the headquarters on the ships."

One of Talley's inventions was to place high-powered radios into small Army storage sheds and mount the whole thing on a DUKW landing craft, usually called a "Duck" by the GIs. Two DUKWs were set up this way, and other radios were mounted on two Jeeps.

A call was put out for volunteers for a dangerous mission. "Three of us were called into an office. They described what they were going to do, sending communications back to the ships. It sounded like a piece of cake to us. We wouldn't even have to do any fighting. It sounded like it was going to be a snap."

Mildenberger was the driver for one of the two communications DUKWs, a vehicle capable of operating both at sea and on land. "After we had practiced a few times, I told them that it would be better if we drove the DUKWs onto the landing craft and backed them off into the ocean. When we drove them off front-first, they had a tendency, because the

engine was in front, to get swamped. But I was told it was against regulations."

On the evening of June 5, 1944, Mildenberger's DUKW was the last to be loaded on the ship because it was scheduled to be the first one off. Again, Private Mildenberger approached the officer in charge with his plan. "He said, 'That makes sense to me. Do it the way you want.'"

At about 4 in the morning, 12 miles off the Normandy coast, the DUKWs were dropped into the water. Mildenberger doesn't know if any of the other boats were lost while being launched, but he does know that several of the other DUKWs, carrying artillery, never made it through the heavy seas.

"There was a guide boat that was supposed to bring us in, but there were six- to eight-foot waves. In

«

JIM MILDENBERGER

At home in Hackensack

»

JUST AFTER THE WAR

Mildenberger worked in Africa right after the war, building air bases.

about five minutes, the guide just went out of sight and was gone. We couldn't keep up with him. I just had to steer the boat into the waves so we wouldn't capsize."

As they made their long journey toward shore — "Ducks don't go very fast." — Mildenberger could see the naval bombardment of the beach and was able to aim his boat at the light from the shelling.

The first troops hit the beach at about 6 a.m., and the communications DUKW tried to go ashore at about 6:30. "I couldn't see any action on the beach. I didn't see any troops. When we got about a hundred yards from shore, we started to attract a lot of machine-gun fire. We backed off to about 500 yards out and radioed in our situation."

Col. Talley had decided to protect the valuable radio and instructed them to continue to keep it out of

range of the machine guns.

Omaha Beach was the most treacherous of the five landing areas along the Normandy shore. The reason Mildenberger didn't see any troops was because the few that had made it ashore were taking whatever cover they could from the withering machine-gun fire and constant Nazi shelling. Many of the troops had gone back into the sea to hide behind the obstacles the Germans had placed to prevent the landing craft from going ashore.

Three times during the morning, the DUKW tried to bring its radio shack ashore, but each time it became a magnet for shelling and machine-gun fire, and the troops that were ashore waved them off in no uncertain terms. "One time, we almost got to the beach, and an officer just told us to get the hell out of there. We had four big antennas sticking out of the top, and I suppose that

was a pretty good target for the Germans."

The American attack finally began to make some headway midway through the morning, and Mildenberger could see the Army Rangers scaling the cliffs to silence a large German gun in a bunker.

The scene on the beach was not pretty. "There were bodies all over the place, and I presumed they were dead. There were tanks stuck near the shore. Not very many of them made it. There was a lot of shelling."

As the battle progressed, the DUKW hovered just out of range of much of

COMING ASHORE

A DUKW comes ashore at Omaha Beach, crammed with gear. *(U.S. Army photo.)*

DUKW
Statistics

DUKW Amphibious Truck

Manufacturer
General Motors

Engines
GMC 6-cylinder, 269 cubic inches and 91. 5 horsepower

Crew
Two or three

Armament
Provision for a machine gun mount. No armor

Maximum Speed (clean)
50 miles per hour on land, six miles per hour at sea

Weight
2.5 tons

Length
31 feet

Range
About 300 miles on land, 50 at sea

the firing, and Col. Talley was able to report valuable information back to the coordinators of the invasion on the ships.

Sometime after noon, the beachhead was finally secure enough to allow the DUKW to go ashore. At 1:10 p.m., it made its way about 50 yards onto the beach and immediately got stuck in the millions of

ing in and dropping off troops, but they weren't taking many wounded back. They'd just turn around and head back out to sea. There were about 15 or 20 of us laying there. Finally someone said that was enough, and he went out and stopped the next boat. They loaded us on board and took us to a hospital ship."

"They asked me if I wanted to go infantry or artillery. I didn't like either one of those choices, and I told them I wanted to go back into a signal battalion. I walked out of the depot and flagged down a truck going down the beach. I'd heard that Col. Talley was now in charge of the beach operation, and I went to see him. He was glad to see me, be-

HEADING ASHORE

A landing craft headed toward Omaha Beach on D-Day gives an idea of the conditions that day.

"Something hit me hard in the back, but I thought it was just a rock. It hurt, but it didn't hurt that bad."

round rocks that covered the shoreline. "We were planning to let air out of the tires, and that should have given us enough traction, but Col. Wheeler told us to wait. He wanted to talk to the officers on the beach."

The second DUKW also made it ashore but was destroyed by shell fire, and the two communications jeeps had their radio equipment drowned as they tried to get to shore.

Mildenberger's DUKW was the only communications link between the beach and the USS Ancon.

Mildenberger and Wheeler and others hoofed it through the constant shell fire over to where the beach HQ was set up. As they were discussing the situation, a shell exploded about 15 yards away from the party.

"Something hit me hard in the back, but I thought it was just a rock. It hurt, but it didn't hurt that bad. But when we started to go, I stumbled, and I couldn't move my arms. I said to Lt. Degnan, 'What's wrong with me?'

"I was wearing a Navy foul-weather jacket that I had swiped from the ship, and Lt. Degnan saw there was a hole in the back. They tore the coat open and he said, 'Hell, you're full of blood back here. There's a hole in you.'"

Mildenberger had been hit by a piece of shrapnel, and he was helped to an aid station on the beach. "The landing craft were com-

After care aboard the ship, Mildenberger was taken to a hospital in England, where the shrapnel was removed. "They said it had severed several major blood vessels, and that's why I bled so much."

Mildenberger carried his souvenir in his pocket with him for some time, a jagged piece of metal about an inch and a half long, but later lost it while he was awaiting transportation in Paris.

The wound took some time to heal, but by July he was released from the hospital and sent to a replacement depot. While there, he was notified that because he had volunteered to drive the DUKW in the first wave, he was going to receive the Silver Star.

"They made a big deal out of it. The replacement depot was located on some rich person's estate. Lady Somebody, I never did get her name, came to pin the medal on me."

While waiting for assignment, Mildenberger volunteered for training with the airborne. "It wasn't because I was any kind of hero. Eisenhower and all those guys were saying that we'd be home by Christmas, and I believed them. I figured that I'd get to stay in England and do the training, and by that time the war would be over."

But the training never happened. Instead, Mildenberger was put on a train, sent to southern England and once again shipped back to France, landing again on Omaha Beach.

cause he had always given me credit for saving his life. I'd been standing between him and that shell burst that day."

After a pleasant conversation, Talley asked Mildenberger what he was doing there, and Mildenberger said he was seeking Talley's help to avoid the infantry or artillery. "Are you AWOL?" Talley asked. "You'd better get your ass back to that depot, and I'll see what I can do."

A few days later, orders came through for Mildenberger to report to the 38th Signal Construction Battalion. "They were pretty amazed at the replacement depot. They'd never seen special orders come in."

Mildenberger's job was to work with teams that were restoring phone line service to much of France. After about three months of this duty, more orders arrived for Mildenberger.

"By this time I'd forgotten all about it, but my orders for airborne school came through. I don't even know how they found me."

For Mildenberger, it was back to England again. A nice break along the way, though, came when he had to wait in Paris for three days to get transportation. "We kept telling the guy, no, we don't need to go today."

In England, he went to 82nd Airborne School and was beginning to learn how to jump out of airplanes and fold parachutes. "They had this training exercise where you would

ACTUAL RADIO TRAFFIC FROM THE BEACH

Jim Mildenberger kept several documents through the years from his time in service. One of those is an actual transcription of the radio messages that were sent from the radio on Mildenberger's DUKW from Omaha Beach to the Corps headquarters aboard the ships. For many hours it was the only communication between that section of the beach and the HQ.

The DUKW was launched at 4 a.m., but the radio circuit was not opened until 6 a.m. as the boat approached the beach. Below are excerpts from the messages of June 6, 1944. The actual message in capital letters is followed by an explanation of the code or Col. B.B. Talley's comments written after the messages were transcribed.

0615 — PETER ITEM KING (DUKW #1 waterborne)

0629 — ROCKETS FIRED (At a pre-arranged signal, thousands of rockets were launched toward the beach by the incoming LCTs)

No time listed — LCI (L) NINE FOUR AND FOUR NINE THREE LANDED ZERO SEVEN FOUR ZERO/ FIRING HEAVY ON BEACH.

0815 — GEORGE NAN NAN (Many damaged tanks on beach.)

0820 — OBSTACLES NOT BREACHED/ FOUR TANKS SEAWARD OF OBSTACLES/ ONE BURNING/ INFANTRY HELD UP/ ENEMY FIRE HEAVY/ CREW ERIC AND CLAUDE HAVE FORCED TO WITHDRAW

0900 — FROM ONE THOUSAND YARDS OFF DOG RED BEACH I SEE SEVERAL COMPANIES/ ONE SIX INFANTRY ON EASY RED AND FOX RED BEACHES/ ENEMY FIRE AND MACHINE GUN FIRE STILL EFFEC-

TIVE/ ABOUT 30 LCTS STANDING BY TO LAND/ OBSTACLES SEEM THICKER THAN IN PHOTOS/ BTY ABLE SEVEN FA IN DUKWS JUST ARRIVED/ LOVE CHARLIE ITEM EIGHT FIVE HIT AND SMOKING AFTER UNLOADING/ HAVE SEEN TWO LOVE CHARLIE TARES BURN/ COUNT TEN TANKS ON FOX/ LANDING RESUMING ON DOG. (Landings had ceased on Easy and Fox beaches and landing was shifted to Dog sector.)

1035 — LCT THREE ZERO FIRING FIVE ZERO CAL MGS AT ENEMY POSITION ONE HUNDRED YARDS WEST OF HOUSE IN MOUTH EXIT EASY THREE

1040 — MEN ADVANCING UP SLOPE BEHIND EASY RED/ MEN BELIEVED OURS ON SKYLINE EASY FOX/ HOUSE AT EXIT EASY THREE SILENT DESTROYER SHELLING LES MOULINS/ THINGS LOOK BETTER.

1055— INFILTRATION APPROX PLATOON UP DRAW MIDWAY BETWEEN EXITS EASY ONE AND THREE.

(Talley indicates in his notes that the situation had reached a critical point at about 10:30 with about 50 LCTs circling at sea, but none landing on Easy and Fox beaches. LCT 30 and LCIL 544 made a heroic charge through the obstacles and landed, silencing enemy fire from the beach. The other craft soon followed, and the beach was taken.)

1140 — TROOPS ADVANCING UP WEST SLOPE EXIT EASY ONE/ THANKS DUE DESTROYER.

No time listed — TROOPS MOVING UP SLOPE FOX GREEN AND FOX RED/ I JOIN YOU IN THANKING

GOD FOR OUR NAVY (About 10:30 a.m., the Navy ships came in as close as possible and rained down artillery on the German positions on the cliff.

1200 — MEN ON SKYLINE FOX RED/ HEAVY ADVANCE UP DRAW BETWEEN EXITS EASY ONE AND EASY THREE.

1205— ENEMY ARTILLERY REGISTERED ON BEACH EASY RED AND FIRES WHEN CRAFT ARE THERE/ BELIEVE CRAFT CAN BE SEEN FROM CHURCH SPIRE AT VIERVILLE. (This message caused the Navy to target the spire and destroy it.)

1310 — EASY XRAY ROGER (The DUKW with the radio finally made it ashore.)

1347— ARRIVED ON BEACH EIGHT ZERO SITUATION DIFFICULT/ INFORMATION LIMITED/ PROGRESS SLOW/ FROM WYMAN TO HEUBNER LIAISON WITH COMBAT UNITS ONLY/ RADIO OUT/ WIRE GOING IN AT PRESENT

1400 — CMDR GIVENS STATES DEMOLITION PARTIES ARRIVED TOO LATE/ BREACHED ONLY ONE GAP/ CLEANUP OF BEACHES JUST COMMENCING/ ENEMY ARTY FIRE CONTINUES ON BEACH/ ATTEMPTING SET UP NEAR EXIT EASY ONE (Talley wrote later, "The situation on the beach was one of extreme congestion. It was impossible to distinguish the living from the dead and in moving up and down the beach it was necessary to step over men without knowing or expressing concern over their condition.") The messages continued throughout the day as the Americans took the crests and moved into the towns beyond.

jump from a platform on the back of a truck going about 15 miles an hour. You were supposed to land and roll. Somehow I came down on my knees, and I spent two days in the hospital."

When he got out, he was told, because he had fallen behind his class, he would have to start all over again with the next group. Instead, Mildenberger decided to volunteer for the 54th Signal Battalion of the 18th Airborne Corps. His job was to ride in gliders, then string phone wire between the front and the headquarters.

"I loved riding in those gliders. You'd sit on the runway, and the plane pulling the glider would take off. We were connected by nylon lines, and they'd stretch and stretch. The plane would be flying away, and we'd still be sitting there waiting for the lines to stretch to their limit. And then, zoom, away you'd go."

At one point, around the time of the Battle of the Bulge, Mildenberger and his team approached an officer at a crossroads and asked him for information about the location of a certain unit that needed a phone line. "He didn't seem to know anything, and we went on ahead. When we came back, we saw the same guy, except this time he had been captured, and they were holding a gun to his head. It turned out he was a German wearing an American uniform."

Another incident along the way to Germany was when a warrant officer flagged them down and asked if they had any gas for two planes that were stranded in a nearby field. "He saw that we were in Airborne, and he asked if one of us wanted to fly one of the planes back to the base. He told us that he'd give us enough

directions to get the plane off the ground, but it was up to us to land it. We passed on that offer."

Near the end, Mildenberger said Germans were surrendering in droves to the Americans — rather than go the other direction and surrender to the Russians. One day, a lone German soldier zoomed into town on a motorcycle and asked where he could surrender. Mildenberger and the others pointed him down the road to the nearest MP station. The soldier, though, said he wanted to go the other way so he could visit his mother before he surrendered.

"I don't know why, but that really hit me the wrong way. I hadn't seen my mother in three years. Why should he see his mother? I took my rifle and smashed the spark plugs on his motorcycle. We told him he could walk to the MP station."

Mildenberger stayed with the Airborne until the end of the war. His last duty was in Schwerin, Germany, near the Elbe River.

Because of his Silver Star and because he'd been overseas for three years, he was second in his battalion with 117 points, and he arrived back in the United States on June 12. He was discharged on June 19, having earned, in addition to his Silver Star, a Purple Heart and five battle stars.

After the war, Mildenberger worked in Africa building air bases. He then worked as a Minneapolis city bus driver before working for Jefferson Bus Lines for nearly 30 years. He was proud of his safety record.

He and his wife, Sally, raised three children in south Minneapolis before retiring to a home in Hackensack in 1984.

PEBBLES ON THE BEACH

When Mildenberger's DUKW finally landed at Omaha at about 1 p.m. on D-Day, it immediately got stuck in rounded pebbles like these.

Paul Norby kept as a souvenir the Bomber Squadron 86 schedule for August 15, 1945. The first strike was called back 50 miles from its target, and the second strike was canceled as the war came to a close in the Pacific.

```
0200   Breakfast
0315   First Flight Quarters
0315   Briefing for C-2
0 347 (about) General Quarters
- - - - - - - - - - - - - - - - - - - - - - - - - - - -
              STRIKE      C-2        (0530-1000)
0430  Flight Quarters   0530  Launch   1000  Recover

NORBY                GITTINGS      SEWALL      NAUGHTON
CURTIN               GOLDEN        PRINCE      PARIS
NASON                WARD          KRAUSE      HENDERSON
UNGER        Strike Recalled  50 miles  from target.
- - - - - - - - - - - - - - - - - - - - - - - - - - - -
0900   Briefing for C-5

                     STRIKE  C-5     (1145-1615)
1045  Flight Quarters   1145 Launch   1615  Recover

LAKE           No go       GITTINGS      MARKS       NASON
GAFFNEY        ────────    GOLDEN        COLLINS     UNGER
EVERDING       War         WARD          DUNKLEE     KRAUSE
BREINHOLT      over
- - - - - - - - - - - - - - - - - - - - - - - - - - - -
                 CANCELLATION ORDER
        WARD                        UNGER
        GOLDEN                      NASON
        GITTINGS                    KRAUSE
- - - - - - - - - - - - - - - - - - - - - - - - - - - -
NOTICES:
      1 Pilots scheduled for first strike that do not get off
will be used on second strike.

NEW PILOTS AND AIR-CREWMEN ARE.
```

Unless indicated otherwise, all photos are from Paul Norby's personal collection.

FROM SEAMAN SECOND CLASS TO REAR ADMIRAL

Paul Norby graduated from Minneapolis Central High School in 1931. In 1935, he joined the Navy as a seaman second class, one rung from the bottom. By the end of the war, much of it spent on an aircraft carrier, he was a squadron commander. By the time he left the Navy, he was a rear admiral.

There are few Navy veterans who can claim to have started as an E-2 seaman second class and ended their military career as a rear admiral.

Paul Norby, who flew dive bombers from carrier decks in World War II, can make just that claim. He began his career at the bottom while learning to fly at Wold-Chamberlain Field and ended it in the lofty hierarchy of the Naval Reserve.

Norby, who just turned 95, lives by himself in Minnetonka, spends time on the Internet and answering his e-mails, and recently got together on a cruise boat on Lake Minnetonka with his World War II buddies.

He grew up in several towns in Minnesota. His dad, Joseph Norby, had graduated from St. Olaf College in Northfield in 1904 and had been a superintendent of schools in Madison and Fergus Falls before becoming the administrator of the Fairview Hospital in Minneapolis.

Norby was born in 1913 and was one of six kids. He graduated from Min-neapolis Central High School in 1931. Since his mother also was a graduate of St. Olaf, there was little doubt about where the children would go to college.

After graduation in 1936, Norby had dreams of going on to Harvard for post-graduate work, and he even had a recommendation by the president of St. Olaf, but he was unable to secure a scholarship.

This was the height of the Depression, with few jobs available, and Norby turned his attention to a special program for aviation cadets. "I said, 'Why don't I try that?' There were 400 who applied, and four of us made it."

Norby reported to the air station and was designated a seaman second class, a rank that now would be called seaman apprentice. He lived at the station and took classes and learned to fly a small plane. "I can't remember what kind of plane it was, but it was a bi-plane and a tail-drag-ger. The field was grass, and it used to be a racetrack. Our solo was just up and around and back."

BOMBER SQUADRON 86

USS WASP

Three of the cadets passed the training and soloed. "But they could only take so many at flight training in Pensacola. So we said goodbye, and the next year they called. We had to pay our own way down to Florida, and we drove down in my Model A Ford."

There were five squadrons at Pensacola, teaching the cadets the different kinds of flying. By 1938, the group was ready for the fleet.

"We got our wings, but we went to the fleet as cadets. We didn't know what to do with ourselves. We couldn't eat in the officer's mess, and we couldn't eat in the enlisted mess. So they had us eat with the chief petty officers, but they sure didn't want us in there listening to their conversations."

Another problem was that the cadets had studied hard at learning to fly, but not at learning life in the Navy. "We were calling the deck a floor; and the ladders, stairways; and the bulkheads, walls. They said, 'Those dumb cadets, all they know how to do is fly airplanes.' "

But sometimes, flying the airplanes was also a challenge. While still a cadet, Norby and another pilot were coming back from a mission when Norby misread the flags being signaled from the flight deck. He thought the landing officer was telling him to circle around and come back and try again.

"So we went round again and came back and the ship wasn't there." It was standard procedure for ships to maintain their planned course so the pilots could find them, but the captain had decided to change course by ignoring a scheduled turn to "help" the errant pilots.

"We did a box, flying further and further out, and then we found them.

They were 40 miles from where we thought they should be." On that particular flight, Norby was flying the executive officer's plane. When he landed, the captain called for the pilot of that plane to come up the bridge, thinking it was the XO. Instead, Norby presented himself.

"The captain said he didn't want to see any damn cadets, and he didn't want to see me. So they called down again for whoever was flying that plane to report to the bridge. So I walked in again. He just stared at me."

The captain was getting ready to let Norby have it with both barrels, but the young pilot spoke first. "I told him that two wrongs don't make a right. I admitted that I'd missed the flag signal, but that it was his job to keep the ship on course. He just looked at me, and finally he said, 'I'll remember that. You're dismissed.' "

«

PAUL NORBY

At home in Minnetonka

»

DURING THE WAR

Norby worked his way up to lieutenant commander and skipper of a bomber squadron before the end of the war.

BOMBER SQUADRON 86

Paul Norby first served on the carrier USS Saratoga, but after it was sunk he went back to the United States and became a trainer. When a new bomber squadron was formed at Wildwood Naval Air Station in New Jersey, Norby became the squadron commander. He is front and center in this 1944 photo.

Norby said he got some unwelcome notoriety as the pilot who told the skipper what to do, but he didn't mean to show up his commander. "He was a good skipper, but he just didn't follow the plan of the day."

Norby remembers one other instance when he might have been a little insubordinate. "There was a new pilot, an Academy boy. Some of those guys were good, and some of them weren't."

"We were going to do some night flying, and I'd been in the ready room with the red lights, trying to get my night vision. After we'd launched, the new pilot was running his plane on a rich fuel mixture, and the red stream gasses were flowing off his engine, and they were very bright. I radioed him to 'lean' it out, but he didn't. Later on, he told me that he had changed his mixture.

"I told him he should have done it when I told him to. If I lose my night vision, I might run into him or another plane."

Norby was assigned in 1938 to Bomber Squadron 4 on the USS Ranger, CV-4. After a year, they finally made the new fliers ensigns, the lowest-ranking naval officer.

The original dive bomber he flew from the Ranger's deck was the Great Lakes BG-1, a plane made in the 1930s. Only 61 were built.

He later switched to the SBD Dauntless, one of the workhorses of the Navy for the next few years. The dive bomber was built by Northrup and had a crew of two, a pilot and a gunner.

Norby was aboard USS Saratoga when the war started. The ship was tied to the pier at San Diego when the Japanese bombed Pearl Harbor.

"We knew war was coming for some time. When the attack came, they froze everybody on the base. We were ordered to load live bombs for the first time. They thought the Japanese would land in Mexico and invade to the north."

The ship immediately set out for

SB2C
Helldiver Statistics

SB2C Data

Manufacturer
Curtiss-Wright

Engine
Wright R-2600 Cyclone radial engine

Crew
Two, pilot and radio operator

Armament
Two 20-millimeter cannons in the wings. Two .30-caliber Browning machine guns in the rear cockpit. The plane could carry 2,000 pounds of bombs

Maximum Speed
294 miles per hour

Ceiling
25,000 feet

Range, loaded
1,200 miles

Number Built
7,140; only one remains flying

Hawaii on its way to Wake Island to deliver Marine aircraft to reinforce the base there. In the end, the rescue mission was a couple days too late, and the Japanese captured the island.

When the ship arrived at Pearl Harbor at night, the harbor master refused to open up the nets that protected the harbor from submarines. "Instead, we spent all night out where the Japanese submarines might have been."

While the ship was in harbor, new metal seats were installed in the SBDs that would provide the pilots with more protection.

The pilots were happy to have them but weren't ready for the side effects. At the end of one flight, Norby said, the squadron looked for the ship and it wasn't where it was supposed to be.

"Our procedure was to drop a smoke

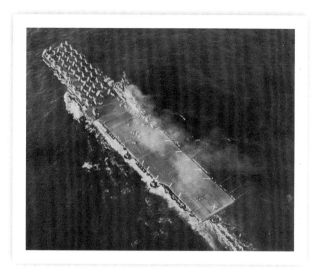

USS WASP

The USS Wasp, CV-18, joined the war effort in late 1943.

They sounded general quarters, and we headed for our ready room for orders."

Because of the damage to the ship, only seven or eight planes could be launched, and Norby was piloting

bomb I had, I went up a little higher to drop it, and it exploded on contact. Shrapnel from that bomb put 14 holes in my plane, and there were skin peels in the wing. I asked my gunner if he was hurt, and he said

---

"You tried to level out at about 3,000 feet. If you missed that by about two seconds, you're in the water."

---

bomb, and then conduct a search from there so we wouldn't get even more lost. We circled around, trying to figure out what had happened to the ship."

Eventually, the bombers found the carrier again. "It turned out that those metal seats had an effect on the compass, knocking it 15 degrees out of whack. We got that fixed in a hurry."

Saratoga was torpedoed southwest of Hawaii in January 1942. "We were eating when there was a thump, and all the planes shook.

one of them. At the last minute, however, the aircraft he was going to take had technical problems, and he took a spare plane.

"When I got in the air, I realized I didn't know what kind of bomb I had attached. I just didn't look."

The little squadron knew the submarine was lurking in the area somewhere waiting for the coup de grace to the carrier. They found the sub, dropped bombs and depth charges on it, then headed back home.

"Because I didn't know what kind of

he was okay, so we started back to the carrier.

"When we got back to the ship, it was dead in the water and the lights were out. When they had tried to level the ship, all the boilers had gone out. The ship was without power. Because they had no power, they couldn't answer our radio calls, and they couldn't talk to us."

Norby and the others circled a few times, and the commander of the squadron finally decided to try and make it to Pearl Harbor for a landing. "He told us to lean-up the mixture until the engines were coughing and get the RPMs down as much as we could.

"We made it there, but we were worried they would think we were a Japanese group. The Japanese planes can't withdraw their wheels, and so when we came over Barber's Point, we kept putting our wheels up and down to show we were Americans."

The pilots landed and waited for the Saratoga to make it to port, which she did a couple of days later. "The guys were already welding before the ship even stopped dead." After emergency repairs at Pearl Harbor, the Saratoga went back to the United States for major repairs.

In late spring, Norby received orders back to shore duty. The war had just begun, but he had been at sea for three years, and the normal rotation was two years.

He was sent to Miami, where, for the next year-and-a-half, he trained dive-bomber pilots. Later, he became an F-4 fighter pilot and trainer at Jacksonville for six months.

In early 1944, Norby, who had advanced to lieutenant commander by this time, was sent to Wildwood Naval Air Station at Cape May, New Jersey, to be the commander of 86th Bomber Squadron. It was to be assigned to the new USS Wasp, just coming out of the shipbuilding yard in Boston.

The squadron joined the Wasp at Ulithi at the start of 1945 and began bombing missions over the Japanese homeland. Norby's group took over the planes of the air group that was being rotated back home.

The bomber pilots were now flying the SB2C Helldiver.

The pilots had to be highly skilled at landing on the carrier, catching the metal lines, and getting their plane out of the way. "Even if it only took you 30 seconds to land and move on, if you've got 70 planes in the air, that still would mean it would take 35 minutes to land them all. Some of those fighters might be short on gas."

As the squadron leader, Norby would always land first and then head up to the bridge to watch the other landings.

"We had a pilot one time who kept coming in and then would just go around, then he'd come in again, and just go around. He was freezing everytime he tried to land. Finally, we got on the radio and ordered him

ON THE FLIGHT DECK

Norby, right, joined fellow pilot Samuel Garjanski on the flight deck of the USS Wasp. Note the wooden deck.

PILOT REGALIA

Norby posed in front of his aircraft in his flying duds.

PLANES IN REVIEW

Aircraft lined up for inspection at NAS Wildwood in early 1944.

to land.

"He made it, and I went out to see him. His flight suit was just soaking wet. I told him if he wanted to quit, he could."

Norby recalls one bombing run over Japan later in the war when he had come in at 18,000 feet and had begun his dive. Suddenly he heard from his tail gunner, "Skipper, I've got butterflies in my stomach."

Norby had little choice but to continue his attack. Later back at the ship, Norby cornered the gunner and asked him why he would say such a thing at such a critical time. "He told me, 'I don't know, I just had to talk to somebody because I was so nervous.'"

On a typical mission, Norby said the fighters would go in ahead of the bombers and clear the way. Sometimes they would even drop chafe, small pieces of metal foil that would confuse the enemy anti-aircraft efforts.

The Helldivers would go in at 70 de-

THE BEAST

The SB2C Helldiver had several nicknames with the Naval pilots and ground crew. It was called "The Beast," the "Two-Cee" and the "Son of a Bitch Second Class."

grees and about 300 miles an hour. "You tried to level out at 3,000 feet. If you missed that by about two seconds, you're in the water."

Not every landing on the carrier was a smooth one. In particular, he recalls one time when he was bringing a 1,000-pound smoke bomb out to protect the destroyer screen, when the mission was canceled and all the planes were ordered back. "We knew we weren't supposed to land with a full tank, but we weren't calling the shots. So when I landed, I ruined the shocks, and the wings were bent.

"They wanted me to sign a piece of paper that said it was 50-percent pilot error, but I said I wouldn't do it. I never did sign that paper."

On one mission, one of the fliers in Norby's squadron got hit and actually had to land at a Japanese air base in Hiroshima. He was taken prisoner and at some point later was put on a train to be taken to Tokyo. The next day the first atomic bomb was dropped on Hiroshima.

Toward the end of the war, the USS Wasp was under regular attack by Japanese kamikaze planes, one of which missed the ship by just a few feet. The carrier was hit by a bomb in March 1945. "The bomb hit right on deck, right back by the second elevator. We came back to Pearl right away."

In July, the carrier returned to the war zone around Japan. On the day the war ended, Norby was flying a mission over Tokyo. "We received messages, 'No go, return to base,' and 'No go, war is over.' "

On September 2, 1945, Norby flew another mission over Tokyo Bay, but this one was in connection with Japan's formal surrender on the

USS Missouri. There were more than 500 planes in the air that day.

After being in the Navy for eight years, many of them at sea, he was done with military life. "I had enough points to go home two or three times. I had been lucky all the way through. I just told them I was leaving."

Norby left the ship in Pearl Harbor. "I took off my flight gear and said goodbye. I got on the first ship heading back to the East Coast. Wouldn't you know it, when we were going through the Panama Canal, I looked behind and there was the damn Wasp."

In all, Norby made more than 380 carrier landings, one of the highest totals by any pilot in World War II. He earned the Distinguished Flying Cross and two Air Medals during the war. His air group earned a Presidential Unit Citation.

After the war, Norby stayed in the Reserves. He had been a lieutenant commander at the end of the war, but as time went by, he moved up the ladder. By the time he retired, he had reached the lofty rank of rear admiral.

He lived in Mabel, Minnesota, for many years after the war, the hometown of his wife, Dorothy, also a graduate of St. Olaf. They had two children.

MUSTANG ADMIRAL

Norby rose through the ranks to rear admiral after starting out as a seaman second class. Officers who rose from the ranks are often called "mustangs."

HEADQUARTERS
ARMY SECURITY AGENCY
WASHINGTON 25, D. C.

WDGSS-94
201-Hedstrom, Arthur C.

25 March 1946

SUBJECT: Commendation

TO: First Lieutenant Arthur C. Hedstrom
Army Security Agency
Washington 25, D. C.

1. You were assigned to Vint Hill Farms Station on 4 December 1944. From October 1945 through January 1946 you worked on a special project for Army Security Agency.

2. Your work consisted of helping in the development of a highly classified complex unit of a special type which has assumed considerable importance in the activities of Army Security Agency.

3. Development of this equipment was carried out with ingenuity and in the face of difficulties imposed by materials and equipment not well suited to this type of development. The equipment which was developed is so well suited to the special type of problem for which it was designed that it is being used as a model to construct additional equipments for Army Security Agency.

4. I want to commend you for your outstanding work in the development of this equipment. I know you will take pride in the material contribution your work has made to the mission of this Agency.

5. A copy of this Commendation will be made a permanent part of your official file.

W. PRESTON CORDERMAN
Brigadier General, USA
Commanding

HE WAS ALWAYS GOOD WITH MACHINES

Arthur Hedstrom had a natural gift for working with electronics and machines. As a youth, he and his brother developed their own hydroelectric system for their rural home. At the end of World War II, Hedstrom helped develop a code-breaking machine that was able to read the messages of the Soviet Union.

Growing up in the remote tip of northeastern Minnesota taught Arthur Hedstrom how to fix things.

"I always figured that if somebody could design and build it, I could take it apart and fix it," he said.

That resolve and skill enabled Hedstrom to rise from lowly enlisted man to first lieutenant during his World War II service and to spend much of his later time in the war building a machine that enabled America to decode the messages of one of its allies – Russia.

Hedstrom was born in 1919 about five miles from Grand Marais in a house along the Gunflint Trail. His father, Andrew Hedstrom, owned a sawmill that provided much of the lumber for that part of Minnesota.

The Hedstrom home was built at the confluence of a small stream and the Devil Track River, about five miles from Lake Superior. He was the ninth of 12 children, four girls and eight boys.

For his first eight years of schooling,

Hedstrom attended a three-room schoolhouse about a mile from home. The children walked to school in the fall and spring and were pulled by horses on a sled in the winter.

There were four or five kids in each class, and Hedstrom said it was a good education. "We had some good teachers."

High school was in Grand Marais, and after hitching a ride with neighbors for the first couple of years, he drove to school in a Model T Ford for the last two.

The Ford became part of his education. "I could take the engine out, work on it, and get it back in the car over the weekend."

His greatest challenge came when he was a junior: he and an older brother decided to provide electricity to the house. The Hedstroms had never had electricity and powered their lights with kerosene and gas.

The brothers took advantage of an existing dam and built a water wheel on the nearby stream. It was about

12 feet high and three feet wide, and it had large buckets to capture the water and make the wheel turn.

"We didn't know anything about electricity, and so we ordered a series of books from McGraw-Hill on the subject."

The first problem was taking a water wheel that turned slowly and hooking it up through a complex series of gears to a generator that needed to go about a thousand revolutions per minute. Once they accomplished

that, they needed to keep the speed of the water wheel constant.

"We got an old flyball governor and hooked it up." The governor would work a lever that would open and close a gate on the stream that brought the water to the wheel. It worked.

"Sometimes, when you turned on a bunch of lights at once, they would all dim for a few minutes until the generator caught up. But it worked for over ten years until the REA came along and brought in regular electricity."

After graduating from high school in 1937, Hedstrom went to work for his father. One job was running a large horizontal saw that made shingles. "There wasn't a guy who ran that saw that didn't lose his fingers. My father told me that one time a worker called him over and said, 'I just cut off my little finger.' My fa-

ther said, 'How did you do that?' And the guy said, 'Well, I was just doing this... Oh, shit, there goes another one.' "

During one summer, Hedstrom was running a small logging camp, where the men were harvesting cedar for his father's mill. "Not everybody knows it, but cedar can be very toxic. That's why it makes such good fence posts — because it doesn't rot. Well, I didn't react very well to it, and I got a rash all over my body. I didn't think I wanted to continue in that business."

He got a job working with a carpenter, building houses and then went to work for Northwestern Bell Telephone Company. He helped put the first telephone line into Grand Portage, Minnesota, and then took over the maintenance of an international line that went into Canada.

"I must have climbed every pole be-

tween Beaver Bay and the Pigeon River."

His next job was to help communities convert from the old magneto or manual phone systems to dial phones. Hedstrom worked in Hinckley, Sandstone, Carlton, Eveleth, and Chisholm over the next year or so.

The work was fairly routine, but yielded some interesting encounters.

At a house in Eveleth owned by a wealthy car dealer, and he was met at the door by the man's wife. "She asked me what size feet I had, and I told her ten-and-one-half. She told me to come back the next day, and she shut the door."

Hedstrom was baffled, but showed up dutifully the next morning. She handed him a pair of slippers she had knitted overnight. "She had beautiful white carpeting, and she didn't want me tracking it up."

«

ART HEDSTROM

At home in North Oaks

»

DURING THE WAR

Hedstrom enlisted as corporal, but was a first lieutenant by the end of the war.

In another case, Hedstrom trimmed what he thought was old telephone wire from a customer's house. Hours later, the phone rang, and the customer reported no heat. Hed-strom had accidentally removed the thermostat wire.

And in one other instance, the lady of the house came into the bedroom where Hedstrom was working. She was wearing only a see-through negligee. "I had to explain to her that I didn't do that sort of thing during working hours."

When World War II came, Hedstrom knew he would soon be drafted. "My boss came to a couple of us and said they were short of experienced telephone men in the service. He asked us to go in. I've always said that I was kind of a 'handcuff volunteer.' "

Hedstrom headed for Fort Snelling where he took a series of tests. They sent him home for about six days to get his personal affairs in order, and then he reported back. He would enter the service as a corporal.

At Fort Snelling, they issued him and others a summer khaki uniform and put them on a train to New York. "We were sure that we were going to North Africa because of the light uniforms."

Wrong. In fact, the destination was Iceland.

For the Allies, Iceland was a key station in the defense of the North Atlantic. It had several radar stations and other facilities, but its phone system was a disaster.

Now telephone technology was something Hedstrom was good at. The rest of his military expertise was lacking somewhat because he had gone right from enlistment to his first duty. "I didn't know how to march, and I didn't know who to salute or even how to salute."

In March 1942, he landed in Reykjavik and was ordered to check over the island's military phone system. "It was the biggest damn mess I'd ever seen. The first thing I had to do was build a main distribution frame with the lines coming in on the outside and the lines going to local phones on the other side."

FIRST DUTY

Hedstrom was originally assigned to northern Iceland to help run the telephone system.

DRIVING TO SCHOOL

Hedstrom drove to Grand Marais High School in this Model T Ford.

By September 1942, Hedstrom had helped straighten out the phones in Reykjavik, been promoted to sergeant, and was sent to the northern side of the island, where a new base and settled in for the winter. The base was situated between two radar outposts, and the base's main function was to plot on maps what the radar stations radioed in and in- major, then a colonel and finally a general. And then commenced an ass-chewing like I never saw in my life. I never did have the nerve to go up to that first lieutenant and tell

---

"Somtimes I'd awake in the middle of the night and I'd have the solution to what had been stopping me during the day."

---

was being constructed at Akureyri – 20 miles from the Arctic Circle.

"They told us the camp was all ready, but, when we got there, all they had done is make a floor for the kitchen."

The men slept in tents, but the mild weather of summer was about to depart for the 24-hour dark and frigid Icelandic winter. "As the days went by, it got colder, windier and more miserable. I went up to the captain and said, 'Look, we're going to be here all winter, we're going to have to build this camp ourselves.' "

The materials for the camp were available, just not the engineers to build it.

"They were just Quonset huts, just like Erector Sets. I figured there wouldn't be any problem putting them up."

First, the telephone troops had to get permission from the Corps of Engineers. They were allowed to build one hut and have it inspected.

"The officer from the Corps of Engineers came up and looked at our work. He told our captain, 'You can build all the damn buildings you want.' "

With Hedstrom in charge, the men built about 14 more Quonset huts

form Reykjavik.

The base was considered the headquarters of northern Iceland, and the Army decided to build a large building for that purpose. To speed up the process, the Corps of Engineers was to tackle one side of the building and Hedstroms's Signal Corps the other. The building was to be made of poured concrete, and the forms had to be built for the walls.

"Every day, the first lieutenant from the Corps would come over and look over our work. He always said we were using too much wire in making the forms. But I knew how heavy concrete was, and so we used a lot of wire."

The so-called amateurs finished their side of the building first, so their side was poured first. It took 20 hours, but, in the end, the walls were in place.

A couple of days later, the teams began the pour on the Corps side of the building. "We had poured for six or eight hours when you began to hear this squeak and other noises. Not long after, the forms just gave out, and the concrete began to collect in the middle of the building in the excavation.

"It only took about ten minutes, but first there was a captain, then a

him he didn't use enough wire."

The General then viewed the side of the building made by the Signal Corps. "Right on the spot, he said he would make me an officer in the Corps of Engineers."

Hedstrom declined and told the general he had already applied for Officer Candidate School and hoped to head back to the United States soon for training.

In fact, Hedstrom only had to pass one more hurdle – an interview by a group of high-ranking officers in Iceland. "I was the last one to be interviewed, and everybody else had come out of the room with sweat running down their faces.

"When I went in, they asked me some tough questions, but I thought I did all right. Finally, a general said, 'Sergeant, we've had a long, hard day. Why don't you tell us a joke?'

"I can't remember what joke I told, but they all laughed." A few days later, Hedstrom had orders to the United States.

He boarded an old luxury liner that had been converted into a troop ship. The skipper was Norwegian, and, when the large convoy set out from Reykjavik, the captain didn't like how slow it was. It was in March 1943, and the Germans still ruled

ARLINGTON HALL

Hedstrom spent much of the war at the intelligence station at Arlington Hall, home of the U.S. code-breaking efforts in World War II. *U.S. Army photo*.

the North Atlantic with their submarine wolf packs.

"He told the convoy he had developed engine trouble, and we returned to Reykjavik. We waited three or four days, and then joined another convoy that was made up of three destroyers, three or four liberty ships and us. The captain was much happier with this arrangement."

In the first part of the trip, though, it wasn't the Germans who posed a lethal problem for the convoy. It was the weather.

"Our old skipper said that he'd spent his whole life in the North Atlantic, and this was the worst storm he'd ever seen. I believed it. There were so many of the ship's sailors seasick that I pulled duty standing next to the captain on the bridge.

"It was so rough, there weren't waves; there were mountains of water there. The captain would look at his instruments and say, 'If this son-of-a-bitch rolls just five more degrees, we won't come back.' "

The storm finally abated, and suddenly the ship was in perfectly calm waters. It was much better for the crew, but also much better for the German subs.

"This captain had the most amazing eyesight. He could see things at sea that nobody else could. One day, he suddenly shouted, 'Ninety degrees left,' and the ship turned sharply. As we looked, we could see a torpedo go right along our side."

It missed the troop ship but hit one of the liberty ships, sinking it quickly. In convoys, there's no turning back, and the remaining ships steamed grimly to a port in Rhode Island. By

the time the convoy arrived, Hedstrom said, only the destroyers and the troop ship were left. Between the storm and the Nazi submarines, the liberty ships were all gone.

Hedstrom went to officer's training at Fort Monmouth, New Jersey, and his adjustment to stateside service wasn't instantaneous. There weren't a lot of German planes attacking Iceland, but there were some, and, when the soldiers there heard a boom, they were conditioned to dive for the nearest low ground.

On Hedstrom's first day at the fort, there was a thunderous boom. Without hesitation, he availed himself of the nearest ditch.

When he looked up, everyone else was standing and saluting. It turned out the boom was a cannon firing to acknowledge "retreat" at 5 p.m.

Hedstrom had to explain his strange actions to a First Lieutenant Peelock, who turned out to be his immediate officer-in-charge of his training unit. It was a rocky start to a relationship that Hedstrom said only went downhill from there. "There was nothing I could do right as far as Lieutenant Peelock was concerned."

The months of scrutiny ended, though, when Hedstrom became an officer and a gentleman in the U.S. Army. His first assignment was to attend a long-line school which taught officers the intricacies of long-distance phone lines.

Because Hedstrom knew more about the subject than the instructor, he was made the assistant instructor in the class. One of the students was Peelock.

Payback can be wonderful. "If there was any kind of bad duty, any stinking job, Lieutenant Peelock got it.

Army of the United States

To all who shall see these presents, greeting:

Know ye, that reposing special trust and confidence in the fidelity and abilities of ___Technician 5th Grade ARTHUR C. HEDSTROM, 17061237, 556th Signal AW Bn___, I do hereby appoint him *___Technician 4th Grade (Temporary)___, ARMY OF THE UNITED STATES, to rank as such from the ___tenth___ day of ___September___ one thousand nine hundred and ___forty two___ He is therefore carefully and diligently to discharge the duty of †___Technician 4th Grade___ by doing and performing all manner of things thereunto belonging. And I do strictly charge and require all Noncommissioned Officers and Soldiers under his command to be obedient to his orders as ___Technician 4th Grade___ And he is to observe and follow such orders and directions from time to time, as he shall receive from his Superior Officers and Noncommissioned Officers set over him, according to the rules and discipline of War.

Given under my hand at ___APO 860, c/o Postmaster, New York, N.Y.___ this ___tenth___ day of ___September___ in the year of our Lord one thousand nine hundred and ___forty two.___

K. F. MARCH,
Lt Col, Sig C, Commanding.

W. D., A. C. O. Form No. 58
March 25, 1924

* Insert grade, company, and regiment or arm or service; e. g., "Corporal, Company A, 1st Infantry," "Sergeant, Quartermaster Corps."
† Insert grade.

16—22676

TECH 4

While in Iceland, Hedstrom was promoted to Technician 4th Grade.

Finally, he came up to me and said he was sorry he had treated me that way in OCS. I told him, 'We're not through with this just yet.' "

When the class did end, he and Lieutenant Peelock shook hands.

In December 1944, Hedstrom was off to Arlington Hall Station in Virginia, the American equivalent of the British Bletchley Park, home of U.S. code-breaking efforts during the war. It was located just outside Washington D.C. in Virginia. Hedstrom's actual duty was at Vint Hill Farms Station, an intelligence-gathering location that eventually had hundreds of acres of antennas and silos.

For the next two years, Hedstrom worked on code breaking, specializing in the complicated machinery that was used to simplify the process.

When the Germans were preparing to surrender, Hedstrom and his mates intercepted a message between Germany and Switzerland about the impending event. "We had the message three hours before Washington knew about it. We all decided to drive up to Washington that night because we thought it would be quite a party. It was."

As the war in Europe and the Pacific came to a close, the cryptographers turned their attention to another code-breaking effort that was critical to the future of the nation – breaking the Russian codes.

Although Russia was officially America's ally, it was becoming clear that the post-war world would be a struggle between the Soviet communist ideology and Western democracy. Knowing what the Russians were communicating was a critical task.

Hedstrom was assigned to create a machine that would duplicate the actions of the Russian code machine. The code breakers discovered that the Russians used a standard five-letter code, they would send three to five messages at a time, making the task more difficult.

It became an all-absorbing problem, and Hedstrom would work on the machine by day and lose sleep over it at night. "Sometimes, I would wake up in the middle of the night, and I'd have the solution to what had been stopping me during the day. It was crystal-clear. And then I'd wake up in the morning, and I couldn't remember the solution.

"That's when I started sleeping with a flashlight and a notepad. When I woke up, all I needed to do was jot down my thoughts. It worked."

It took many months, but Hedstrom came up with the machine the Army was looking for.

The officer in charge of the project wanted to thank Hedstrom by putting something in his file to show how important the assignment was, but in a top-secret world, such memos were difficult.

The final letter achieved new heights of ambiguity: "Your work consisted of helping in the development of a highly classified complex unit of a special type which has as-sumed considerable importance in the activities of Army Security Agency." And, "The equipment which was developed is so well-suited to the special type of problem for which it was designed that it is being used as a model to construct additional equipments..."

One of the things that made Hedstrom happiest was that the machine he built to replace the Russian code machine could fit on a kitchen table. Some time later, the Americans captured one of the real Russian code machines, and it was much larger. Hedstrom had managed to build a better, or at least a more compact, mousetrap.

Because of his projects, Hedstrom was kept in the Army until late 1946. He had to sign papers saying he would not disclose any of the work he had been doing. He was offered a job on the White House staff at that point, but he decided it was time to be a civilian again.

When he did get home to Minnesota, he took back his old job with Bell Telephone. He worked his way up the company ladder, ending up in Minneapolis as the general switching manager at the divisional level. He retired in 1981.

He married his pre-war sweetheart, Marian — whom he had met in Grand Rapids — at the chapel at Fort Monmouth, New Jersey, in November 1943.

They have two children, two grandchildren and two great-grandchildren. And, on Saturday afternoons, Hedstrom and his son and a friend gather to work on a Model T Ford they're restoring. It's the exact model of the car he used to drive to school in Grand Marais some 70 years ago.

MARRIED HIS SWEETHEART

Marian and Arthur Hedstrom were married at Fort Monmouth, New Jersey, in 1943.

As a young officer in Alaska, Hogan clowns around with a captured Japanese knife while sitting astride an unexploded Japanese bomb.

Unless indicated otherwise, all photos are from Patrick Hogan's personal collection.

THE BOMB DISPOSAL SQUAD

Patrick Hogan of Gilbert, on Minnesota's Iron Range, was one of the first Minnesota men drafted into the Army during World War II. He volunteered for a bomb disposal unit and served in Alaska and Europe, finding and defusing bombs and mines. "You never had to worry about making a mistake."

It's usually a good thing to be first – unless it involves your local draft board.

Patrick Hogan Jr. of Gilbert was a 25-year-old car mechanic working at the Montgomery Ward service station on University Avenue in St. Paul when he got the historic communication in March 1941.

Hogan became one of the first men drafted in Minnesota prior to World War II. For this distinction he received an all-expenses-paid trip to Fort Snelling, a new set of olive drab clothing and his picture on the front page of the St. Paul Pioneer Press.

The picture showed Hogan's feet being examined, with the caption: "Dogs of War Being Measured."

Hogan says he was "quite shocked" by getting the notice. The nation wasn't at war, and he had not made plans to spend time in the military.

Hogan was born in 1916, the second of six children. His father had emigrated from Canada to be a steam shovel operator, first in the iron mines near Hibbing, and then later near Gilbert.

His father later went into the livery business, then converted his horse business into the area's first horseless carriage business. Patrick Sr. also purchased the first car on the eastern Mesabi Range in 1911.

"I've always been impressed by what he did," Hogan said. "Here he had a livery barn full of horses, and then overnight he switched over to servicing cars. He didn't know the difference between a magneto and a coil, or anything else. But he made it go."

Patrick Jr. graduated from Gilbert High School and went to Eveleth Junior College before finding out there were few jobs on the Iron Range in the late years of the Depression. He eventually took the job at Ward's in St. Paul.

Hogan's mother and father accompanied him to his induction in St. Paul, and then he was off to Fort Leonard Wood and later Fort Knox for training.

"There were openings at Aberdeen (Maryland) for volunteers for bomb disposal training. My friends thought I was goofy, but I thought it would be a chance to do something a little bit different. I figured you'd never have to worry about making a mistake because you wouldn't be there to find out about it."

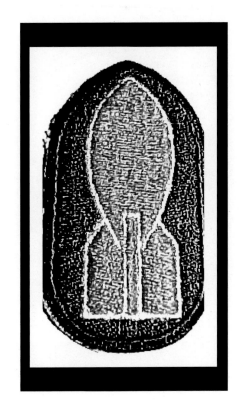

At Aberdeen, Hogan was chosen for officer's training, and he completed his bomb disposal training as a second lieutenant.

"There was a lot of training. There were a lot of different fuses you had to learn. Some of them were not meant to be touched."

When the war started, the Japanese began sending helium balloons across the Pacific with a bomb attached. Hogan's squad was sent to San Francisco for a short period to be available in case one of these balloon bombs came to rest on the West Coast.

After the bombing of Dutch Harbor in the Aleutians, Hogan and his team were moved to Adak, one of the desolate islands that trail away from western Alaska. When the Japanese were ousted from their strongholds at Kiska and Attu, further west, Hogan's bomb squad was sent in to clear the formerly occupied territory of explosives.

"There was a lot of mine sweeping. They had entrenched themselves in the caves, and the caves were full of big gun emplacements. They had railroad tracks where they could roll out the guns to the cave openings and shell the beach. If they had opposed the landing, it would have been a disaster for us."

Instead, the Japanese departed quietly, leaving the dried fish still hanging in the caves. The bomb squad initially had to check for booby traps, then diffuse and destroy the artillery shells. A bonus for the bomb squad was that they had first crack at the myriad knives, flags, guns and other souvenirs left behind by the quickly departing enemy.

Hogan's memories of living on Adak are not pleasant. "It was a very bad environment. For over a year we stayed in tents and slept in sleeping bags, and they weren't the kind of cold weather bags you see these days. We just had to wrap ourselves in GI blankets."

There was a small pot-bellied stove in each tent, and the men would have to go down the hill to the beach to retrieve coal the Navy would drop off every now and then.

"When there was a blizzard, you had to follow a rope to get out to the latrine behind the tent. There were guys who lost contact with the rope, and they never came back.

"Sometimes the wind would blow so hard, it would knock the tent down. There wasn't much you could do but just lay there all night in the collapsed tent and hope you could put it back up in the morning."

Originally, Hogan's bomb disposal team was slated to head for the South Pacific, but as the United

«

PATRICK HOGAN JR.

At home in Gilbert

»

DURING THE WAR

Hogan was drafted, but then went through officer's training school and joined a bomb disposal unit.

States gathered its forces for the invasion of France, the team was given orders to cross the United States and depart for England. They had a few days to stop off in their hometowns along the way.

Earlier, the squad had adopted a blue fox as a mascot on their Alaskan island, and he had become part of their family. "I drew the longest straw and I got to keep the fox," Hogan said. He concealed the animal in his coat for the long journey from Alaska to Minnesota. The fox was named "B.D." for Bomb Disposal.

"When I got to Minnesota, they put me up at the St. Paul Hotel. I knew the fox would never be able to handle the warm temperatures in the room, and so I tied him to the flag pole in front of the hotel."

During the night, some of the hotel's other customers saw the fox and raised a ruckus with the hotel management about cruelty to animals. Hogan was summoned from his room.

"I had to explain that this was the fox's normal habitat, being outdoors." The Minneapolis Tribune sent a photographer over, and for the second time in his military career, Hogan made the front page of a Twin Cities newspaper.

Hogan left the fox with his parents, and one day it got loose. He made his way north and was captured, nearly starved, at Winton, near Ely.

"I was very sad when I got a letter from home some months later that a dog had gotten over the fence and had killed the fox. It was such a beautiful animal."

The bomb disposal squad was loaded aboard the Queen Mary for the trip over the Atlantic. "There was nothing but the best for us going over there."

In England, the squad was assigned

HOME SWEET HOME IN ADAK

Early in the war, Hogan was stationed at Adak, Alaska, one of the islands in the Aleutians. The unit's mascot, a silver fox named "B.D.," is on top of the doorway. Hogan brought the fox home to northern Minnesota, but the fox was later killed by a dog.

to bivouac with English bomb disposal experts. Following the Blitz of England, there was probably nobody who knew more about dealing with bombs than the British. The team

Third Army. It was not assigned to any particular division or unit, but was moved to wherever it was needed as the Third Army advanced. Usually, that was right with the front

Some of the land mines could be detected with mine-sweeping equipment, but for others, the only way was the old-fashioned method.

"You'd just crawl on your belly and

"We were very, very lucky. We never lost a man. There was 100-percent wipeout in some squads."

---

lived in Coventry, just on the outskirts of London.

"They were very hospitable, very nice to us," Hogan recalled. "They taught us everything about bomb disposal. They knew it all. We even went out on calls with them."

Hogan's unit was called the Fifth Ordinance Bomb Disposal Squad, and it was attached to the

lines.

The unit landed on Omaha Beach on D-Day plus 1. "It was a sad mess. It was a variety of hell. There was still plenty of action on the beach, and there were still many mines to clear away." Some mines were in the sand, and others were floating in the surf just outside the beach.

tap the sand in front of you with a trench knife. You'd just probe gently with the knife, and if you hit something, you knew it was a mine. You'd have to carefully push the sand away. You learned to be very careful."

The bomb disposal expert would then have to, ever so carefully, remove the mine from the ground and, if there was enough room, detonate it with a charge or blasting cap. If there was no room, the mines were simply stacked up and the area was secured with red tape to warn off any troops.

Some of the mines were wooden or plastic, undetectable by metal detectors. The only way to find them was with the trench knife, and too hard a tap would reveal the mine in a way that was not approved.

As the U.S. troops moved inland, the bomb disposal people would be the first ones in once a town had been secured. "It was our job to get the troops out of the weather, and so we had to go through all the buildings looking for booby traps or bombs."

The bomb experts would usually break a window first to visually inspect the inside of a building. If it appeared that there might be a booby trap attached to the door, plan

BOMB TRUCK

Hogan takes a break on the fender of a truck the bomb disposal unit used to carry equipment.

B went into effect. "We would tie a rope to the door and tie the other end to a jeep and drive it around the corner. If it was a little bomb, the building might be damaged. If it was a big bomb, the whole building might come down."

Once a building was determined to be free of explosives, the GIs could settle in for a night's sleep out of the rain or snow.

The team was generally in the forefront of the troops, and, if a minefield was suspected in the line of a column of troops or tanks, Hogan and his men were called in. "The infantry would often have to give us covering fire as we tried to clear a minefield."

Once a corridor was made through a minefield, the men would mark it with tape so the vehicles and foot soldiers could pass through safely.

To dispose of a mine or bomb, a charge was set on it and electrical wire was run back a few hundred yards, from where detonation would be safe. "All those explosions for all those years really took a toll on my hearing."

Sometimes, Hogan was called upon to help out a local farmer. "He might have had a small herd of cows, and now he might only have two left because they keep stepping on mines in his field. The dead cows would lie on their backs with their feet in the air. The GIs would use them for target practice, and the cows were so bloated and full of gas that when a bullet hit them, you could hear the air whistling out."

Often the farmers were so grateful for having their farms de-mined that they would share their precious hoard of food or wine with the Americans. One time, a farmer served up a delicious meal, then asked Hogan and his men how they liked the food. The farmer used a word the Americans didn't know, and they had to look it up in their French dictionary. The word was "cat."

"One of my sergeants realized what he had just eaten and his face turned red. He bolted for the half door, leaned over it, and let everything fly. It didn't bother me; I thought it was very nice that this farmer had sacrificed his pet cat for our dinner."

In France, the bomb team received further instruction from the French underground, also experts in bomb disposal after five years of war. "They knew about all the fuses. I remember the worst one was 'ZZAK.' And you didn't touch that one with anything. The Germans were very ingenious on how to kill a person."

The squad of six people traveled mainly in a jeep and a 4x4 Dodge truck that carried their equipment. In front of the jeep, the men rigged a boom to pick up bombs that were too heavy to lift.

A major portion of the squad's work came when Patton's army was about to cross a river. The team would be called in to make sure a bridge wasn't wired for demolition by the retreating Nazis.

On one occasion, the team was creeping down a path to a bridge when they heard a snap in the brush beside them. The team reacted quickly and captured a German soldier.

"He was so young. He had on him a flare pistol, a Luger, and an American .32-caliber pistol that he must have gotten from one of our guys. If we'd gone past him, he could have picked us off very easily."

Hogan relieved the German of his Lugar and American pistol, two souvenirs he kept after the war. The prisoner was turned over to an engineering company nearby. "His job was to fire a flare at night to show the German bombers where the bridge was."

At another bridge, the squad came under fire from a German 88 artillery piece. "We hid on one side of a wall, and the shells came down on us. We jumped over the wall, and the Germans adjusted and the shells came down on that side of the wall. That was a very accurate gun, that 88 howitzer."

The work the men did required a great deal of training and know-how, Hogan said. "If you turned a fuse the wrong way, it would go off." Bombs that were too big to move had to be donated on the site. "You'd use little blocks of TNT or blasting caps.

"We set off one bomb, a huge one that, instead of creating fragments, flattened out the metal jacket and sent it flying. It was just like an airplane propeller, and it went whoosh, whoosh, whoosh right over our heads. It scared the hell out of us."

When the Battle of the Bulge broke out, Patton's Third Army was heading toward Germany. The army wheeled and headed north to help the 101st Airborne, encircled at Bastogne. When the Third Army reached Bastogne, the bomb disposal squad was one of the first into the area that had been controlled by the Germans.

"We had to get in fast to clear the buildings and get these guys out of the cold. It was a sad mess. They didn't have boots like we do today. The boots just soaked up the water like a sponge, and then they'd

FAMILY REUNION

When Hogan was in training, he met his cousin Loretta at Fort Leonard Wood.

HOME ON LEAVE

Hogan stood in front of the family business in Gilbert.

freeze. I spent Christmas in Bastogne, and they were playing Christmas music. It wasn't a Christmas I wanted to remember, though."

In some places, the bomb disposal teams found where the Germans had stockpiled socks, underwear and other clothing. "We just threw it out the windows to the soldiers. And then we got out of there before they caught us."

One day, while heading toward a French village, the jeep hit a small mine. "I went flying up in the air and came down by the side of the Jeep.

The driver got blown the other way. We got up, and you should have seen how fast we changed that tire. We could see activity in the windows of the town. We thought it was Germans.

"Just then, an old man came walking down the road, and it turned out he was a priest. He told us that the Germans had left that morning. To me, that old priest was just like a saint. I always wanted to go back and thank him."

Another time, the men were sweeping a field to clear it of mines and a

Jeep containing General Patton roared up. Patton took one look at the bomb squad and summoned them over. "The general wanted to know what we were doing without our helmets on. We told him that we couldn't wear any metal because of the mine sweepers. He didn't care. He said that if we got hurt it would take six guys to get us off the battlefield, and he didn't want to spare those six guys. He said, 'When I put out an order, I expect it to be obeyed.' We put our helmets back on."

Hogan said that he knows that many soldiers didn't like Patton, but he had no problem. "He was quite a general. He didn't believe in sitting still. You'd always hear him saying, 'Get those tanks moving.'"

The team made it all the way to Austria before the war ended in Europe.

"We were very, very lucky. We never lost a man. There was 100-percent wipeout in some squads. They either didn't have the training, or they got a little careless. I always kept in mind what the English taught us: 'Don't become too familiar with your work. Familiarity breeds disaster.' "

Hogan has some sad memories of the war. "One of the worst was this mother and her daughters, three or four of them, scavenging for food in an ammo dump. We told them to get out of there, but these people were starving. Well, they must have set off a mine, and the whole thing went off. It was the complete annihilation of them. We'd always try to give these people food and tell them to get out of the dumps when we could, but they were always scavenging. They had to."

Another sad memory was toward the end of the war when his squad saw German prisoners being shipped to a POW camp. "There were just truckloads of these young Germans, and they were all just kids. They had run out of troops, and they were using Hitler youth by that time. They were so disheartened. They were just dirty-faced young boys. They looked like Boy Scouts coming back from a camping trip. They were demoralized. They were crying. They had been brainwashed into thinking they were the master race."

Hogan has a strong opinion on land mines. "I can't believe they didn't outlaw them after World War II. They saw what happened in France with all these young people without arms or legs. They should never allow land mines again."

Hogan left France at Camp Lucky Strike, crossed the Atlantic in a liberty ship, and made it to Camp McCoy in Wisconsin, where he was discharged. He had spent 36 months overseas.

His father's garage in Gilbert had been closed during the war because there were no parts or tires to be had. Hogan helped his father reopen the business. Hogan operated it until about three years ago, when a blizzard dropped enough snow on the roof to collapse the building.

In 1950, he married Gertrude Sevruk of Floodwood. "She was a home economics teacher, and I wanted somebody who could really cook," Hogan said. From another room, Gertrude answered back, "Boy, did I fool him."

The two have three children, and they now spend the cold-weather months in Florida.

Hogan has been active in the American Legion since the war and has been post commander for the past 15 years.

A few years ago, Hogan went back to Omaha Beach for the 50th anniversary of D-Day. "It was so peaceful, I took my socks and shoes off and rolled up my pants and walked in the water. It was so nice. Not at all like I remembered it."

AT HOME
Hogan posed with his parents in Gilbert during a visit home during the war.

U.S. Army photo. Unless indicated otherwise, all other photos are from Jack Finnegan's personal collection.

LAYING WIRE
ACROSS EUROPE

John Finnegan, who later became the executive editor of the St. Paul Pioneer Press, found a job in the Army laying wire across Europe. His regiment, the 311th, part of the 78th Infantry Division, became the first full regiment to cross the Rhine into Germany on the famous bridge at Remagen.

John R. Finnegan grew up helping his family run a large hotel in northern Minnesota. In the Army he trained as an engineer. When he got to Europe during World War II, he became a communications-wire layer.

And, as he completed his service time in occupied Germany, he finally got to do what he wanted to do all along — be a journalist.

Finnegan eventually became executive editor of the St. Paul Pioneer Press in his newspaper career, but in 1944 and 1945, his skills were mainly applied toward making sure the commanders at headquarters could talk to the outlying companies. He also learned how to fire his bazooka. Well, he fired it once anyway.

Finnegan's family owned the Chase Hotel in Walker, a 130-room classic set next to Leech Lake. Finnegan would work at the hotel in the summer and go to school in Minneapolis the rest of the year.

In January 1943, he graduated from Central High School in Minneapolis.

He had been co-editor of his high school newspaper, and after graduation, he became the editor of the Robbinsdale Post. He was 18.

"They were shorthanded because of the war. I did a little bit of everything, including selling advertising."

He was soon drafted, however, and was first assigned to be trained as a medic. He entered the Army's ASTP (Advanced Specialized Training Program) program, though, and applied to work in intelligence.

The Army, in its wisdom, however, decided he would become an engineer. "I figured it was typical Army to put me in an area I had the least interest in — math."

Finnegan was sent to Rhode Island State College, where he studied algebra, calculus and advanced calculus. He also reverted to form and started his own newspaper for the students in the ASTP.

"Eventually, though, they closed the program down because they were short of infantry." Finnegan was assigned to the 78th "Lightning" Division, which had served for some time as a training division. By this time, it was being reconstituted as a full-fledged infantry division and was being readied for action in Europe.

Many of those transferred into the 78th came from the closed-down ASTP or from the Air Corps cadet training program, another casualty of the need for infantrymen. "There were so many sergeants and staff sergeants that it was impossible to get a promotion in that division. I went in as a PFC, and I came out as a PFC."

Finnegan did accelerated training in radios and Morse code, but then was made a member of a wire-laying

team and assigned to the 311th "Timberwolf" Regiment, 2nd Battalion Headquarters Company. His job would be to lay telephone line between the headquarters and the outlying infantry companies so there would be direct communication.

The 311th Regiment boarded the SS Carnarvon Castle in late 1944 for a 12-day trip to England. "We didn't encounter any submarines, but we were weaving and bobbing all the way over. I spent a lot of time up on deck, and a couple of times I slept up on deck because a lot of guys in the hold were sick, and the stench down there was something awful."

The ship arrived in England on October 25, 1944, and the division bivouacked in Bournemouth, about 100 miles south of London. The training continued, but the men were soon loaded on LSTs (Landing Ship, Tanks) at Southampton for the trip to France.

"The English Channel is just awful at that time of year, with huge waves and lots of rain. We didn't get very far before our LST was rammed by a hospital ship. It stove in the side of the LST pretty good, and the side curved around the boxes of ammunition."

The landing ship had to be towed back to Southampton, and all the gear and men were loaded into another LST.

It wasn't the end of LST worries, though. The pounding of the ocean was beginning to rip apart the second LST as it plied the English Channel. "A weld had broken on the deck, and you could look through the seam into the hold."

Just as the LST was about to make harbor in Rouen, the ship ahead of it hit a mine, causing further delays.

Finnegan's unit eventually landed and caught up with the rest of the regiment. They were transported inland to a small village named Duclair.

The stay in rural France was anything but a vacation, though, as the rains quickly changed the pastures into mud. "That was awful. The mud was four or five inches thick. You had to move around in the mud, sleep in the mud, and we didn't have our overshoes or rubber boots yet."

Soon the 311th was transported, via the same 40-and-8 boxcars that had been used in the First World War, to Tongren in Belgium to serve as a reserve unit for a time. On December 9, the 78th Division was ordered forward into the Hurtgen Forest to take over a section of the Allied front line.

The 78th arrived at the end of the fighting in the Hurtgen, one of the

«

JOHN FINNEGAN

At home in St. Paul

»

DURING THE WAR

Finnegan's regiment drove all the way to the Ruhr Valley in Germany.

bloodiest battles of the war. Their first greeting was the occasional screeching of Nazi buzz bombs overhead. "Once the engine stopped, you could count one, two, three, four, five... before the explosion. That would tell you how many miles away it was. Of course, if it hit you, you would never know it was coming."

Finnegan was ordered to raise a wire over a road so trucks could pass underneath.

"Sitting beside the road were these guys who had been through the battle. They were all these Bill Mauldin types, dirty and unshaven. We all were still fairly clean. I got my spurs on and was walking over to where I had to climb a tree to raise the wire, and one of these guys says, 'See you later.' "

Finnegan puzzled over the cryptic message, but set out to do his duty. "I climbed up one tree and moved the line up about three feet. All of a sudden, I could hear something whizzing through the air. And then I heard it again.

"I went over to the other side and moved that line up about three feet, and I heard something else whiz by."

Finnegan finished his chore and was heading back when one of the Hurtgen veterans called him over. "Hey, kid," he said. "Did you notice anything strange up there?" Finnegan told the GI he had heard this whizzing sound, and the soldier replied, "Yeah, we've lost a number of guys to snipers right there."

"I said, 'Thanks a lot.' He could have at least told me before I raised the wire. But, then again, thank God he didn't tell me."

The 311th stayed in the Hurtgen for three or four weeks. Finnegan ran

A SNOOZE ALONG THE WAY

In the parlance of the GIs, this was called a 10-minute break -- ETO style.

the switchboard, which was installed in one of the pillboxes left over from the Siegfried Line.

The conditions were snowy and very wet, and the foxholes and trenches were filling with water. "I think we lost more men to frostbite and trench foot than we did to battle wounds. The medical tent was near my pillbox, and there were scores of guys who were barefoot over there. You couldn't even put a blanket on their feet because it was too painful."

Finnegan's pillbox had a foot of water on its floor, so he had to raise the switchboard above the water line. "I did what they told me and took off my boots every day. It was a crank-operated switchboard, and, since I couldn't put my feet down, I figured, what the heck, I might as well make use of my feet. So I turned the crank with my foot. Then I would move the wires with my

hands."

He became adept at the procedure. "But I still have a little space between my big toe and the next toe where I would turn the crank."

The division was just on the edge of the German offensive in the Battle of the Bulge. "Just south of us, we did lose some guys. The Germans captured them in their foxholes. They must have wanted them for intelligence purposes. But, other than that, they went right by us. We were like a thumb sticking out there."

As the Bulge wound down, the unit advanced to Simmerath and came under constant enemy shell fire, about 300 rounds a day. They called one intersection that the German's had zeroed in on ".88 Corner." Because of the intense shelling, the phone lines were constantly being cut, and Finnegan and the other wire men found themselves often in no-man's land stringing new wire.

"The way we would do it was to get in a Jeep with a big wire reel and take off and go as fast as we could go." The men tried to lay the wire at the edge of the road where it

primary weapon, but he also had been issued a bazooka, just in case. While training one day, Finnegan was called upon to fire his bazooka at a cardboard tank.

windfall by quickly getting a regiment across it.

The regiment chosen was the 311th. It was the first complete American regiment to cross the Rhine. "By the

"That was the only time I fired my bazooka, and I almost burned down the headquarters."

wouldn't get run over by the vehicles.

At one point, the HQ lost contact with F Company. Finnegan and his crew were ordered in the middle of the night to lay some new wire. "We got about a quarter of a mile down the road. It was one of those cold, crisp nights where you could hear the crunching of the Jeep on the snow for miles. They started lobbing in mortar shells at us. One landed right in front of us, and that stopped us pretty quick."

The men bailed out of the Jeep and dove into the ditches on either side of the road with mortars exploding all around them.

"All of a sudden, something hit me hard in the back. I thought it might be shrapnel, but when I reached around there was no hole and no blood. I looked down and saw I'd been hit by a frozen hunk of the road that the mortar had kicked up."

The men yelled back and forth to each other to see if they were all right. One of Finnegan's companions yelled back that he was okay, but that his face was wedged up against the rear end of a dead horse. They continued running the wire and got back without further incident.

Finnegan was assigned a rifle as his

"My loader tapped me on the head, and I fired it. Then somebody said there was a hole starting to burn in the tent behind us. I guess we had been standing a little too close. That was the only time I fired my bazooka, and I almost burned down the headquarters."

The division played a key part in several actions, including the capture of the Schwammenaul Dam. On March 8, 1945, the Allies were surprised to have captured the Ludendorf Bridge across the Rhine intact. It was known as the Bridge at Remagen, and the Allies took advantage of the

time we got to the bridge, it was in pretty bad shape. I rode across the bridge on a tank, and I remember hoping that the bridge would hold together until I reached the other side."

Once across, the Americans began getting ready for a push up the east side of the Rhine. First things first, though. It had been reported that there was a warehouse nearby containing wine and spirits. Finnegan and others were ordered to take a jeep and investigate.

"The warehouse was stacked with

WELCOME TO SCHMIDT

The 78th Division took credit for the liberation of Schmidt.

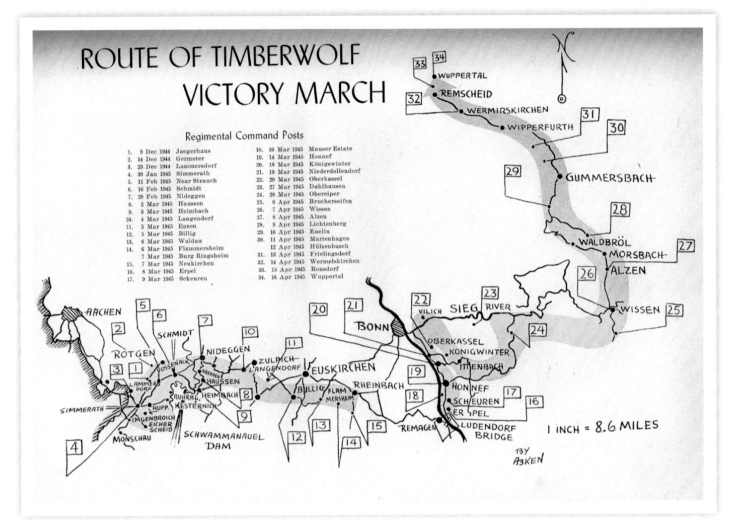

ROUTE OF TIMBERWOLF VICTORY MARCH

Regimental Command Posts

1.	9 Dec 1944	Jaegerhaus	
2.	14 Dec 1944	Germeter	
3.	23 Dec 1944	Lammersdorf	
4.	30 Jan 1945	Simmerath	
5.	11 Feb 1945	Near Strauch	
6.	16 Feb 1945	Schmidt	
7.	28 Feb 1945	Nideggen	
8.	2 Mar 1945	Haussen	
9.	3 Mar 1945	Heimbach	
10.	4 Mar 1945	Langendorf	
11.	5 Mar 1945	Enzen	
12.	5 Mar 1945	Billig	
13.	6 Mar 1945	Waldau	
14.	6 Mar 1945	Flammersheim	
	7 Mar 1945	Burg Ringsheim	
15.	7 Mar 1945	Neukirchen	
16.	8 Mar 1945	Erpel	
17.	9 Mar 1945	Scheuren	
18.	10 Mar 1945	Mauser Estate	
19.	14 Mar 1945	Honnef	
20.	18 Mar 1945	Königswinter	
21.	19 Mar 1945	Niederdollendorf	
22.	20 Mar 1945	Oberkassel	
23.	27 Mar 1945	Dahlhausen	
24.	28 Mar 1945	Obereiper	
25.	6 Apr 1945	Brucherseifen	
26.	7 Apr 1945	Wissen	
27.	8 Apr 1945	Alzen	
28.	9 Apr 1945	Lichtenberg	
29.	10 Apr 1945	Eueln	
30.	11 Apr 1945	Marienhagen	
	12 Apr 1945	Hülsenbusch	
31.	13 Apr 1945	Frielingsdorf	
32.	14 Apr 1945	Wermelskirchen	
33.	15 Apr 1945	Ronsdorf	
34.	16 Apr 1945	Wuppertal	

1 INCH = 8.6 MILES

BY A3KEN

ROAD TO VICTORY

The 78th Division marched across Germany in 1944-45 as the Third Reich collapsed.

German and French wines and champagnes. The sergeant and I took a look, and then he loaded me up with wine bottles, stacking it like cordwood. On the way back to the Jeep, though, I looked up and a Stuka began strafing the road. Normally, you'd dive for cover, but I carefully got down on one knee and then on the other knee. I didn't drop one of those bottles. The Stuka flew right over, missing me. I got back with every one of those bottles, and I got a lot of thanks from the guys. For the next couple of days, we were drinking champagne out of our tin cups."

Another part of the encounter was not so happy. One of the Stukas was hit by American fire, and the pilot bailed out and was parachuting down. "As he floated down, guys opened up on him from both sides. He was killed before he ever touched the water. I was shocked by that, but that's what war is like. He was trying to kill us, and some of the guys figured he had it coming."

To this day, Finnegan has never seen the movie based on the capture of the Bridge at Remagen. "There was a time when I never wanted to see any war movie. I'm over that now, and maybe someday I'll see it. Probably not."

The last major assignment for the 78th Division was to take part in the capture of the Ruhr Valley, Germany's industrial heartland. "We

MAZE OF WIRES

This bombed-out building was headquarters for a battalion. The wires indicate the difficulty in keeping in touch with outlying infantry companies.

were taking in prisoners by the droves by that time, but they were usually either 12- or 13-year-old boys or old men. I suppose they were part of the home guard.

"We interrogated some of the prisoners, and they said they had been told if they were captured by the Americans, they would be re-armed and sent against the Russians."

The Ruhr was the last major action for the regiment after more than 130 days of continuous combat. The unit set up as an occupation force near Fulda and Hunfeld. "The people were very gracious. They were thankful that the war was over for them. They were very cooperative."

As the rigors of battle were taken away, Finnegan again started his own newspaper for his battalion. He

PRISONERS

By the end of the war, many of the German prisoners were old men and young boys.

was soon called on the carpet, though, and questioned about why he was doing a newspaper when there was already a regimental newspaper. The commanding officer decided Finnegan's skills would be better used by creating a regimental history.

The book was done over the next several months, and Finnegan was able to pick his own crew. "I got six or seven guys. Some were photographers, some were artists, and a couple were people who spoke German because we had to deal with the local printers. And one guy was a scrounger, and his job was to find enough quality paper to print it on. He did it, and I never asked him how he did it."

The local Linotype operators didn't speak or understand English, so the Americans had to stand over their shoulders and correct the copy as it was typed.

The book traced the progress of the 311th in its journey across Europe and recorded such things as the number of killed-in-action, 414; wounded-in-action, 1,785; and total casualties, 2,454. The 311th started with 3,207 men, and 1,863 of those were still in the company at VE Day. The regiment captured 17,178 prisoners in the war and accounted for 618 enemy dead.

Before the book was done, though, Finnegan's father died, and he was sent home on an emergency discharge to help his family run the hotel.

In 1946, since neither he nor his brother wanted to be in the hotel business, the property was sold, and Finnegan entered the School of Journalism at the University of Minnesota. He graduated in 1948 and began work at the Rochester Post

Bulletin. He also married his wife, Norma, that year.

In 1951, he joined the staff of the St. Paul Pioneer Press and covered the Legislature and city politics. He eventually became an editorial writer and then assistant editor of the editorial page.

In 1969, he made the big leap from that job to assistant-to-the-executive editor, and, a year later, he became the executive editor of Minnesota's second-largest newspaper. He served on the boards of Associated Press Managing Editors and the American Society of Newspaper Editors. He retired from

newspapering in 1989.

Finnegan has kept very busy serving on the legislative committee for the Minnesota Newspaper Association and on the board of the Catholic Spirit newspaper, serving the Twin Cities area. He has won a host of Freedom of Information and Freedom of the Press awards through the years, and is considered a national expert in those areas. He also was an adjunct professor at the University of Minnesota. He is currently working on a book.

He and Norma have six children, and they reside in St. Paul.

THE VICTORS

The 78th Division marched trimphantly through Berlin at the end of the war. *Deutsche Fotothek photo.*

25 MISSIONS IN AN AVENGER

Leon Frankel grew up in St. Paul wanting to fly airplanes. World War II gave him the chance. He flew 25 missions in the South Pacific in torpedo bombers from two different carriers, the Lexington and the Yorktown. Along the way, he earned the Navy Cross and participated in the first Navy raid on Tokyo.

Leon Frankel knew he wanted to be a flier from the time he was a young boy growing up in St. Paul.

Little did he realize as he played with his toy planes and read books about aviation that he would one day fly airplanes off aircraft carriers, help sink a Japanese cruiser, or do his part in founding a new nation.

Frankel was born in a neighborhood in St. Paul that no longer exists. Just to the east of the State Capitol, land that once was houses and stores and neighborhood streets has been replaced by Regions Hospital and other developments.

In the 1920s and '30s, though, it was a tough little neighborhood. Most of the people living on Frankel's street were Jewish, and there were two synagogues in the neighborhood; one with a red brick façade and the other with white bricks.

"Of course, we called them the red shul and the white shul, and you didn't want to accidently go to the wrong one. My parents went to the red shul."

Frankel was born in 1923. His father supported the family during the Depression as the owner of a small grocery store on the corner of Mount Airy and Lorient. Memories of growing up include spending a great deal of time at the Central Community House, a neighborhood center that was next to his home.

"There was a woman who ran it named Faye Biederman, and she ran it with an iron hand. She kicked me out for a whole year at one point because I called her 'Warden Biederman.' She made me apologize to her in public."

Frankel recalls that he wasn't overly religious in his youth, and he refused to go to Hebrew school. Getting his bar mitzvah was a challenge, and his mother hired a series of tutors to give him the wisdom to fulfill the requirements.

"They were all old men and I went through three of them. Two of them died, but the third one got me through. And then he died."

Frankel attended Mechanic Arts High School, and managed to graduate in 1940 while he was still only 16 years old.

"I had this grandiose idea that I wanted to be a doctor. My parents scraped together enough money to pay my tuition at the University of Minnesota for a brief period. I used to get a ride to Folwell Hall every day from the Blommer Beer truck. I'd have to take the streetcar or hitchhike to get home. In the end, I dropped out. I couldn't handle it."

The government started drafting people in 1940, but for a while Frankel was protected because he was working for a defense industry plant in Rosemount. "I was a shovel operator," he said with a smile. "That means I was using a shovel to put the sand back on top of this huge pipeline they were building."

Frankel got the job by going to a relative who happened to be head of a union. "There were guys all over the office trying to get into the union, but I walked in and told him who I was. He had me fill out an application, and I was working the next Monday. It taught me that great lesson: It isn't what you know, it's who you know. I was making $65 a week, which was huge money in those days."

Later, Frankel went to work for a machine shop that built dies for the New Brighton arms plant.

He knew, though, that the military was in his future. On December 7, 1941, he was at Bilbo's Pool Hall, his daylong haunt every Sunday, when he heard the news of the Japanese attack on Hawaii.

Frankel had thoughts of joining up, but he was sure he didn't want to be in the infantry. "I had grown up right after World War I, and I used to hear all these horrible stories from my relatives and others about the trenches, the gas, the bullets flying everywhere. I knew that wasn't for me."

Frankel loved to fly. Once he and a friend had pooled their resources,

two dollars, and had gone for a ride in a Piper Cub at Holman Field. "I knew, after that, that this was it. I had all the model airplanes, and read all the pulp magazines about the World War I aces like Rickenbacker and the Red Baron. I was really fascinated with the thought of flying."

One day, he decided to head over to Fort Snelling to see if he could enlist in the Army Air Corps.

"Of course I had to stop at Bilbo's Pool Hall on the way over, because it was right on the streetcar line. I ran into one of my buddies, Red Fogerty. I told him what I was doing, and he said, 'Why don't you join the Navy instead?' And he told me about the V-5 program."

The program aimed at taking young men and making them ready for flight school. So Frankel changed his direction from Fort Snelling to

the Wold-Chamberlain air base, where the Navy was headquartered. He found he would need three character references, and he got one of them from his old nemesis at the neighborhood center, Faye Biederman.

"I had to go before a board of review where they all sit at a desk while you stand in front of them. That was a trying experience. It was like an inquisition team. They keep firing questions at you to see how you stand up to it."

Frankel passed all the tests and was sworn into the V-5 program, but there was a problem. There was no room in the program in early 1942 with so many people volunteering for the service.

Finally, that fall, Frankel was put in the Civilian Pilot Training Program, and he ended up at Hibbing Junior College in the dead of winter. The

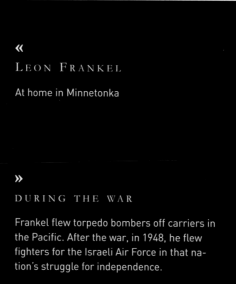

« LEON FRANKEL

At home in Minnetonka

» DURING THE WAR

Frankel flew torpedo bombers off carriers in the Pacific. After the war, in 1948, he flew fighters for the Israeli Air Force in that nation's struggle for independence.

Avenger
Statistics

TBF/TBM Avenger Data

Manufacturer
Grumman, General Motors

Engine
Wright R-260-20 Radial engine, 1,900 horsepower

Crew
Three

Armament
Three .50-caliber Browning machine guns, two on the wings and one in the tail. One .30-caliber machine gun mounted in the belly. The Avenger could carry up to 2,000 pounds in bombs, or one 2,000 pound torpedo.

Maximum Speed
276 miles per hour

Ceiling
30,100 feet

Range
1,000 miles

AVENGER DROPPING A TORPEDO

The TBF Avenger became one of the most important Navy planes during the war, carrying payloads of either bombs or torpedoes.

training was in Piper Cubs, and it resulted in Frankel's first chance to solo.

One flight didn't go very well. "I was on my third solo one morning when it started snowing out. Everything was covered with snow, and I couldn't find the field. I knew I was getting low on gas, and I thought it would be prudent to come down and land somewhere.

"I found what looked like level land, and I put her down. I was doing all right for 50 or 100 feet, but then I hit a furrow or something. It flipped the airplane right over, and I was hang-ing upside down by my seatbelt. I opened the seat belt and went crashing right through the canvas roof of the plane."

There was minimal damage to the aircraft, and the instructors were able to attach skis, fix a few broken parts, and fly the plane back to the airport.

"One thing I remember clearly was that there was no indoor plumbing at the airport. It was a one-hundred-yard dash to the outhouse, and, boy, was it cold out there."

Frankel finished his training in Hibbing and went back to Wold-Chamberlain. His next training stop was the University of Iowa at Iowa City, where he joined the 18th battalion to go through the cadet school there.

It was Frankel's first taste of real military training. "I was walking down the street one day and I passed up this guy. It turned out to be Bernie Bierman, the former football coach at the University of Minnesota. Now he was a colonel in the Marine Corps. When I went past him, I didn't say, 'By your leave, sir,' and he spun me around and gave me a good dressing-down. After that I saluted cab drivers, anybody who was wearing a cap."

There were about a dozen Jewish students in the program, and the college Hillel organization offered Sunday services for the cadets. "I didn't know about it, and I was just going along to the Protestant services every week. You had to go somewhere. But a friend, Martin "Ham" Ginsberg from Hector, Minnesota, told me about Hillel. I thought it was great because there were a lot of sorority girls down there."

Frankel joined the boxing team because he was the only one in the program in the under-130-pound weight class. "We would wear these helmets and 16-ounce gloves and just pound each other. At the end of one fight, the referee brought us to the center of the ring and raised my hand. I walked over to the corner and collapsed. The guy who had lost the fight walked away okay."

Primary flight training was at Olathe, Kansas, for three months learning to fly Stearman trainers. The next phase was at Pensacola, Florida, where the cadets flew the Navy version of the AT-6 trainer, the SNJ.

Part of Frankel's instrument training was taught by WAVES, and that wasn't his only connection with the distaff side of the Navy. His room in the barracks at Pensacola faced a hallway in an adjoining barracks where the WAVES lived.

FRANKEL IN HIS AVENGER

Leon Frankel looked every inch the tough, Navy pilot in this photograph.

slipping. She couldn't have landed the plane, but she sure could fly."

Advanced training was at Barin Field

man and General Motors, was the heaviest single-engined airplane in the military. It had a crew of three,

---

"It's funny because the guys who were out there couldn't wait to go home. We couldn't wait to get there."

"Every night when the WAVES would go by heading for the showers, I couldn't even get in my room because it was filled with cadets taking in the show. You couldn't get another person in there. Of course, the WAVES knew what was going on, and sometimes they'd wave their towels and laugh."

Frankel once took a woman instructor up for a flight. "She taught us how to use the simulators. She had never actually flown in an airplane before, but once we were in the air I let her take the controls. She could do perfect turns, no skidding, no

in Alabama, known in the cadet corps as "Bloody Barin," in part because the Royal Navy pilots trained there. "They were reckless. There were so many accidents and so many killed there."

Frankel was set for a naval career of flying fighters, but then one day at Barin, a British pilot landed a TBM Avenger, a torpedo bomber. It was love at first sight for Frankel.

"The officer in charge spent an hour with us trying to talk me out it, but in the end he signed off."

The TBM, manufactured by Grum-

and it could carry torpedoes, bombs, mines, or rockets.

Frankel was off to Fort Lauderdale to train in the Avengers, but after graduation he was faced with the classic "hurry up and wait" syndrome common to the military. There were no slots for TBM pilots at that time.

He and some other flyers were sent to New York finally to ferry some new TBMs to San Diego, a trip that included five stops along the way. When flying into El Paso, the new TBM being flown by Frankel's friend,

JAPANESE CRUISER YAHAGI HIT

Frankel earned his Navy Cross for participating in the attack that sunk the Japanese cruiser Yahagi on April 7, 1945. *U.S. Navy photograph*

Grady Jean, lost power just before landing and crashed. Jean was unhurt, and Frankel flew him the rest of the way to San Diego.

"When I saw him go down, I hovered over him to make sure he was all right. Later he said I was only concerned because he owed me $200."

At San Diego, it looked like another long wait for orders, but it turned out that Jean was from the same town in Arkansas as the assignment officer. "It was again one of those cases of 'it's who you know.' "

The two were soon assigned to Torpedo Squadron 9 and sent to Pasco, Washington, where a TBM squadron was re-forming after a cruise to the South Pacific. While there, he was summoned to the commanding officer's office. The skipper asked if he would take a car to the train station and pick up his wife.

Eager to please, Frankel told the skipper he'd be happy to do so. What he didn't say was that he didn't know how to drive. "Yes, I learned how to fly airplanes before I learned how to drive. I went and got his car, and I practiced driving it around the airfield for a half hour, hoping nobody would see me. I managed to get his wife back without any incident, and I gave him back his keys. I hope he didn't see the sweat pouring off me."

The training was moved back to San Diego, where Frankel learned how to land a plane on an aircraft carrier, no small endeavor.

Then there was training on how to take off from an aircraft carrier. "The first time I did it, I was hooked to the catapult. You just put your head back on the headrest and go to full throttle, full power. You do

everything the opposite of what you'd been trained. You did your trim tabs the opposite, you go to right full rudder, and full nose down. Otherwise, that catapult will send you right into heaven."

Frankel found he was adept at landing on the moving target. "I had 67 landings on carriers during the war, and I never even blew a tire. I was only waved off once, and that was because the deck was fouled. I was good, I really was, and that's not just a bunch of ego."

The pilots took a ride on the carrier Yorktown to Hawaii for yet more training, and then were shipped to the Admiralty Islands and finally to Ulithe in the Caroline Islands, where they joined the air crew of the famed USS Lexington.

All the training made the pilots some of the best in the world, but it was also frustrating. "It's funny because the guys who were out there couldn't wait to go home. We couldn't wait to get there."

On February 16, 1945, Frankel participated in the first Navy raid on Tokyo. The plan was to take out as many Japanese airplanes and airplane plants as possible prior to the landing at Iwo Jima.

The Japanese were anxious to defend the homeland, and Frankel's group was met by about 40 or 50 fighters and heavy anti-aircraft fire. "It was the wildest thing you ever saw, and one of the Japanese planes ran right into the skipper's airplane and damaged his propeller. I flew alongside him and tried to defend him. That's where I got my first DFC."

The citation for the Distinguished Flying Cross says, in part: "Flying through intense and accurate anti-

YAMOTO EXPLODES

As Frankel and his group returned to the carrier after sinking the Yahagi, they had a bird's-eye view of the result of another American attack on the battleship Yamoto. *U.S. Navy photograph*

aircraft fire, Lieutenant Junior Grade (then Ensign) Frankel pressed home damaging attacks on an important Japanese aircraft factory and, when two planes in the formation suffered crippling damage over the target, fought a running battle with enemy fighter craft across eighty miles of the Japanese homeland while flying at a reduced speed in order to protect the impaired planes."

As the missions went by, the excitement of finally being in combat diminished. "After you've been there for a while, the edge wears off. You look forward to when you can go home."

The TBMs were a large, stable plane, and Frankel enjoyed flying them. They were even equipped with an ashtray in the armrest for those

long, four-hour missions. Everybody on the plane smoked, except when they were at a high altitude and using oxygen.

Torpedo Squadron 9 changed ships from the Lexington to the Yorktown in March, as the Lex was scheduled to go home for an overhaul.

On a mission over Iwo Jima, Frankel ran into a hornet's nest. "I don't know if it was the Japs or the Marines, but when I got back we counted over 50 holes in the plane. I was trying to make a low pass to drop some bombs."

By this time in the war, the Japanese had starting using kamikaze missions extensively against the U.S. fleet. "Everybody says, 'Oh, you were at the end of the war. You had it easy.' Well, the kamikazes were coming at us morning, noon and

night. It kind of got on your nerves."

The pilots were ordered to disperse about the ship and to take shelter in the wardroom, three decks down. If there was an attack, they were told to hide under the tables.

"You could tell by which guns were firing as to how close the kamikazes were. When the five-inch guns were blasting, they were still 10,000 or 12,000 feet away. When the 40-quads began booming, they were getting close. And when the 20s started firing, you knew they were right on top of you."

Frankel didn't always obey the orders to disperse. He remembers one kamikaze attack on a neighboring ship during which he and some other pilots went up on deck to take in the spectacle. When three of the four attackers were shot down, "We were all cheering like crazy."

Another time, he and a buddy were playing cards in the ready room, near the flight deck, when an attack came. "We definitely weren't supposed to be there. The kamikaze hit the other side of the ship, just opposite of where we were. It was a tremendous jolt. The fluorescent fixture above my head came crashing down and hit me. I looked at him, and he looked at me, and, boy, did we run."

There was supposed to be no liquor on board the ship, but it was common practice for pilots to get a two-ounce shot of brandy from the medical personnel after a mission. "It was supposed to settle our nerves. Some guys would save it up from a half-dozen missions and then really tie one on."

A bunkmate of Frankel's had family in the canned-food business, and now and then a package from home

TIME OUT FOR FUN

War wasn't always serious business. Members of a training group gathered for some recreation at "Jake's Farm" in 1944. Frankel is third from the right.

would arrive. "The cans would say they contained fruit or something, but when you opened them up they had these exotic liquors inside like Grand Marnier. He was a good roommate."

All the packages from home were greatly welcomed by the pilots, although by the time they found their way to the South Seas, their condition was sometimes not good. "There would be mold on the salami, and the cookies were nothing but crumbs, but it was okay. The folks at home were doing their best to support you."

The most memorable day of action for Torpedo 9 came on April 7, 1945, when it joined a huge wave of about 400 airplanes sent to intercept a Japanese task force led by the battleship Yamato. The Japanese fleet had been bottled up for some time,

and this foray was basically a suicide mission to Okinawa. The Japanese admirals wanted to beach the immense battleship on Okinawa and use it as a stationary platform for its huge 18-inch guns during the American invasion.

Frankel took time before the mission to inscribe one of the torpedoes "From Faye Biederman and all the gang at CCH" (the neighborhood house where he spent his childhood). "It turned out to be one of the torpedoes that hit the cruiser Yahagi. I told her about it when I got back, and she broke down in tears."

The Navy was tracking the Japanese fleet carefully. "We took off about noon, and it was a long ways off, about 300 miles. They gave us an extra fuel tank. Our planners gave us a tremendous vector. They had a hunch where the Japanese might

be, and we went right to them. Other squadrons that day never did find them."

Frankel's group was ordered to attack the Yahagi and an accompanying destroyer. Other American fliers that had attacked earlier had done their job, and the Yahagi was dead in the water with the destroyer pulled up alongside, perhaps to take sailors off the wounded ship.

The fighters attacked the ship first and dropped bombs on the stricken cruiser. In a well-coordinated attack, the torpedo planes moved in less than a minute after the fighters had done their work.

As the Avengers turned for the attack, Frankel ended up in the lead. He told his radio operator, called a "tunnel man" in the parlance of the TBM crews, K.V. Kistler, to concentrate on the Japanese cruiser and give him readings on the radar.

"We had very good radar on the TBMs." The torpedoes had to be released at exactly the right time to hit the water and be armed by the time they found the target.

"I hit the pickle, and felt the torpedo release. It was running hot, straight and normal and was heading for the center of the ship. I was going as fast as I could go. I couldn't jinks on the way in because we had to go straight. In the end I was so close that I couldn't turn. We probably didn't get hit because we were going so fast.

"I had to go right over the cruiser, and I went about 50 feet above the bow. We almost hit the mast, we were traveling so low. Then I started jinksing like crazy, and we got out of there.

"As we headed for the rendezvous, one of the pilots who had been behind me came up beside and gave me the thumbs up that my torpedo had hit its mark."

The result below was hellacious. In all, five torpedoes struck the Yahagi within a few seconds. The large ship simply broke into fiery pieces and sank within a minute.

Frankel continued on, and by chance the rendezvous point brought him close to the Yamato. When he was about a mile away, the torpedo and bombing attack on the battleship had its conclusion.

"I saw this unbelievable explosion. It was like pictures I saw later of the atomic bomb. The sea around the ship was just blood red from the explosion."

The Yamato broke into two large pieces and quickly sank.

Frankel and the others now had to make their way back to the Yorktown while running very low on fuel. It was the longest mission any of the pilots had flown.

"In my logbook, it says the mission lasted six hours. Even though we had left at noon, I got credit for a night landing because the sun had set before we got back.

The attack on the Yahagi earned Frankel a Navy Cross, the second highest honor in the American military. The citation read, in part:

"For extraordinary heroism... Frankel broke through the clouds and pressed home his attack to point-blank range in the face of intense antiaircraft fire to score a di-

rect hit and contribute materially to the sinking of the hostile cruiser a minute later. Subject to a cross fire of intense antiaircraft fire from the cruiser and destroyer during his retirement from the strike, he brought his plane and crew through unscathed."

Those weren't Frankel's only moments of trepidation in his 25 combat missions.

"We had been told to always switch to a full tank before going in for an attack so that we wouldn't have any fuel problems during the attack. One day we were attacking these Japanese-held islands, and I saw I still had 40 gallons in the tank. I thought that was enough."

FRANKEL'S OTHER WAR

Leon Frankel took a leave of absence from the Air Force reserves in 1948 to join the Israeli Air Force as that nation, created that year, struggled for its independence. Frankel and other volunteers from around the world flew many planes including this German ME-109, made in Czechoslovakia. Frankel is third from the right. He was in the 101st Squadron.

It wasn't.

"I was about 200 feet off the surface when my engine stopped. It just quit cold. I thought, 'Oh, no, I'm going in the drink. I'm going to be a POW. Oh, my God, why is this happening?' I switched tanks, and the emergency fuel pump worked, and the engine caught."

Later his fellow pilots inquired why his plane suddenly appeared to be standing still in the air. "I just told them to forget it."

One of Frankel's strongest and saddest memories came in an attack on the Japanese troops on Okinawa. The group was to have close fighter support as it made its run, but the fighters got too close. Frankel was flying right behind Commander Byron Cooke, the commanding officer of Torpedo 9.

"I saw a fighter sweep across and hit the skipper's plane. It was right in front of me. I pulled back and I saw the wing fall off his plane. He was such a great guy, we all just loved him.

"I was so unnerved by what I just saw that when we got to the target, we were supposed to fire our rockets two at a time, but I just fired a salvo, all of them at once."

Another time, Frankel's squadron was ordered to bomb a target on Okinawa. The Avengers were in formation waiting for orders about where exactly the target was, and the waiting went on for some time.

"I was just sort of playing with the pickle (the device that unlatches the bombs from the bomb rack) when I heard a thud and there was a sudden lurch in the plane. I asked the radio operator to see if he could see what had happened.

"A few minutes later, he came back on the intercom. 'Sir, I found out

what it was. The bombs are laying on the bomb doors.' "

Frankel had accidentally dropped his load of bombs, but since the bomb bay doors were closed, they only dropped a few feet. They had partially split open the doors and the air was whistling in, perhaps enough wind to trigger the device on the bombs that armed them.

"It was pretty scary. I opened the bomb bay doors, and they tumbled out into the water. Of course I still wanted credit for a mission, and so I went in with the group but only strafed the target."

Frankel's final Distinguished Flying Cross was given to him when he completed his 25 missions. He had a large chunk of leave coming, and he took it at home in St. Paul. He was

home on leave when the war ended in August 1945.

After his active service, he stayed in Navy Reserve until 1958 with one leave of absence. In 1948, he got a call asking if he would fly for the newly born nation of Israel.

That's another story, for which there is no room here, but suffice it to say that he flew another 25 combat missions, this time mainly in Messerschmitt 109s that were built in Czechoslovakia. Once again, he survived a war.

Frankel spent time in car sales, and later as a manufacturer's rep. He married in 1951, and he and Ruth had two children. He retired in 1987, and he and Ruth now live in Minnetonka.

The President of the United States takes pleasure in presenting he NAVY CROSS to

LIEUTENANT, JUNIOR GRADE, LEON FRANKEL
UNITED STATES NAVAL RESERVE

or service as set forth in the following

CITATION:

"For extraordinary heroism as Pilot of a Torpedo Bomber in Torpedo Squadron NINE, attached to the U.S.S. YORKTOWN, in action against major units of the Japanese Fleet off Kyushu, Japan, April 7, 1945. Flying by instruments through a heavy overcast in a daring attack against an enemy light cruiser and a screening destroyer, Lieutenant, Junior Grade, Frankel broke through the clouds and pressed home his attack to point-blank range in the face of intense antiaircraft fire to score a direct hit and contribute materially to the sinking of the hostile cruiser a minute later. Subjected to a crossfire of intense antiaircraft fire from the cruiser and destroyer during his retirement from the strike, he brought his plane and crew through unscathed. By his superior airmanship and gallant fighting spirit, Lieutenant, Junior Grade, Frankel upheld the highest traditions of the United States Naval Service."

CITATION

Signed by Secretary of the Navy James Forrestal, Frankel's citation for his Navy Cross speaks to his action in sinking the cruiser Yahagi.

Marvin Hackbarth, center, bending over, was learning to shoot a mortar in this hometown press release photo printed in a Minnesota newspaper.

These Hutchinson, Minn., men, shown at Camp Claiborne as they learned how to operate a 61-millimeter mortar, may be among the American units landed in northern Ireland. The instructor is Corporal Roy C. Krasean, and the others, left to right, are Privates Milton Stoll, Marvin Hackbarth, Myron Carrigan and Clarence Veenhuis.

Unless indicated otherwise, all photos are from Marvin Hackbarth's personal collection.

WAR REALLY WAS
HELL

Marvin Hackbarth can tell a war story with the best of them, and he has a deep reservior of experiences to draw from during his 14 months of combat in Italy during World War II. But not all his stories are funny or poignant. Some of them are about the truly dark side of war. Some of them still give him nightmares, 60 years later.

Marvin Hackbarth hates war.

His experiences as an infantryman in Italy in World War II left him convinced there is no greater evil on Earth than war.

He saw things he would rather have not seen. He did things he didn't want to do. And he lost friends who can never be replaced.

And he still has nightmares. "Now they call it PTSD. I know people expect that it would get better with time, but it hasn't. It hasn't at all."

Hackbarth grew up in the Minnesota rural community of Cosmos as a "town kid," the son of the area's farm implement dealer. He graduated from Litchfield High School in 1939, but even before graduation he enlisted in the Minnesota National Guard.

"Part of the reason I joined was that I was patriotic. I thought it was the right thing to do for my country. Both my brother and sister joined the service. That's how people were in those days.

"The other part was because it was the Depression and the little bit of money you could get from the Guard meetings was important. Money was hard to come by."

The approach of war was clear to him. "There was the tremendous bombing of England. We'd turn on the radio every day and hear news of Hitler marching through Belgium, France and Poland. It was just a matter of time before we were in the war."

On February 10, 1941, Hackbarth's unit, Company B of the 135th Infantry, was called to active duty. The unit was headquartered in Hutchinson.

Company B trained and slept in the old Hutchinson Armory, then was sent to Camp Claiborne, Louisiana, to join the Thirty-Fourth Division, made up of men mainly from Minnesota and Iowa. "It was a brand new camp with lots of mud. We slept in five-man tents." The training went on for ten months as the United States teetered on the brink of war.

On December 7, 1941, the bombing

of Pearl Harbor settled the matter, and Hackbarth's company was sent to Pensacola, Florida, to guard the communications centers there for two weeks.

During his time at Camp Claiborne, Hackbarth decided he wanted to get into the action a little faster, and he tried to transfer to the Marines. When that failed, he applied to get into the newly formed 101st Airborne, but his company wouldn't let

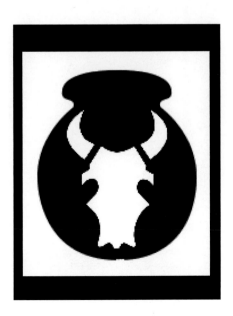

him go. Finally, he applied to be a pilot in the Army Air Corps and passed the test.

"I got my orders to report, though, when we were in Northern Ireland. Naturally, they wouldn't let me go. At the time, I didn't realize how fortunate I was. If I had gone to any of those places, I probably wouldn't be here today."

The Thirty-Fourth Division, in 1942, traveled to Fort Dix in New Jersey and then on to Northern Ireland for more training and waiting. "Company B was all broken up by that time. I was assigned to Company H in the 133rd Infantry. It was a heavy weapons company, and we trained on machine guns, mortars, and BARs (Browning Automatic Rifles). Most of the company was from Iowa, and they called me the 'stump-jumper from Minnesota.' "

The training intensified in Northern Ireland, with the company running at least ten miles a day, seven days a week. On one forced march, the men went thirty-six miles without a break.

"We slept in sleeping bags. They gave us straw to put in mattress covers. And the food was absolutely terrible. It was British rations. They gave us sugar once, and, the next day, we asked for more. They asked us how we had used a whole week's ration of sugar in one day."

On one exercise, the company broke all the existing Army records for a speed march, and word filtered up to Gen. Eisenhower. As a reward, he made the company his headquarters' guard when the division went to war. "They called us the 'Palace Guard.' We didn't think too much of that. We were a fighting unit."

After a long stay near Swindon, England, the division shipped out to North Africa. Because the company was assigned to headquarters, it didn't land until about two weeks after the initial landings in Algiers.

Hackbarth was a sergeant by this time, and his platoon was given a number of different jobs around Algiers. At one point, it was the fire-guard for the headquarters at the St. George Hotel.

"We had some guys who had been in reform school before they got in the Army. In fact, they joined the Army to get out of reform school. One of these guys came up to me one night and gave me a brand new Reader's Digest. He said, 'I just stole it from General Eisenhower's room.' He thought he was doing me a big favor. I told him to put it back right away and hope he didn't get caught doing it."

Hackbarth did have one major en-

«

MARVIN HACKBARTH

At home in Litchfield

»

DURING THE WAR

Hackbarth spent 14 months in combat in Italy in World War II

counter with Eisenhower. "Our rooms were in the attic of the St. George, and Eisenhower was on the second floor. I was heading up to my room, taking two or three stairs at a time, when Eisenhower came around the corner of the landing. I hit him square in the chest with my shoulder. He just went, 'woof,' as the breath went out of him. I really hit him hard. I picked myself up, saw all those stars, saluted, and got the heck out of there.

"I can truthfully say that I made contact with General Eisenhower."

Hackbarth's also remembers when General of the Army George C. Marshall came to visit and held a press conference. "I wasn't in the room, but I talked with the reporters afterwards. There were about forty reporters, and Marshall went around the room and allowed each of them to ask a question. Marshall didn't answer, he just listened and didn't take notes. When each one had asked his question, Marshall went around the room again and answered each question. The reporters were just shaking their heads. It was an incredible feat of memory."

The company spent ten months in Algiers and, at one time, was guarding the Allied Forces intelligence unit, about fifty miles from the city. "They had some visitors one time, and they asked if my platoon could put on a firing exhibit. So we set up our machine guns and fired them all at the same time into a hill nearby. It was pretty impressive. But then we found out later that we had killed three Arabs who were on the hill."

Another time, Hackbarth was called into company headquarters. "The captain told me to pick four other men who weren't afraid to do some shooting if they had to."

They left in five trucks and went to a fort near Algiers where the trucks were loaded. "They told us to shoot anybody who came near the trucks." The trucks were driven through Algiers, down to the docks where the material was loaded on ships. At one point, a local civilian approached the convoy, seeking a cigarette. Hackbarth said he was able to warn him away before he was gunned down.

"We found out later that we had been guarding the invasion maps of Sicily and Italy. They said we'd get medals for that, but of course we never did."

The company was sent to Oran, where they joined a convoy of ships headed to Italy. The unit quickly joined the fighting at Monte Casino. "Some of the Thirty-Fourth Division saw action there. Thank God, we didn't. We got there just as they bombed the monastery. It was the most devastated place I've ever

GROUP PHOTO

The men in Hackbarth's unit pose for a group photo at some point during their service in Italy.

seen.

They had to use road graders just to find the roads. There were no buildings, nothing but dust, sand, and stumps of trees. And it turns out

would be coming back with him.

"I told them flat out I didn't want him there, but they told me it was an order. I told the officer that it was my opinion it would bring death

ging at the wire. He quietly asked if anyone had stepped on the wire, but no one had. He quickly ordered the men to take cover in a nearby shell hole.

"Who's going to get those medals — their mothers? I never thought much of medals after that."

---

they really didn't have to bomb the monastery. I talked to German prisoners later, and they said they were never in the monastery."

The company's next stop was at Anzio as replacements for troops who had gone in earlier. Company H was sent immediately to the front lines at the perimeter of the beachhead. The famous 442nd "Go for Broke" Regimental Combat Team, made up of Japanese Americans, was right next to the Thirty-Fourth Division. "It was really cold out, but they all took a bath in the cold water. I don't know if it was tradition, or what. I know they were tremendous fighters."

Hackbarth's platoon was occupying a house that had been ninety percent destroyed by shelling. The men could look through a hole in a remaining wall to observe the German lines in the distance. "In between our lines were two dead German soldiers. Nobody ever did anything with them. You can imagine what they looked like after a while."

Telephone wires led back to the company's headquarters about a mile away. Each night, Hackbarth would have to head back to the command post to get his team's rations for the next day. On one of his visits, he was told an artillery spotter

upon us, and it nearly did."

The artillery spotter brought a long telescope with him, and the next day called Hackbarth over to look through it. In the distance, off to one side, the telescope revealed four Germans working their way through the grass carrying mortar shells. The spotter communicated back to the big guns. "They brought the artillery in on those guys. There was just a big cloud of dust. They killed everybody."

After the artillery man left, the Germans sought revenge, knowing the observation had come from the American outposts. "They hit another house with Americans about 150 yards away from us. They just flattened it. No one could have lived through it. That would have been us if they had picked the right house."

As time went by, the weather was miserable, but the rain may have saved Hackbarth's life. "A shell came in and hit right next to me, but I wasn't hit. I could reach out and touch where the shell had gone into the ground, but the ground was so soggy that it absorbed the impact."

Another night, Hackbarth was ordered to take a gun crew to another position. In the dark, they followed the telephone wire. As he led the men, he could feel something tug-

"There was a blast of automatic fire. You always hear about bullets whizzing by, and I suppose they do. But they also make a loud crack as they go by, sort of like a small sonic boom. They're as loud going by your ear as they are when they come out of the rifle." The German patrol soon moved on, and the Americans had been saved because one of the enemy had tripped over the phone wire.

Still out on the perimeter at Anzio, Hackbarth and two other soldiers were playing cards one day, hidden by the wreckage of the house that was their shelter. "I was leaning back on the sandbags when a mortar shell came in and hit a tree right next to us. One of the guys got hit four times in the guts with shrapnel. The other guy was hit in the shoulder. We had to carry the first guy out, and both of them went to the field hospital. I never saw either one of them again. I was only saved because I was leaning against those sandbags, and they shielded me from the blast."

After leaving Anzio, H Company and the Thirty-Fourth Division joined the long, slow push up through northern Italy, fighting through some of the most mountainous terrain in the world.

At one point, in walking just a few yards, Hackbarth recalls he had to step over seven dead Germans. "War is such hell."

One of his jobs was to fire heavy weapons into caves the troops encountered to make sure there were no enemy troops lurking inside. As his unit approached a small Italian village in the mountains, they came upon one of the most horrific scenes of the war.

"The Germans had just pulled out of the town, and the Americans were coming in. Evidently the townspeople had dug this cave in order to protect themselves from the fighting. Apparently the whole town had gone inside this cave.

"The American troops that went before us did what we always did. They fired into the cave. When they went in to look around, they found bodies, lots of bodies.

"They started bringing people out. They laid the men in one row, and the women in another row, and the children in a third row. By far, that third row was the longest. When they got everybody out, there were 200 bodies.

"If I had been there, that would have been my job. But I didn't do it, thank God. It wasn't me. But somebody did. I don't know how he lived with himself after that.

"And the amazing thing, nothing about it ever appeared in the newspapers or anywhere else that I saw. It happened, but it was like it didn't happen."

Another time, Hackbarth was called in and sent to a prison compound. "They told me one of my men had deserted. Sure enough, he was there, but while I was looking for him, I found one of my old friends

from Cosmos. He had also deserted.

"You know, those guys all got dishonorable discharges, but it wasn't their fault. They had been in all the shelling, and their nerves just went all to pieces. They were sick people; they couldn't help it. My friend had seen so many of his comrades killed, his nerves just went. I know they have a policy, but he was a brave man, and he should have been treated better."

At one point, the Americans came up against a hill that may have contained German soldiers. "They asked for volunteers, but this was getting late in the war, and there weren't any. They asked again, and promised medals to anybody who went. Still nobody volunteered. Finally, they picked a handful of men, and up the hill they went. I was a sergeant and so I had binoculars, and I watched three of them get gunned down trying to get up that hill. I said to one of my buddies, 'Who's going to get those medals — their mothers?' I never thought much of medals after that."

Hackbarth spent some time in a hospital in Naples after he was injured. "My men were digging in, and, of course, I didn't think they were doing it fast enough, so I grabbed a pickax to help them. Just then a shell came in, and I jumped down in the hole and got a big gash on my foot."

Much to his surprise, he found that most of the beds in the Naples hospital were taken up by American GIs with venereal disease. "We didn't think much of that. They were using our beds. But then while I was there, the Army brought in the first penicillin in the war. Some of these guys had been suffering quite a long time. There was a real celebration. They

all got relief finally."

While recuperating, he wandered over to a nearby racetrack. He stepped through an open door and realized he was in a makeshift hospital wing. "It was a ward for guys who had lost their legs. Every guy in there had lost at least one limb, and many of them had lost both. So here am I walking through, and they can hear my boots hitting the floor. I wanted to get out, but I couldn't find another door. Those guys were completely silent and just staring at me. Finally, I found my way out. That's another reason I don't like war."

Back at the front, Hackbarth was approached by an officer. " 'Sergeant Hack, move your squad a mile and a half up the road,' he told me. So I got in my Jeep, and with four trucks behind me, we headed up the road. After we had gone for a while, we came to a gate blocking the road. I pulled my Jeep over and went and opened the gate and motioned for the first truck to move on through. It didn't go very far before it hit a mine and killed everyone in the truck.

"Why that gate was closed I don't know. But if it had been open, that would have been my Jeep that hit that mine."

As the war wound on, the Thirty-Fourth Division came up with a morale booster. Each month, two men from each company were allowed to go home on furlough. The second month, Hackbarth's name was picked.

It was great being home in Minnesota, but there was a price. "After I had been there a couple of weeks, and my time was short for heading back, I would go to movies with my friends and just sit there and shake. I was dreading going back."

When he did get back, the war seemed even more deadly than before. "I was with the guys, and they were shooting artillery over our heads. They did that all the time. On this day, they were shooting what we called radar shells because they were set to explode before they hit the ground. Well, sometimes they'd get too close to each other in the air and they would set each other off. That happened right over our heads. I jumped for cover, while the other guys just stood there looking at me. They wondered why I was so jumpy, but I had had a taste of normal life. They were so used to war, but now I wasn't."

Going out on a death detail was the job Hackbarth hated the most, but he and his men were assigned that duty three times while in Italy. Somebody had to pick up the bodies and bring them back.

"The worst was one time when we were in the mountains, and it had snowed. Our soldiers were all dressed in white, but during the day all the snow melted, and they were sitting ducks as they tried to get up a hillside. There were thirty-seven men killed. Because I had been raised in the country, they thought I could handle the horses. It was so steep there that that was the only way to get the bodies out."

The dead men were to be put into rubberized body bags. "But, often, they had died in strange positions, and, if an arm or leg stuck out, we just had to break it to get the body into the bag. That was kind of tough. I knew some of those men.

"We got them all into the bags, but when we tried to get them on the horses, it was a disaster. The horses were rearing up and throwing the bodies into the mud, and then the

GERMAN LEAFLET

The Nazi government used propaganda leaflets during the war, and this was one that Hackbarth picked up along the way. The messages were often anti-semetic.

horses were trampling them. Finally, I said to the other fellows, 'I wonder what their mothers would think if they could only see their sons now? What would they say?'"

On another night, Hackbarth was ordered to take a truck with about fifteen infantrymen down a certain road. "As we traveled along, all of a sudden there was a big bonfire in front of us. What was going on? Why was it there? There was something very mysterious going on.

"We stopped at a farmhouse and woke the people up to find out if they knew about the fire. I left a couple of guys to guard the road. Soon, one of them came back and said there were Germans marching on the road. I went out there and hid behind the pillars by the gate. A whole company of Germans went right by me. I was scared to death. I was just a few feet from them, and our truck was sitting right there in the farmyard."

Hackbarth was able to make his way back to the farmhouse and send a message that it appeared that an entire German division was going down the road. "It was one of those nights when you hope daylight will never come because then they'll be able to see you." Eventually, he ordered his men in groups of twos and threes to find their way back to the American lines.

"I was the last to leave, and, as I went down this small road, all of a sudden this German on a motorcycle came around a bend and was there, right in front of me. I aimed my rifle at him three times, and each time I put it down. I was an expert shot, and I would have had him. But in the end, he went past me."

That humanitarian decision made the horror of the war easier to bear

in future years. "Thank God, I didn't shoot him because I would have had that on my conscience all these years. I've thought about that so many thousands of times through the years."

Because of his earlier warning, though, the Americans were able to rain down artillery on the Germans. "We tore up that column pretty badly."

In the end, the Thirty-Fourth Division accepted the surrender of the German Thirty-Fourth Division. The Americans, by this time, had pushed all the way to the Swiss border. Hackbarth volunteered to drive a Jeep back to Naples, and the terrain that had been so devastating for the prior fourteen months now seemed beautiful and serene.

This respite was a taste of what was to come. Hackbarth would soon be discharged and finally return to Min-

nesota for good.

Back home, he considered going to the University of Minnesota, but instead took over his father's farm-implement business. He ran it until 1980, when hard times in rural Minnesota forced him to get out of the business.

He has been retired since, living in Florida in the winter and on a lake near Litchfield in the summer. His wife of fifty years died several years ago. They had two sons and a daughter.

His war experiences remain with him daily.

"I often think about, what if that gate had been opened? What if I had joined the airborne? What if a hundred other things hadn't happened? But here I am, alive. I feel like there's something that God wanted me to do in this world."

CLINKING BEER BOTTLES

Hackbarth and his buddy offered each other a toast in Chicago while they were on their way back to Minnesota for furlough. They nearly got into a fight in a Chicago theater, but the friend, who was a Golden Gloves champion, ended the fisticuffs quickly.

PONTOON BRIDGE
Although one of the easiest and quickest to build, the pontoon bridge had its problems -- like its tendency to toss tanks into the river.

Unless indicated otherwise, all photos are from Earl Hall's personal collection.

BRIDGE BUILDING,
ARMY STYLE

Earl Hall was a young officer out of East Texas when he became a company commander in an Army bridge building regiment in World War II. The 1303rd Engineer General Service Regiment built bridges all across Europe and was primed for the invasion of Japan when the war ended in 1945.

The problem is that tanks can't swim.

When George Patton's Third Army came to a river blocking its path, the American blitzkrieg came to a thundering halt until the engineers could build a bridge. During World War II, hundreds of bridges, great and small, were built across ditches, streams, canals, and raging rivers.

Earl Hall helped build a few dozen of those bridges as a company commander in the 1303rd Engineer General Service Regiment.

Hall's bridge-building career started with an interest in science as a schoolboy growing up in Beaumont, a city in southeast Texas not far from the Louisiana border.

"During the 30s and 40s, there was a widespread belief that engineering could change the world. People told me I was good at math, physics and science, and there was some idealism there," Hall said.

He graduated from Beaumont High School in 1939 and went straight to college at Texas A&M.

"It was a poor boy's college. It cost $50 tuition for the entire year. My mother was a widowed school teacher who had lost her job when the Depression started."

Hall's mother scraped by, teaching courses funded by the Works Progress Administration. "We were in pretty sad straits, but I had a pretty good paper route, and we put together a little money to go to school on."

In the end, it cost about $600 for the college year, including books, housing, meals, and the rest.

At that time, Texas A&M was one of a handful of schools across the country that was totally made up of Reserve Officer Training Corps cadets. "Everybody on the campus wore a uniform. Every semester we had to take military science and tactics, and we all marched to the mess hall for lunch and dinner, and sat in an organized fashion for the meals."

Hall was grateful that this early service to his country had a monetary benefit. The Army paid him ten cents a day for his ROTC status.

The United States went to war when Hall was still a junior. The bombing at Pearl Harbor incensed Hall and his roommate so much that they marched down to the recruiting office in Bryan, Texas, and volunteered.

"The recruiting officer told us that we couldn't volunteer. He said we'd been in the Army since we were freshmen, and that the Army would tell us when it was time for us to go."

Texas A&M sped its education

process because of the war, and the students took their first semester of senior year during the summer. By January 1943, they graduated.

Hall got his second lieutenant commission in Virginia, and he was sent cross country to Camp Ellis in Illinois to be part of the cadre as the 1303rd regiment was being formed. "It was a most unusual unit," Hall said.

The heart of the unit was formed around men who had construction experience in the civilian world. Several general foremen or construction managers were given direct commissions into the unit. "A lot of men knew an awful lot about what we were doing."

Hall's experience wasn't bad, either. In addition to his engineering degree, he had spent one summer building highways and other summers working as a roughneck in the Texas oil fields.

The cadre was formed in July 1943, and grew to 1,700 men by March of 1944. The men trained by building bridges across the famous Spoon River in Illinois.

No one knew, of course, where they would be sent once they were ready, but some of the officers were taking a side course in Japanese, Hall said. Instead, the 1303rd was ordered to Massachusetts, where the men boarded a troop ship for England.

"We didn't take our equipment with us. Our equipment met up with us in England."

Their training continued, and Hall, who was the commander of Company B, did some special training with the British commandos. Hall's area of expertise was explosives, and a major job of the engineering units was to lay or remove mine fields.

The unit also stayed busy in England by building airstrips and laying concrete platforms for buildings called hardstands. "They said that every time we poured another hardstand, they had to run up another barrage balloon to keep the island from sinking.

"We poured a lot of concrete while we were there."

D-Day came and went while the engineer regiment waited its chance. Hall took part in the landings personally but will not talk about his activities, noting that it was top secret at the time. He rejoined his outfit in time for its own landing at Normandy on July 28, 1944.

By August, the 1303rd had been assigned to Patton's Third Army and was part of the full gallop across France toward the German border. The engineering regiment was in the 12th Corps and served as flank

«

EARL HALL

At home in Woodbury

»

DURING THE WAR

Hall led a company of bridge builders in the Third Army's race across Europe.

TRESTLE AND I-BEAM BRIDGE

One of the most permanent of the bridges the Army built, the trestle and I-beam bridge was often built on the debris left over from a bridge destroyed by the retreating German Army. The beams were usually scrounged from the local scene.

guard for the right side of the racing army.

Bridge builders are expected to be in the rear of the front lines, but the 1303rd spent the next nine months almost continuously in the combat zone.

Hall's company became something of an independent unit. "We went across Europe as an individual unit, never together as a battalion or regiment. They just put us to work as engineers, and we rarely stayed anywhere for more than a few days."

The unit cleared minefields, built a prisoner of war camp, and did extensive roadwork. "But more than anything else, we built bridges. We crossed the major rivers in Europe, and got pretty good at it."

There were three general types of bridges the engineers would build. One was called a Bailey bridge, which was mainly a gigantic erector set. The main pieces were six-by-10 foot panels with crossed steel braces. Each panel weighed 600 pounds.

"We figured it took six men to lift one and put it in place. If a man couldn't carry 100 pounds, he didn't belong in an engineering unit."

To construct the bridge, crews built a section at one end and pushed it out on rollers over the river until it reached a pier. "You always had to have enough built behind to support what you were pushing out."

The second type of span was a pontoon bridge. Pontoons were floated down the river and captured and put in place with treads above them. "First, you'd build an abutment on either side of the river. You'd attach the floats one at a time. They were clumsy, clumsy things."

To keep the bridge from floating downstream, anchors were dropped upstream and the structure was lashed down with cables fixed to the anchors.

A third type was the wooden trestle bridge, built with thick trestles topped with steel I-beams.

Whatever the type of bridge, it had to support the 70 tons of load needed to get a tank to the other side.

The bridges were often built on the rubble of bridges the Germans had destroyed in their retreat. The engineers would construct wooden cribs to hold the rock and rubble, and would let that support the new bridge.

Heavy equipment was at a premium, and the B Company made do with one small crane, big enough to lift I-beams, and a small bulldozer. All wood was sawed by hand. "There weren't any Skil saws in those days."

In general, a bridge could be erected in two or three days. "That's if you're working very hard, and you know what you're doing."

The type of bridge they built depended on the water to be crossed and the speed at which it was needed. A pontoon bridge was the quickest, but also one of the hardest to build in fast-moving water. The tankers also disliked pontoon bridges intensely because of their instability.

With no weight on a pontoon bridge, the carrying surface was five feet above the water. When a tank rode out on the bridge, the surface was only a foot above the water. "It bounces up and down, and they were known to dump tanks in the river. They were tricky to build and tricky to drive across. You never sent two tanks in a row over a pontoon bridge.

BAILEY BRIDGE

Like a giant erector set, the Bailey bridge was assembled out of pieces, such as these six-foot by eight-foot panels, and then pushed over the river.

But bridge-building wasn't the only thing the engineers did. Because the 1303rd was on the flank of the army, its members often did reconnais-sance in small vehicles, searching for German units that had been by-passed by the lightning advance.

the Battle of the Bulge, the engineers were deployed as infantry troops. "We did our duty, but we weren't very good at being infantry.

"At the Bulge, they sent us up, and we were assigned a sector at the corner of the Bulge to keep the Germans from expanding. We dug into our fox holes and waited. The Allied cause was very fortunate the Germans didn't choose to attack us. It's one thing to be deployed, and another to perform well in action."

"Here I was a 22-year-old talking to the general of the army, but somehow that didn't bother me a bit."

"The pontoon bridge was not your ideal bridge."

Hall noted that his company never actually brought the materials for the bridge to the site. Special Bailey or pontoon companies did that.

If I-beams were needed, they would have to be found locally. "You know we didn't ship I-beams overseas to make bridges. We didn't ask; we didn't pay; we just took it. Sometimes the French would get a little disturbed when we took them, but all we could tell them was that we were fighting a war."

"If you drove into a French town, and all the people came out with flowers and flags and wine, you knew the Germans were nowhere around. But if the town was all shuttered up, and nobody was in sight, you knew the Germans were close at hand."

Once an enemy position was encountered, the engineers would call in 8th Air Force support, and P-47s would attack the German units. On at least two occasions, including

Hall said Patton's logistical skills were never more evident than in getting his army up to that battle. "We had orders for which roads to follow, and when we'd go over a crossing, a unit coming the other way would follow right behind us. It was beautiful logistics, but that was Uncle George."

Hall did have one close encounter with the American general. "Patton had a habit of coming up to the front in a Jeep, with the flags flying and his entourage in tow. He really didn't belong in a combat area."

Hall was overseeing the construction of a bridge when he noticed the presence of another officer next to him. "Patton immediately told me when he wanted that bridge done, and he said, 'If you can't do it, I'll find somebody that can.'

"Here I was, a 22-year-old, talking to the general of the Army, but somehow it didn't bother me a bit. I don't know why. I simply told him how long it was going to take for each phase of the project. It was a lot more hours than he wanted.

"But, you know what? Nobody could take our place, and nobody could do it better. The general just walked away without saying a word."

Following a trip to the front lines, Patton would often return to his headquarters in a spotter aircraft, Hall said. That way, the soldiers would never see the general heading backwards from the front.

Hall said a lot has been written about Patton since the war. "But we respected him, and we loved him. He took care of us, and that meant equipment, supplies, and recognition, too. And I've read about that special discipline he enforced, but at that time I didn't notice anything special about it."

One part of the Patton operation that Hall always remembered was when a leading element of the Army would capture a German rest camp and liberate a quantity of liquor. "He always shared it with the troops. We

THE ORIGINAL CADRE FOR 1303RD ENGINEERS

B COMPANY

Hall was lower left in this photo of the officers of B Company, 1303rd Engineers.

would get our ration every so often. I think sometimes we built those bridges when some of the guys were half drunk."

When the Bulge was halted, the Third Army's advance to the heart of Germany continued. "It was a moving event, and we just tagged along."

When there were no bridges to build, there were often minefields to clear. "It was nerve-wracking business, but you had to do it.

"Once a mine was detected, you could blow it up or dig it out. If you dug it out, you'd use your bayonet to scrape the dirt away from the mine.

"But the Germans didn't want us to remove their minefields. The main mines were Teller mines that had about 12 pounds of TNT in them. But they would also plant smaller anti-personnel mines that would go off with just a footstep. Sometimes they would attach the anti-personnel mines to the bigger mines. You'd have to search with your bayonet to see if the mine was booby-trapped.

"We didn't have enough training at it, and most of the training was on-the-job experience. We lost a few men out there. When one guy was blown up, another guy had to take his place. Wars are like that."

Getting supplies could be difficult when the pressure was on to build a bridge because the armor was waiting to press on. "You were supposed to fill out a requisition, and it would go upstream to corps headquarters, and then you waited until they brought it to you. That was a little slow.

"What you really did was find out where a heavy equipment depot was and go steal one. Nobody got terribly upset with us."

Hall said he had the ideal motor

sergeant. "He knew his stuff about rebuilding vehicles and fixing them. It turns out he ran a car ring in Detroit that stole cars in America, redid them, and shipped them over to Canada. He was perfect as a motor sergeant for our company. He knew how to get parts."

The bridges were generally built without enemy resistance, but, on occasion, there would be a mortar attack. Once, a German 88 opened fire on a project.

And sometimes an airplane would strafe the engineers.

"One time, out of nowhere, a plane came over and strafed us. It was going like hell. I jumped up in the Jeep where we had a ring-mounted .50-caliber and waited for him to come back. When he did, he came too fast for me to even swing the gun around.

"It turned out it was a Junkers two-engined jet. It's a good thing they didn't have too many of those."

Hall's most dangerous incident, though, came without enemy fire. "We were going to build a bridge

across the Moselle, and we had to take an assault boat across to the other side to look at the ground over there.

"Assault boats have flat bottoms and are powered by paddles. The current was taking us downstream pretty quickly, and we couldn't control the boat."

The boat struck a sunken island with trees sticking out of it and tossed the men into the fast moving river. "When the boat went off and left us, I was holding onto a tree for dear life. I had more clothing on than I would have liked for being in a river, and I just wasn't a good enough swimmer to reach the shore.

"Private McDaniels saw us. He had grown up in Tennessee, and he knew how to navigate fast rivers in small boats. I don't know how he got out there, but, if he hadn't, I would have drowned. Nobody told him to come out and rescue us. He just did it. We took care of each other."

The 1303rd finished its war in Europe at Passau, Germany, in the spring of 1945. For two weeks, Hall,

REFUELING

The 1303rd learned how to build bridges at Camp Ellis in Illinois.

now a captain, was the military governor of Passau.

Not much later, though, the 1303rd mounted up and headed for Marseilles, where the men were loaded on to a Navy troop ship that quickly took them across the ocean, through the Panama Canal, and to the Philippines.

While in the Philippines, Hall learned there was a difference between the European war and the Pacific war in terms of what you could get away with. "Some other company saw us with a piece of equipment that had once belonged to them. Before I knew it, I was up for general court marshal. Fortunately for me, our C.O. went and explained that's how we'd done that in France. They let me go, and told me not to do it again. I could have been in Leavenworth."

The regiment set up camp near Clark Airfield and got ready for its next duty, the invasion of Kyushu, Japan. When the atomic bombs ended the war, the regiment was sent as an occupation force to Japan, and then its members slowly began to go home.

Hall had enough points to go home early, but he was considered essential personnel by the Army, and he was kept on to guide the unit through being disbanded.

He arrived home in Beaumont, Texas, on Christmas Eve 1945.

For several years, Hall worked for General Electric as a jet engine specialist. He still has patents with the company for mechanisms he invented. His love affair with engineering, however, was waning.

"I began to see that engineering couldn't save the world."

In mid-career, Hall quit his job and went to the Boston University Theological Institute. One of his classmates was Martin Luther King Jr., who became a lifelong friend.

General Electric helped out with Hall's new endeavor by keeping him on as a part-time specialist.

In the end, Hall became deeply involved in the civil rights movement, and participated in such activities as the Selma to Montgomery marches. In the following years, as an ordained Methodist minister, he served churches and communities across the country.

Control Data, a Minnesota company, hired him at one point, and that was his passport to the state. Once in Minnesota, he became the director of business management at the University of St. Thomas, a position he held for eight years before retiring.

He still lunches with colleagues at the university.

Hall wrote a book on integrated project management with fellow scholar Juliane Johnson, and the book is still considered a standard in the field.

Hall has three sons and lives in Woodbury, where he has been using his master gardener skills.

Hall is now working on a book called Finding the Footprints of God, a perspective on spirituality from the mind of a scientist.

"I consider it a tremendous privilege to have done the things I've done, to have known the people I've known and to have gone the places I've gone – and to have that little gal, Carol, my wife, with me."

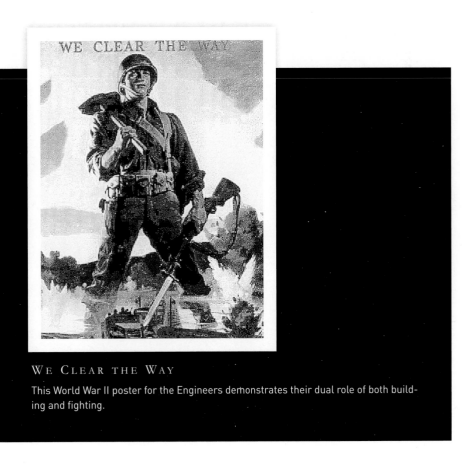

WE CLEAR THE WAY

This World War II poster for the Engineers demonstrates their dual role of both building and fighting.

HIDING OUT

After bailing out over Belgium, Cupp and three other crew members were taken in by this family near Lessines. The family kept this photo throughout the war, even though possession of it could have meant instant death. From left, in front, are Navigator Robert Donahue, Abel Coton and Ghislain Boucher. In back are: Co-Pilot Douglas Hooth, Hortense Boucher, Berthe Delaunois, Bombardier Richard Wright and Ball Turret Gunner Bill

Unless indicated otherwise, all photos are from William Cupp's personal collection.

EVADING THE ENEMY

William Cupp of Northfield was a ball-turret gunner on a B-24 Liberator. On his third mission, the aircraft was shot down, beginning an extraordinary three months of evading the Germans in occupied Belgium. Once he was captured, the adventure wasn't over. Cupp took part in a 500-mile walk across Germany to his freedom.

William L. Cupp grew up on a farm near Tipton, Iowa. He graduated from high school in 1941 and was ready to enlist in the Army immediately after the Pearl Harbor attack in December of that year. "I told my folks I was going, but they said I was too young. I was 17 at the time."

Instead, he got a job at a defense plant in Clinton and was quickly promoted to inspector when they found out he could read blueprints.

Cupp took a test to get into the Army Air Corps in late spring 1942, and signed up in July. His interest in aviation went back to the family farm where the U.S. Post Office had placed an emergency landing field that Cupp's father watched over. Cupp wanted to be a pilot.

Although he was signed up and eager to go, the Army made Cupp wait seven more months before finally calling him up in January 1943. He was sent to air cadet screening and then pre-flight school in San Antonio. At Uvalde, Texas, he began flight school on PT-19s.

"I was doing all right until my in-structor was assigned somewhere else. I was given another instructor, but in the end I washed out. There were a lot of washouts."

After basic training at Wichita Falls, Texas, Cupp was sent to Tyndall Air Force Base in Florida for aerial gunnery school. "I passed the test to become a navigator, but it looked as if the school would take forever. I was anxious to get going."

The next stop was El Paso, where he became part of a crew.

"We were flying the B-24Ds, and most of these planes were not in really good shape. There was usually a fire coming out of one engine or another. On our first few flights, the radio operator couldn't reach the radio because he was always wearing his parachute on his chest. He was scared to death. Eventually, they transferred him to the mailroom on base. The bombardier also got into some sort of trouble, and he was shipped out."

The crew of 10 finally began to mesh, and Cupp volunteered to be the ball turret gunner, traditionally one of the most dangerous jobs on the plane. The turret was suspended beneath the B-24 Liberator. It could be retracted into the airplane for landings and takeoffs.

"I didn't want any of the other guys in there. I didn't trust them. Besides, I was smaller than some of the guys."

Still, the accommodations were not very comfy. "You sit with your knees up all the way and the gun sight be-

tween your knees. After eight or nine hours, it gets pretty uncomfortable. And there was no way you could get a parachute inside the turret. Believe me, I spent hours trying to figure out a way to do it."

On its way overseas, the crew had to fly to Iceland. It was almost the last trip for the new crew.

"The Germans had stolen our radio channel for our fix on the base in Iceland, and they were sending out bad information from Norway. By the time we figured it out, we were a hundred miles or more off course. We didn't have enough gas to go back, and our navigator was given the job of finding out where we were. He found one star to get a fix on. He was able to get us to the base, but one of our engines had run out of gas before we landed."

Several other crews did not make it and were never heard from again. "It gave us a little confidence in our navigator."

Cupp and the crew were assigned to the 861st Bombardment Squadron, 493rd Bombardment Group of the Eighth Air Force. It was May 1944, just a month before the D-Day landing.

Their first mission was on D-Day, but instead of getting their new B-24, the crew was assigned an older version. "It was a real junker. The guns were limp from being fired too many times. When it flew, the tail didn't line up with the nose."

Worse than that, the bombing mission had to be aborted because the target was locked in with heavy cloud cover. The only good news was the chance to have a bird's-eye view of the world's largest invasion. "It looked as if you could walk across the English Channel on all those ships. There were so many of them."

The second mission was even worse.

"We got another junky plane, and we were over Holland, and the oxygen supply started to malfunction. After the bombardier fell asleep, the pilot said, 'Well, we can't do that,' and we came back. It was so embarrassing."

The third and last mission again featured another "veteran" plane called Won Long Hop. "The ground crew guys told us that the plane was supposed to have been sent to the salvage yard that day, but instead we were flying it."

The first run over the target — an airfield in France — at 20,000 feet found the B-24s above the cloud cover with the target obscured. A second run at 12,000 feet put them right over the target, and the payload was released. Because there were no enemy aircraft around, the

«

WILLIAM CUPP

At home in Northfield

»

DURING THE WAR

Cupp was part of a crew assigned to the 493rd Bomb Group. The crew's B-24 was shot down on its third mission.

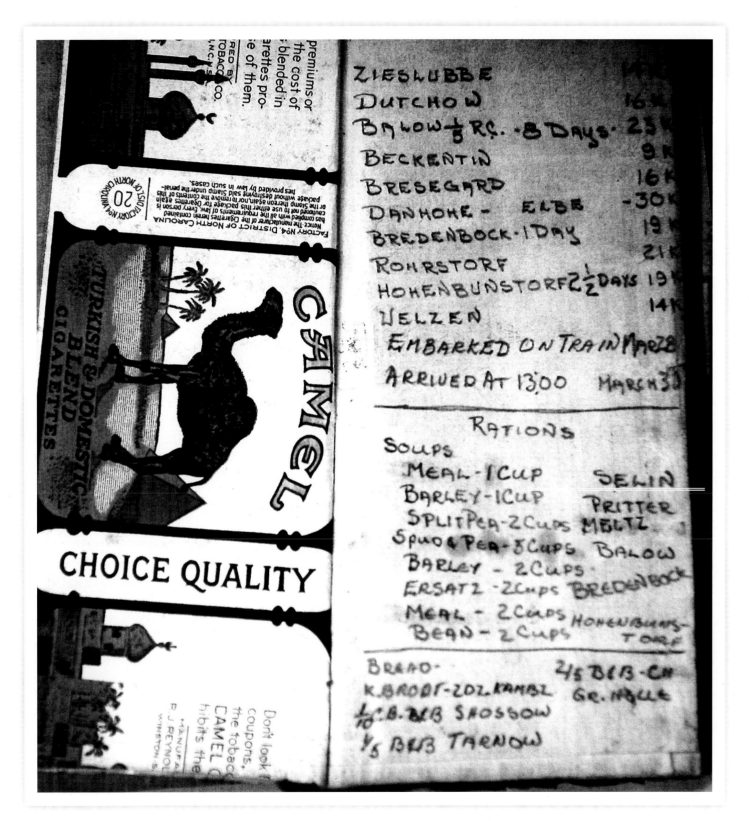

ZIESLUBBE

DUTCHOW   16 K

BALOW ⅕ R.C. - 8 DAYS - 23 K

BECKENTIN   9 K

BRESEGARD   16 K

DANHOHE -   ELBE   -30 K

BREDENBOCK - 1 DAY   19 K

ROHRSTORF   21 K

HOHENBUNSTORF 2½ DAYS 19 K

UELZEN   14 K

EMBARKED ON TRAIN MAR 28

ARRIVED AT 13:00   MARCH 30

RATIONS

SOUPS

MEAL - 1 CUP   SELIN
BARLEY - 1 CUP   PRITTER
SPLIT PEA - 2 CUPS MELTZ
SPUD & PEA - 3 CUPS BALOW
BARLEY - 2 CUPS
ERSATZ - 2 CUPS   BREDENBOCK
MEAL - 2 CUPS   HOHENBUNS-
BEAN - 2 CUPS   TORF

BREAD -
K.BROT - 2 OZ. KAMBZ   ⅖ B/13 - CM   GR. MUHLE
4/10 B. B/13 SHOSSOW
⅕ B/13 TARNOW

KEEPING TRACK

When he reached Stalag Luft IV, Cupp began to keep track of information in a little book he created out of cardboard and cigarette packages. On the right is a listing of how many miles the American prisoners walked each day on their journey across Germany. Below that is a list of the rations they received.

pilot had ordered the ball turret retracted, so the plane could make more speed. Cupp was sitting next to his turret, listening to the radio traffic.

flak again. The tail gunner was sprayed with Plexiglass as the rear of the plane shattered. One of the tail rudders was blown off.

"By this time there were holes all

A group of trees was coming up from below at a rapid speed. Cupp hit a tree, bounced into the air, then hit the ground like a ton of bricks. "I didn't have the strength to pull down

---

"A soldier came and poked a pitchfork around the hay pile I was in, but I was down about 12 feet."

On the bombing run, the plane had been struck by flak, and the number one engine was hit and put out of action. The pilot was also slightly injured.

"I could look down after the run and see the bombs make a perfect pattern on the runway below. But then the squadron leader said, 'Let's go back and see what we did.' So here we are, flying basically the same pattern over the target for the third time. The German gunners were good to begin with. They just shot the dickens out of us."

This time the rickety plane lost its fuel tank for the number four engine, and now the air power was down to two engines. "We couldn't keep up with the rest of the planes, so we just headed straight for the coast. That may or may not have been a good idea."

The plane was hit again by flak as it traveled over occupied Belgium. "The pilot was doing a good job of manhandling that big behemoth. I went up to the cockpit, and I could see the sweat marks coming right through his leather flight jacket."

The pilot tried some evasive action, but, by the time the navigator could figure out where they were, they were flying over another German air base and they were besieged with

over the plane. You could hear the whistling as the air blew through the plane. Even with all that, we were still hoping to get to the coast."

The crew dumped everything it could out of the bomb bay, including all the guns and ammunition. But still the plane was losing its fight to stay in the air.

"The pilot said we had two choices. We could stay with him, or we could parachute out. All nine of us chose to bail out. I put on my heavier shoes and strapped on my parachute. By this time the plane was at about a 45-degree angle, and there was some doubt about whether it was safe to jump out of the bomb bay. I was wondering, 'Do I want to do that?' Then the other two engines conked out, and the plane went into a steeper dive. I just said, 'Oh,' and I stepped out."

Afraid of having his parachute observed, Cupp free fell as long as he thought he could. "It was actually quite peaceful for a change. The roar was gone. There was no more firing."

As he entered a cloud bank at about 1,200 feet, he pulled the rip cord. "I didn't know that I was upside down, and when the chute came out it flipped me around and really gave me a jolt."

my parachute from the tree. It would be a beacon to any German observers, but I didn't care. I got out of my flight suit, and I saw a fellow coming at me, waving. I wasn't sure what to do, so I hid myself in the field. When I looked back, my parachute was gone."

A couple of farm workers waved Cupp to a nearby farm home, and there he found two other members of his crew. The farm wife gave him a large bottle of beer, and all three men changed into civilian clothes that were provided by the farmers. Then, it was out the back door and into a wheat field for the night.

The plane had been shot down near Lessines, Belgium, about 40 miles west of Brussels.

Cupp learned later that the pilot stayed with the plane as he tried to maneuver it over a church and village. He tried to bail out much too late and was killed. The local priest finished the mass he was saying to schoolchildren at the church the pilot had saved, and then went out and gave the American his last rites.

In the next few days, Cupp and the others were dispersed around the countryside by the Belgian underground, the Comète Line. In one house, the woman of the house kissed Cupp and wept. "I didn't know much about the European tradition of kissing. I was pretty impressed."

He stayed there three weeks, passing as a member of the family. On one occasion, at 5 a.m., the household was awakened by heavy pounding on the door. It was the Gestapo.

"I was in bed in my green Army underwear. Out the back door I went. We had been making hay in the barn, and I dove into it. I could hear a lot of loud voices. The Germans questioned why there were unmade beds in the house, but the housewife told them that the men had gone off to a neighboring farm to work very early.

"A soldier came and poked a pitchfork around the hay pile I was in, but I was down about 12 feet. It did make me a little nervous, though. And the hay made me scratchy."

Cupp spent the next three days in a field while the Germans continued their sweep of the area.

"The Belgian people were so brave. They would have been shot instantly if they were caught. But they were determined to make it awkward for the Germans."

The ultimate goal for the evaders was to reach Spain or Switzerland, and there were several underground lines set up to guide the men, mainly American air crewmen, to safety.

With the help of the guides, Cupp made his way south to the French border. The last hurdle getting across the border was solved when one of the resistance fighters, a young woman, flirted with guards while Cupp and Robert Donahue, the crew's navigator, slipped into France.

Aboard a train, the two enjoyed the ride. "We had just walked about 50 miles, so we were pretty sore. We stuck our feet out the window."

In the small town of Aniche, the two Americans had lost their escort of resistance fighters. "We didn't know what to do, so we went into a church, and, when the service was over, we planned to approach the priest and ask him for help."

Donahue was in another part of the church, and when he came out, in his farm clothing, one of the local boys yelled, "robber." "We weren't dressed right for church, and so we made people suspicious."

The airmen fled, and when a German with a gun approached them and asked where the robbers were, they pointed in a different direction. As they hustled down the dirt road leading out of town, they heard a rattling sound behind them. The priest had followed them on his bicycle.

He directed them to another town, but as they walked through the town, all the townspeople stood in the doorways and watched them pass. "It was spooky because nobody said anything. We said, 'Let's get the heck out of this town.' We were just going past the last house, and it was getting pretty dark and we heard a voice say, 'I wouldn't go that way if I were you.' We asked why, and he said, 'There's lots of Germans down that way.'"

In the end, the Americans were invited inside a house and given bread and jam and milk. They spent the night in a haystack and headed south again the next day.

South of Amiens, they hitched a ride on a truck, and when they climbed in, they found they were sharing it with a German soldier. "It was raining, and we just pulled our jackets over our heads. In the end, it was probably good he was there because other Germans inspected the truck, but when they saw the soldier, they just left us alone."

That night they ended up at a farm. "We had gone about two days without sleeping. They gave us some beef sandwiches, and I fell asleep with my head in my plate."

After about four days at a farm, the French resistance showed up. There had been problems with Germans infiltrating the escape and evasion system, so the resistance member grilled them at length to be sure they were really American air crewmen. He also took their dog tags.

When it was time to head south again, they were put in a panel truck with a blanket thrown over them. Their two escorts were mechanics at the German air base in the town, and they drove the truck right through the base, saying hello to all the Germans and fellow workers. They passed through two guard stations along the way.

Cupp and the navigator stayed on a local farm for a month. "There were a lot of Germans retreating through that farm, and we could hear the bombardment in the distance."

It was time to leave again, and the two decided to try and reach the American lines, which were not far away by this time. Unfortunately, to get there, they had to go through the German lines.

"We spent the night in a haystack, and we walked in the dark through a bombed-out German airbase. We kept falling into the craters."

The next day, they worked their way through the German lines in the rain. "There were lots of German soldiers everywhere, but everybody looks the same in the rain. We were doing okay, but then the sun came out, and there we were. There was no place to hide. A guy at a machine gun on the next hill sent a bullet our way, and we decided we'd better stay."

They were 200 yards from the American lines.

The two were apprehended and taken in for a very intense questioning. This time, no one was buying their story that they were Belgians looking for work in the war factories.

The future looked grim for Cupp and Donahue. "They told us that we were not in a good place, and that it was time to shoot us. They stood us up at the edge of a woods and put a hood over our heads. They started saying, 'Ready... aim...'"

"I yelled, 'Wait, we're Americans,' and the officer ordered the men to halt. After that everybody became friendly. They offered us candy and cigarettes. Well, not everybody was friendly."

Americans caught in civilian clothes are liable to be shot as spies, and Cupp had foreseen a problem after the resistance had taken their dog tags. They begged to get them back, but instead were given a set from other soldiers. "Mine said I was Sergeant Green. I had to tell the interrogator that I really was an American soldier, but that I wasn't Sergeant Green. It was pretty hard to explain. They were pretty sure that we were two observation pilots that had been shot down.

"Some people took us and tried to do us harm. They worked us over a little bit." As a final bit of convincing, the Germans put Cupp and Donahue on the front of a Jeep and drove it straight at a wall, hitting the brakes only at the very last second. "I didn't know I could hold onto a Jeep like that, but I did. They must have done it 20 or 30 times."

The interrogators finally decided to bring the two Americans, still clinging to the front of the Jeep while they zig-zagged all the way, to the German command post at Pontoise.

It didn't get much better there as Cupp and his comrade were interrogated separately. Apparently unsatisfied with the results of the questioning, the officer began to assemble a firing squad and, after a while, had 11 men gathered in the headquarters. "They were having a tough time finding enough people to shoot us. Everybody had cleared out."

Just as the firing squad was ready to go, though, U.S. shells began to rain down on the German HQ, and plaster was falling from the ceiling. The firing squad quickly dispersed.

Cupp and the navigator were loaded on a truck heading away from the fighting, and over the next few days the truck was strafed 28 times. Cupp kept count. "The driver got to be pretty good at hiding between buildings when we heard the planes coming. One time, though, we were heading down a road, and an American tank was heading right for us. The driver took to the ditches, and we got away. I was thinking it would be nice to be captured, but I didn't know if I'd be alive when it happened."

The truck traveled up into Belgium, and Cupp thought he had a good

chance of escaping when they neared Brussels. "Everything looked good. All I had to do was wait until everybody fell asleep and then just walk away from the truck. Unfortunately, I fell asleep with them."

As the truck headed away from the fighting, it began to pick up German soldiers who were fleeing the collapsing front lines. A new guard was put in charge of the two prisoners, and he called Cupp and Donahue "Isadore" because he assumed all Americans were Jews.

The truck sped on into Germany, and the guards attempted to unload their prisoner burden at a local air base.

The Luftwaffe officer was not pleased to see the Americans. "He wanted to shoot us right on the spot, right in his office. In fact, he pulled out his gun and pointed it at us. The guards pushed us out the door, and we all ran down the hall. When we all got back to the truck, everybody started laughing. They thought it was a great joke."

For the next couple of weeks, the guards were never able to solve their problem of what to do with the Americans. Meanwhile, the truck began a cruise around Germany, dropping off the soldiers in their hometowns. Each night, the guards would put the prisoners in the local jail, and every day the truck would head out to another German town.

The final destination for Cupp was Stalag Luft IV in Poland, one of the more feared prisoner-of-war camps in Europe. They arrived on September 21, 1944, more than three months after they had bailed out over Belgium.

After five months at the prison, the sound of the Russians advancing on the German lines could be heard. But rather than abandon the camp, the German guards, on February 6, 1944, began marching the men back toward Germany.

"We marched out on the edge of the Baltic and crossed the Oder River." Cupp estimates that there were 10,000 Americans in the camp at one time, but that number had shrunk to 8,000 by the time of the long march.

"We were very hungry. We were in bad shape when we started, but in good shape compared to what came later." The men marched and marched, clear across Germany, staying in barns or out in the open at night.

In the end, the prisoners were marched for 504 miles until they reached a point where they could be loaded on a train, where the journey continued in a circuitous route that avoided both enemy lines.

Why did they drag the Americans clear across their country in order to surrender?

"I think they wanted us in hand, so it would give them something to negotiate with at the end. And I also think they didn't want us to be turned over early because we could come back and fight against them.

"There was some speculation, too, that they just intended to slaughter us."

As the war ground to a close, the Americans got new guards — Poles who had been forced to fight on the side of Germany. "They brought us to a place where the Americans had backed up to the river Mulde as part of the agreement with the Russians at the end of the war.

"One of the guards took the ammunition out of his rifle and handed it to me. He said, 'Now march me to the Americans.' " Cupp was happy to do so. "We came across the river. There were about a thousand of us in our group. We went one way, and the guards filed off to the side." It was April 26, 1945.

There was plenty of food for the freed prisoners, and Cupp just kept eating. It was two weeks after he was freed that he finally was able to weigh himself, and despite eating ravenously, he still only weighed 89 pounds

The long trip back ended in a train ride to Jefferson Barracks in St. Louis. Cupp estimates he was gaining weight at an average of two pounds each day, and he weighed 168 pounds by the time he got home.

He went back to the farm for awhile, then enrolled at the University of Iowa, where he earned both his bachelor's and master's degrees. He completed his doctorate in sociology at the University of North Carolina.

He also married his childhood friend, Elizabeth "Penny" Penningroth, and the two had two children, a boy and a girl. Cupp taught at Upstate Medical School in Syracuse, New York, at Butler University in Indiapolis, Indiana, at St. Olaf College in Northfield, and at Kearney State College in Nebraska. His academic focus was on criminology. The Cupps moved back to Northfield after their retirement.

He has made 10 trips to Europe and has personally thanked many of the Belgians and French who risked their lives by helping him during the war.

With the exception of the pilot, all the other nine crew members survived the war.

THE CREW

The men who made up the crew of the Liberator that was shot down over Belgium in June 1944, included, from left, front: Irving Norris, nose gunner; Hugh Bomar, armorer; Frank McPherson, radio operator; Robert Mathie, tail gunner; Bill Cupp, ball turret gunner. In back: Robert Donahue, navigator; Richard Wright, bombardier; Floyd Addy, pilot; Douglas Hooth, co-pilot; Cecil Pendray, engineer.

LST-620

Somewhere in the Pacific, LST-620 unloads its cargo on a sandy beach. Jim Downey served 19 months aboard the ship.

Unless indicated otherwise, all photos are from Jim Downey's personal collection.

IT WAS A
TWO-OCEAN WAR

If Jim Downey joined the Navy to see the world, he got his money's worth. During 1944-45, his ship, LST-620, hauled troops and supplies to the beaches at Normandy and then traveled across the globe to do the same thing at places like Iwo Jima and Okinawa. Downey was a radioman on the ship.

The Atlantic, the Pacific – Jim Downey definitely got in his ocean time during World War II.

The Navy radioman spent the war on LST-620, and that ship did everything from landing supplies on Omaha Beach to landing troops on Okinawa. If Downey joined the Navy to see the world, he got his money's worth.

Downey grew up in Yonkers, New York, an industrial city on the Hudson River north of New York City. His dad was an electrical engineer for Bell Telephone and commuted into the city each day for work.

"During the Depression, he was a good provider," Downey said. "We always had food on the table and shoes on our feet."

Downey graduated from Gorton High School in 1943 and joined the Navy on September 20, four days before his 18th birthday. "I didn't want to be a foot soldier. I talked my dad into letting me join early. My brother was already in the service, and my dad dreaded me going in."

Boot camp was at Newport, Rhode Island, and then Downey was on to radio school. "I knew Morse code, and I had some background in radio. I always had an interest in radio."

Most of the three months of school was spent improving the young sailors' typing and Morse Code skills, and then it was off to the fleet. For Downey, it meant being sent to Seneca, Illinois, to become part of the inaugural crew for LST-620.

"It was that time of the war where it was all young guys going in. I would guess that 90 percent of the men on the ship were under 20 years old. It was my first time away from home. I'd led a pretty sheltered life, but I grew up fast."

It was at Seneca that Downey learned with the routine that was to make up his life for the next 19 months. There were three radiomen on the ship, and each would take a four-hour shift and then get eight hours off before taking their next four-hour shift.

The relatively short shifts helped overcome the tedium of listening to the dits and dahs coming over the radio set and typing them onto sheets of paper. They would later have to be decoded so the message could be read.

"When the ship wasn't really doing anything, the boatswains and others could take it easy, but the radiomen had to keep working." Downey said it was fortunate that throughout the time he was on the ship, none of the radio guys got sick. "I suppose we would have had to do double shifts."

The new crew took the ship down the Mississippi River and then out into the Gulf of Mexico, around Florida and up to Norfolk, Virginia. "We called the LST a 'Large Slow Target' because it had a top speed of about 12 knots, and it usually cruised at ten knots."

The LST actually stood for Landing Ship, Tank and was designed to carry tanks and other war materiel. The ship was 328 feet long and 50 feet wide. The bridge and control areas, including the cramped radio room, were in the stern, and large cargo decks were in the bow.

There were eight officers and 100 enlisted men. The captain and the executive officer were both former chief petty officers who had been promoted to ensigns.

The ship was part of the 11th Amphibious Group, and it loaded up a hold full of medical equipment, including ambulances, in the summer of 1944 and headed out to sea.

"You know a ship like that is always fighting on the front line. It's always out there where the U-boats are. I never thought of that when I was in the Navy, but I think about it now," Downey said. "We were such a big and slow target, they wouldn't have even needed to use a torpedo on us, they could have just taken us out with their guns."

The trip over was in the largest convoy ever to cross the Atlantic during the war, Downey said. It was mainly bringing troops and supplies to back up the recent invasion at Normandy. The convoy was escorted by Canadian corvettes and U.S. sub chasers.

"Now and then, we could hear the depth charges going off, but we couldn't see anything."

LST-620 delivered its medical supplies to Normandy in France, then began a routine of heading to British ports to pick up another load before returning to France.

"We would come in at a high tide with empty ballast tanks. We would drop this very large anchor on our way in. When we hit the beach, we would fill up the ballast tanks, and that would hold us on the beach. The anchor would keep the stern

from moving."

When it was time to go, the ship would wait for high tide again, dump its ballast, and then use the anchor to help drag it off the beach and back to sea. The LST dumped men and supplies at Omaha, Utah and St. Michel beaches.

"One night, on a crossing, our lookout shouted 'Torpedo!' and he jumped overboard. It turned out that it was only a porpoise. They loved to come straight at us and then dive under the ship. But we thought we had lost a shipmate."

Luckily, the "man overboard" was signaled back to a trailing patrol boat. Downey said he didn't find out until 50 years later at a reunion that the man had been rescued. "So he lived to see another day, but not on our ship."

«

JIM DOWNEY

At home in Burnsville

»

DURING THE WAR

Downey had been interested in radios since he was a kid, and the Navy put his skills to use aboard an LST.

On one of the stops in Plymouth, England, Downey and the ship's quartermaster, another young sailor, were invited by the crusty old chief boatswain's mate to accompany him to a local pub.

"I was embarrassed to admit it, but I'd never had a drink before. We got there about noon, and they kept feeding us this hot beer. By two o'clock the quartermaster and I were not feeling too good, and we needed a place to go."

The men staggered to a Red Cross facility and passed out. "Everything was going round and round. After that, I never went to another English pub."

At another stop, in Londonderry in Northern Ireland, Downey came back to the ship deathly ill. "The doctor said I had food poisoning, and he asked me what I had eaten. I told him I'd ordered steak and chips. He said, 'They don't have any steak over here. You probably had horse meat.'"

In late 1944, LST-620 was ordered back to Norfolk, Virginia. The trip took 19 days, and the convoy en-

SOUTH SEAS WARDROBE

The captain on Downey's ship was not a stickler for proper uniform, provided the men did their jobs well. A fellow radioman on the LST wore nothing but swimming trunks for the duration. Downey is at the center of the picture.

LST
Landing Ship, Tank Statistics

LST

Manufacturer
Chicago Bridge and Iron Shipyard (LST-620)

Engines
Two General Motors 12-567 diesel engines

Crew
Eight officers, 100 enlisted men

Armament
One 76-millimeter gun, six 40-millimeter guns, six 20-millimeter guns, two .50-caliber machine guns, four .30-caliber machine guns.

Maximum Speed
12 knots

Cargo Capacity
2,100 tons of tanks and vehicles, or 140 troops

Length, Width
328 feet long, 50 feet wide.

countered a hurricane-force storm.

LSTs are flat-bottomed boats and, even in relatively calm seas, have a tendency to roll. In a major storm, they can be hell on wheels.

And then we had to crawl through some garbage in our skivvies while they paddled our backsides. At the end was the chief boatswain, and we had to kiss his belly. And then we

Shellback."

LST-620's first mission in the Pacific was to offload supplies at Guadalcanal. From there, it became a routine of shuttling troops and supplies

"And when we hit a big wave, the twin screws would come right out of the water. But I wasn't scared. It never crossed my mind to be scared."

"Our crew's quarters were down the starboard side of the ship, and normally you can see all the way down the passageway several hundred feet. During that storm, I was heading for my rack and I looked down the passageway and all I could see was the second hatch down. That's how much the ship was bending.

"And when we hit a wave, the twin screws would come right out of the water. But I wasn't scared. It never entered my mind to be scared. When you're young, you think you're invincible and you have little fear. I never felt I was in danger. I think about it now.

"I never got really seasick. I got a little woozy sometimes. But when I was a kid I was always carsick. I'd have to sit in the front seat so I wouldn't get sick. My dad wondered why I would ever go in the Navy."

Back in Norfolk, most of the crew took leave. Then it was down through the Panama Canal and up to San Diego and then across to Hawaii. At ten knots, these were not speedy voyages.

The ship then headed for the South Pacific. "I remember when we crossed the equator. I had curly hair, and they were really waiting for me. They cut it off right down the middle and just left the curls at the sides.

had to sit in an electric chair where we got a shock. We had to do all of that for the honor of being called a

from one island to another across the Pacific.

The ship could hold 140 troops in the

A FULL COMPLEMENT

This U.S. Navy photo shows a full deck of equipment aboard an LST in wartime.

INVASION AT NORMANDY

LSTs disgorged troops, equipment and supplies on the beach at Normandy in June 1944. LST-620 was part of the armada. *U.S. Navy photo.*

sleeping compartments on one side of the ship, but for short jaunts, many more soldiers could be accommodated, and they would simply be out on the large deck.

The ship landed at Saipan, Guam, and Iwo Jima to bring in men and materiel after the islands had been secured. Downey remembers one supply run where a fleet of Jeeps was dropped off. The sailors on the LST appropriated one of the Jeeps, painted it battleship gray, put Navy numbers on it and dubbed it the ship's Jeep.

After that, when the ship's captain needed to go visit the LST group commander, he did it in style.

The captain was an easygoing sort. "We never saw him much. He never bothered us; he just expected us to do our job. That's why you see in the pictures a lot of bare chests. One of the other radiomen, Stan, only wore a swimsuit the whole time we were in the Pacific."

In April 1945, LST-620 finally saw its first combat action at Okinawa. The ship was loaded with ammunition and patiently waited for several

LST CREW

Downey is standing, second from left.

days, anchored off the beach until it was allowed to land. "I suppose it was a little dangerous, but I didn't think about it."

Downey said the Navy had established a picket line made up of destroyers between Okinawa and Japan to give an early warning when the Kamikazes were coming in.

"When they were 50 miles out, the spotters would radio us the Kamikazes' positions and headings and we would go to general quarters. They had fogging machines, and they would fog up the harbor pretty good. The hospital ships were especially well protected by the fog."

Later, LST-620 brought troops to the little island of Ie Shima off the northwest coast of Okinawa. On this

BUDDIES

Wearing their hats back, sailor-style, part of the crew of LST-620 poses. Downey is sitting at right.

mission, a Kamikaze was headed right for the LST, but it was blown out of the air by a destroyer before it could complete its mission. Famed World War II journalist Ernie Pyle was killed at Ie Shima.

Back at Okinawa, all the ships in the fleet were ordered to sea to weather a massive typhoon. "If we'd been in the harbor, we'd have washed up on the beach."

On another day, LST-620 was heading out of the harbor to get supplies. Downey was heading to his rack, his four-hour shift over. As he looked out to the ocean, he saw a large mine go by, very close to the ship's hull.

"I don't know whose it was or what it was doing there. It just went by like that. I was too young to be afraid. I just went to my bunk and got a good night's sleep. It wouldn't have done any good to tell anyone. It was gone.

"The Lord has taken care of me all my life. I'm 82 now, and He's still taking care of me."

When the war ended, LST 620 was sent to Sasebo, Japan, as part of the occupation force. "My memory is that it was a desolate place. I never saw a soul, no one. When they saw us landing, the people all stayed inside."

Next up for the ship was Shanghai, China. Now it was the duty of the landing ship to bring Chinese troops up to Manchuria to fight the communist troops. "We put the troops on the top deck. They were a ragged lot. I watched them pulling the lice off their bodies. We were glad to have them off the ship."

Downey earned enough points to go home, and he took a troop transport back to San Diego and eventually to Lido Beach, Long Island, where his folks were waiting for him.

He worked in New York for a department store. Downey didn't join the reserves after the war, but he later was persuaded to join up because the extra money would allow him to buy a car.

"The next thing I knew, I was recalled for the Korean War, and my little brother was driving my car." He was later assigned to Lubbock, Texas, where he met his wife.

Downey later moved to Texas, still in the department store business as a buyer and merchandise manager, and he retired when he was 61. One of his two daughters moved to the Twin Cities area, and the Downeys followed her several years ago.

He says he has acclimated well and is a regular member of the "Grumpy Old Men's Club" that shares coffee regularly at Apple Valley Post 1776. Four years ago, Downey was honored with a Jubilee of Liberty Medal, authorized by the people of France and presented by Congressman John Kline, for his participation in the invasion at Normandy.

DOWNEY AT SEA

Jim Downey served in both the Atlantic and the Pacific during World War II.

DIRECT HIT

One history book said Dunn's B-26 Marauder was the most heavily damaged plane to be safely landed in World War II.

Unless indicated otherwise, all photos are from Ed Dunn's personal collection.

ON TWO WINGS
AND A PRAYER

Lt. Ed Dunn was piloting his B-26 Marauder over Germany on a bombing run in early December 1944 when a German .88 shell exploded amidships. The explosion killed the turret gunner and ripped out the main beam of the aircraft, leaving the tail section held on only by the plane's skin. Dunn aimed his plane back toward France.

On December 2, 1944, Lt. Ed Dunn and his crew set out on what was supposed to be a pretty standard mission. The B-26s in the 391st Bomb Group, 573rd Squadron, were to hit an oil storage depot in Saar-lautern, Germany.

Because of foggy weather, a "pathfinder" lead aircraft was to guide them to their target using radio beams.

The B-26 was carrying 16 250-pound fragmentation bombs, a full load of 4,000 pounds for the Ma-rauder.

The crew took off from its base in Roi Ami in central France at about 8 a.m. The clouds were thick up to about 7,000 feet, and it was difficult plowing through them. Once above the clouds, the group of 18 planes, six in a flight, formed up behind the pathfinder, which had come from a different base.

"By this time we were all hoping that the war would be over pretty soon," Dunn said. "It seemed like the flak was getting heavier and the weather was getting lousier on every mission. Of course, I never said anything to the crew about it. It didn't make much difference how you felt — you still were going to fly another mission."

Edward B. Dunn was born and raised in the eastern South Dakota town of Flandreau. Known as "Ebby" in his youth, he wasted little time in getting his life in order. By age 16, he had his own job, his own apartment, his own car, and he was dating "the prettiest girl in town."

He also attended high school and was the drummer for his school's award-winning band. Dunn was a member of the South Dakota National Guard, which he joined by lying about his age when he was 15. He earned $1 for meetings and $15 for the two-week summer camp. By 1940, his enlistment was completed.

When the war started, Dunn had already traveled over most of the West, and in 1942 he moved to Omaha to get a job with the Martin Aircraft Company which was planning to open an assembly line for the Martin B-26 Marauder.

In the meantime, Dunn passed the test to get into pilot training, and he was on a waiting list. And, no longer willing to live apart, he and his sweetheart Betty were married in June 1942. Betty moved with him to Omaha, where he was earning as much as $100 a week at the aircraft factory.

In October, he finally got his orders

to report to San Antonio for pre-flight training. In November, he found out he was going to be a father.

Dunn received his wings and was commissioned a second lieutenant in August 1943, and he was sent to B-26 Marauder transition training at Del Rio, Texas. On D-Day, June 6, 1944, Dunn and his new crew began a flight with a new B-26 across the Atlantic on the northern route to England. Their payload was 3,000 pounds of K-rations.

By December, Dunn had flown 32 missions.

There was a crew of six on the B-26: Pilot, copilot, bombardier, turret gunner, waist gunner, and tail gunner. On that December 2, Dunn's regular turret gunner, who had been involved in a fracas, was in the stockade.

Before the flight, a young turret gunner, Staff Sergeant Jesse Elerbee, approached Dunn and asked if he could join the crew that day. He was eager to get in his 65th and final mission. Dunn told him, "Welcome aboard."

"It was the only time he flew with us. I'd never seen him before."

Dunn's B-26 was in the four slot, or the plane directly behind the lead aircraft and directly in the middle of the flight of six planes. It was a brand new plane, the first new plane that Dunn had ever flown in combat. The plane was only on its fourth mission and hadn't even been named. The pathfinder was directly in front of this lead group, and a flight was on either side.

The pilots flew as tightly as they could, trying to minimize the target for the German gunners. Often, the wing tips of the planes would be

only three feet apart. As the planes approached the target, and the group took evasive action, maintaining the formation would get even tougher.

It took about seven seconds for a German 88 anti-aircraft shell to travel from the ground and explode into the formation at 10,000 feet, the normal bombing altitude. The Americans tried to avoid the flak by turning every 45 seconds or so. There was no pattern, so the Germans couldn't adjust.

The problem was that even the planes in the formation didn't know which way the lead plane would go. They could only follow. For the planes on the wide edge of the turn, it meant full throttle and the hope of holding on. On the inner edge of the turn, it meant cutting the throttle and hoping not to get crunched. With only a few feet between the

«

ED DUNN

At home in Bloomington

»

DURING THE WAR

Dunn earned the Distinguished Service Cross and a Purple Heart on his 31st mission in Europe.

wings, it was a little nerve-wracking.

"You're just so busy flying, though, that you have total concentration. If you don't have total concentration, you won't be able to do it. Still, nobody likes to be shot at. My hand would be shaking on the throttle."

In fact, that type of flying had brought on an incident in Dunn's crew not too many days before. The turret gunner (who later got in a fight with an officer and was jailed) had been known to have a drink now and then, and he showed up at Dunn's tent, where the officers were playing cards.

He said he wanted to see Dunn.

The gunner was obviously drunk, and he was in officers' country, where he shouldn't have been. Dunn's copilot, Second Lieutenant Edwin Armstrong, tried to handle the situation, but the man was adamant about seeing Dunn. When he got his chance to speak, he slurred, "I want to tell Lieutenant Dunn that he's chickenshit. He flies too close, and he scares me."

The man was guided back to his barracks, but the next morning Dunn gathered the crew and gave everybody a chance to change crews if they wanted. "They all said, 'No, no, no.' They wanted to stay. I told them we fly the airplane close to the others because that's the orders, and it's the safest way to fly. Flying like that was skillful, but it wasn't chickenshit."

The crew on the mission to Germany that fateful morning had been told that the target was completely clouded over, and that the bombing would be done from above the clouds, using the pathfinder's electronic gear. When they got near the target, though, that was hardly the case.

"The clouds broke away, and there was the Saar River. We were perfect targets for the German gunners. You know the salvos are getting close when you can see the red fire in them. They'll bang you around a little bit. You can hear that rain of shell fragments against the airplane."

The Pathfinder needed a minute or more of straight and level flying at the end of the bomb run to find the target. Without the evasive action, the B-26s are in their most precarious position. The Germans opened up.

"The first salvo was really close. On the second salvo, a shell entered my rear bomb bay and exploded." The shock was incredible, and the middle of the aircraft was blown to pieces. Bits of shrapnel flew throughout the plane.

The top turret gunner, Elerbee, trying to survive his last mission, was blown away. Only parts of him were left in the aircraft. The waist gunner, Staff Sergeant James Sims, next closest to the explosion, was riddled with shrapnel. The main supporting

BRAND-NEW SHIP

The B-26, 334165, was nearly brand-new when Dunn and his crew took it on its fateful flight in December 1944.

B-26
Marauder Statistics

B-26 Data

Manufacturer
Glenn L. Martin Company

Engines
Two 1,900-horsepower Pratt and Whitney R-28-43 radial engines

Crew
Seven (two pilots, bombardier, navigator/radio, three gunners

Armament
12 .50-caliber Browning machine guns; 4,000 pound bomb capacity

Maximum Speed (clean)
287 miles per hour

Ceiling
21,000 feet

Range, loaded
1,150 miles

beam of the fuselage was gone, and only the skin of the airplane was holding the tail section on.

In the cockpit, Dunn was struck in both the right elbow and right ankle

gaping holes all over the plane. The top gun turret was gone. The tail gunner, Sgt. John Wagner, was trying to help Sims.

There was no way to get to the

The bombardier, Staff Sgt. Oliver Hartwell, crawled through his tunnel from the nose of the B-26 back to the cockpit. Dunn showed him his leg, and the bombardier stuffed

---

"Oh, Lord. I've come this far. If I demolish the colonel's plane, he'll kill me."

---

by shrapnel. "My body felt like it was hit by a sledgehammer. I was strapped into my seat, but the explosion spun me around in the seat. It was a big jolt."

The plane banked sharply to the left. Dunn tried to correct by pushing hard on the right rudder, but there was no response. He signaled to Armstrong to also lean on the rudder, but the plane continued its steep left bank.

Dunn was able to get the plane under control by adjusting the power of the engines and using the ailerons, the small, hinged sections of the wing that can turn the plane by being raised or lowered. After the slow, wide turn, the plane was now coming in over the target again, but they had no idea if the bombs were ready to drop or even if they were still there. "It's not healthy to land an airplane with 16 fully armed 250-pound bombs."

Armstrong left his seat to survey the damage, and what he found as he entered the mid section of the plane was chaos. About 10 or 12 feet of the main beam of the plane was gone. The bombs, whose arming pins had been pulled earlier, were hanging lopsided from the racks or strewn on the floor.

The catwalk was gone. There were

bombs, or to even get past the first bomb bay. Their mission now was survival. If they were able to land, it would have to be with the bombs on board.

Dunn kept the plane on a heading out of Germany, but as the tail section swayed back and forth, it seemed as though it would tear away at any moment. The cables to the rudder had been severed as had the hydraulic lines for the landing gear and the propeller control. There was no radio. "Both engines seemed to be running fine, bless their hearts."

bandages into Dunn's boot to staunch the bleeding. After that, apparently overcome with the peril they were in, Hartwell sat down between Dunn and Armstrong and did nothing but whimper for the rest of the trip. Sending him back to the nose of the plane, Dunn knew, with the chance they would have to bail out at any second, would be a death sentence. So he let him sit. "Besides, I was too busy to pay any attention to him."

There was some thought of abandoning the plane, and Dunn gave the crew that option. Armstrong carried

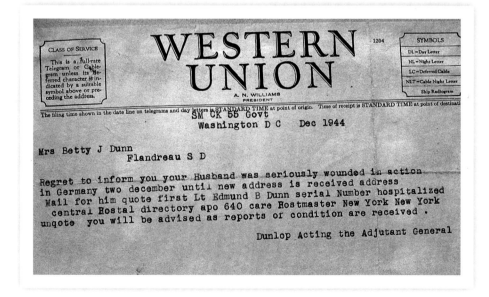

TELEGRAM TO DUNN'S WIFE

The Army Air Corps informed Betty that Dunn had been seriously injured in the Dec. 2, 1944, flight.

DUNN RECALLS ONE OTHER MISSION

Ed Dunn's piloting of his devastated B-26 back from a bombing run on Dec. 2, 1944, is an amazing story. One official history of the Army Air Corps said it may have been the most damaged B-26 that ever landed safely during the war.

Dunn, however, like most wartime pilots, was involved in several other hair-raising flights during the war. At least one is worth mentioning.

It happened on Dunn's seventh mission. He was flying in the six slot, the second airplane back on the left of the six-airplane flight. They were just getting to the target when another flight flew directly over them and released its bombs.

Each plane was carrying four one-thousand-pound bombs, and the 24 bombs came screaming through the formation Dunn was part of. One of the bombs cleanly took off the right engine of the plane in the four position. The plane immediately veered drastically to the right and slammed into the plane in the five position. Both planes hurtled to the ground.

At about the same time, another bomb took off the prop of the lead plane in the formation, taking him out. Dunn, who was just dropping his own bombs, watched the carnage take place around him. If any of the bombs that hit the aircraft had detonated, the whole flight would have been destroyed.

By the time they were past the target, Dunn realized he was alone in the sky, flying over occupied France without fighter protection. They had been warned not to approach any other flight of American planes because they might be mistaken for Germans who had captured an American plane. He and his co-pilot plotted a course back to England, and, circling carefully around the fortress of London, landed at their base at Matching Green.

Dunn heard there were pictures of the disaster and he tried to get them from the photo lab. He was informed that the pictures had been destroyed at the order of an officer in charge. Forty years later, Dunn saw the pictures in several World War II history books.

a big sign back to the middle of the plane with "Bail Out?" written on it. The crew declined. It seemed the only way to get Sims immediate medical attention was to fly back to the base.

Meanwhile, the flight leader, Lt. Joseph Boylan, flew his plane back to find the crippled B-26 and help guide it home. Boylan could see that Dunn's plane was on the verge of breaking into pieces.

"All this time, the tail was swaying back and forth a foot or more. Boylan stayed at a respectful distance."

Dunn began a slow descent into the clouds, and the flight leader disappeared. They were on their own. Dunn had to fly on basic instruments: needle, ball, airspeed, compass, and altimeter. He was able to maintain about 200 miles an hour, and he came down slowly, hoping to break through the clouds and find a place to land. When the altimeter read zero, they were still in the clouds. The descent became even more slow and cautious.

In the back of the plane, Wagner had tied a parachute onto Sims in case they were given the order to abandon ship.

When they finally caught a glimpse of land, they found they were flying through a valley, with 800-foot hills on either side. In the valley was a canal they thought looked familiar. If they were where they thought they were, the plane was only about 100 miles from the base. Dunn thought

they had enough fuel, but he couldn't be sure that the tanks hadn't been ruptured by a piece of flak.

Dunn brought the B-26 up to 1,000 feet and flew in the general direction of the base. When they descended, they saw a landing strip. Dunn and Armstrong could see nothing out of the windshield because of the rain, so they leaned out of the side windows to observe the airfield. As they made their final approach, however, they found it was full of bomb craters. Dunn gave the engines full power, and they pulled up just in time. The landing strip was not the American base after all. Armstrong tried to plot their course on a map, and they followed a railroad track

CRASH LANDING

The props on Dunn's B-26 show the effects of landing without wheels.

they guessed would take them to their base.

By now, the brakes on the props were slipping because there was no electrical power. The propellers were beginning to speed up, and Dunn was again losing control of the plane. If the 13-foot props sped up too much, they would hurtle themselves from the engines. "The engines were revving about 5,500 rpm. We were very close to losing the props."

The situation was desperate, but suddenly, in the gloom ahead, they could see the distinctive church tower at Roi Ami. Quickly, Dunn found the field. The landing had to be perfect because the plane had no landing wheels, and the bombs were armed and loose in the back of the plane. There would be no second chance.

At 50 feet, Dunn cut the power. Un-

SIDE VIEW

Technicians were unsure what held the B-26 together on its flight home.

fortunately, as soon as the power was gone, so was his control of the aircraft. It veered suddenly to the right, and began to zero-in on one of the aircraft parked alongside the runway. Dunn saw with horror that it was the group colonel's plane.

"Oh, lord," he thought. "I've come this far. If I demolish the colonel's plane, he'll kill me."

Dunn dropped the right wing, adjusted the heading, and the plane crunched down on the runway and began a 4,000-foot slide down the concrete. Dunn and Armstrong pounded each other on the back, shouting for joy. The rain helped to keep the airship from catching fire. "Of all the landings I ever made, that was the only good one."

Dunn and Armstrong exited through the top hatches. "I'm feeling no pain, just jubilation." It had been nearly two and a half hours since their plane was hit.

Medics came and removed Sims, who was barely alive. "It was hell for us up in the cockpit, but can you imagine what it was like for two and a half hours in the back with the tail swaying like that?"

Sims survived, but was paralyzed. He died two years later. Dunn has a letter from Sims' mother thanking him for bringing her son home that day.

At the aid station, Dunn was told he would be taken to the hospital at Amiens, about 30 miles away. Still pumped with adrenaline, he turned down both morphine and a shot of whiskey. He even persuaded the ambulance driver to drive out to the runway to see the plane, and the driver opened the back doors for Dunn to see what was left of his new B-26.

"This flight was a miracle. Thank you, God, for our lives."

The rush of excitement began wearing off, and pain began to take its place. Dunn told the driver he'd have the morphine now, but the driver didn't have any. The ambulance plowed over the rough roads for nearly two hours to get to the hospital.

The next weeks were a series of train trips and surgeries as Dunn was moved across France to Cherbourg. "Those guys were doing surgery over there in the most difficult circumstances, and they did a fabulous job. The way they could repair things was just amazing."

On Christmas Day, he was aboard a hospital ship en route to England. Christmas dinner was potato soup.

Dunn recuperated in England, and later rejoined the 391st for four more missions aboard a Douglas A-26 light bomber. The B-26s had been phased out by late in the war.

In civilian life, Dunn went into the insurance business in the early 1950s, and that led to various other business ventures. Over the next several decades, Dunn and his partners became some of the largest land developers in the Twin Cities.

Ed and Betty had seven children, 22 grandchildren, and 14 great-grandchildren.

"I wasn't the best pilot in the 391st, but I was the luckiest."

For his effort on bringing his plane home on December 2, 1944, Dunn was awarded the Purple Heart and the Distinguished Service Cross, the second-highest decoration awarded by the U.S. Army.

YOUNG SOLDIER

Dunn originally got into the service by joining the South Dakota National Guard after lying about his age. The 15-year-old Dunn is in the center, at bottom.

EVACUATING THE WOUNDED

Jim Anderson is one of the Marines at the left evacuating a comrade using a blanket. The Marine at the right has just fired off a smoke grenade.

Unless indicated otherwise, all photos are from Jim Anderson's personal collection.

ONE COMPANY'S STORY
K-3-5

Jim Anderson of Dallas, Wisconsin, joined the Marines when he was 17 years old. By the time he was 20, after three major invasions in the Pacific, Anderson was one of 19 original Marines left in his company, K-3-5. There were 235 Marines when the company first went overseas.

When Company K of the Third Battalion, Fifth Marine Regiment, First Marine Division, known by the parlance of the Corps as K-3-5, stepped ashore at New Britain in 1944, there were 235 men.

When that same company was assigned duty in China at the end of the war, there were 19 Marines from that original group who went ashore.

Jim Anderson of Cameron, Wisconsin, was one of those 19.

Anderson was born in 1925 and grew up in the rural town of Dallas, Wisconsin. He attended high school at Barron, and in those days, if a student was doing well, he was allowed to enlist in the military with the assurance that he would still get his diploma.

And so, on March 9, 1943, at age 17, Jim Anderson joined the Marine Corps. Several months later, his diploma was sent to his parents.

Basic training was in San Diego, followed immediately by infantry training at nearby Camp Elliot. In

October, he went on board the troop transport Rochambeau and was moved to New Caledonia.

"I remember that you had to stand in the chow line three-fourths of the time aboard ship. And I remember the powdered eggs that stunk. I had to put a lot of ketchup on them to camouflage the smell."

After they spent a brief time at New Caledonia, an Australian ship took them to New Guinea.

"Now, we were having mutton twice a day."

K Company got to New Guinea after the main action was over. "I never fired a shot. We went up in the hills, looking for the Japanese, but we never found any."

They stayed on New Guinea for a month, then boarded an LST (Landing Ship, Tank), a means of transportation that was to become common to the Marines in the following months.

Anderson said he was amazed at how the LSTs could get right up on shore. The large landing ship would

drop anchor a short ways out, then run onto the shore, disgorging its loads of tanks and troops, then use the anchor rope to pull itself back into deeper water.

Company K arrived at Cape Gloucester, New Britain, about three or four days after the landings. "It was very, very, heavy, dense jungle. And it would rain every afternoon. Bull-

dozer tanks would have to cut roads into the jungle."

The company arrived just after Christmas 1943. The Marines were trying to take a Japanese airfield, so U.S. forces could use it to bomb the Japanese stronghold at Rabaul on the other side of the large island. New Britain is northwest of New Guinea and Australia.

The Marines fought their way inland, and on the first day Anderson's company encountered only the thick jungle. "The first night, I dug in with my buddy. Well, you couldn't actually make a hole in the ground, but we got behind a big tree. One of us would stay awake while the other slept. You always guessed that you were getting the short end of it because nobody had a watch. It rained so much that watches wouldn't last."

The two could hear noises in the jungle, but they usually were caused by enormous land crabs or wild pigs. The way to solve the problem was by throwing a hand grenade at it.

The second day, the Marines started to encounter some fire, but Anderson said he never saw the enemy. The company was approaching Suicide Creek, a few miles inland.

"I was the second scout. The first scout was out in front of me. All of a sudden, there was a burst of machine-gun fire, and down he went. I crawled up to him, but I could see he'd been hit three or four times, and he was dead. They say you learn more in one week of combat than in a year of training, and, if I had more experience, I would have known not to stand up, but I did."

Anderson immediately took a bullet in his left side. It had ricocheted off his cartridge belt and entered his abdomen.

"It knocked me over. I managed to drag myself out of there, and I got back a ways. I was practically passed out, I suppose from the shock. And then the Japs threw a mortar in there, and it filled my left leg with shrapnel."

He lay there about 20 minutes before a couple of Marines dragged him out. He was taken on a stretcher back to the battalion aid station where his wounds were stabilized. "They tied off my leg. That was the worst of my problems at that point."

An amphibious tractor, or amtrac, took him back to the beach after which he was transported on an LST to an Army hospital back on New Guinea.

"It was a very good hospital, built out of tents. What I didn't expect

«

JIM ANDERSON

With a war souvenir at his home near Cameron, Wisconsin.

»

AS PART OF COMPANY K

Anderson looked pretty jaunty in this portrait at the end of World War II.

was that there were female nurses. I was all covered with mud and blood, and she cut all my clothes off me and gave me a bath. I was kind of embarrassed."

Doctors operated on Anderson's leg and took out the larger pieces. They left the wound open, hoping other pieces of shrapnel would work their way out as time went by. A few days later, they operated on his stomach and took out the bullet that was lodged there.

A month later, Anderson was sent back to his unit on New Britain. "It was pretty amazing that I was sent back to my company. They often put wounded men in casual companies, and they ended up as replacements here and there."

The wound was not healing well, and Anderson could hardly leave his cot. One of his comrades would bring food to his tent each day. The pain was getting worse. Finally, they sent him back to the hospital.

"I think later in the war they would have just sent me back to the States, but at this time they needed bodies over there."

This time at the hospital, the doctors closed up the leg wound with stitches, and after a few weeks discharged him again. Actually, the medical people just let him walk out of the door of the hospital.

"I was thinking I could go to Australia for a few months and enjoy myself, but the more I thought about it, I knew I couldn't leave my buddies."

Anderson had to walk down to the dock and make his own arrangements to find a ship back to New Britain. The final humiliation came when he did arrive back at K-3-5 in an Army uniform he had borrowed

MARINES ON PELELIU

Marines of the First Marine Division hunker down at Orange Beach during the Battle of Peleliu. *National Archives photo*

and had to endure the ribbing of his friends.

Not long after, the First Marine Division was sent to Pavuvu, an island rest camp near Guadalcanal. The camp was at a coconut plantation. Anderson was assigned to light duty as his leg healed. The men were al-

lowed about six cans of beer a week as part of their ration. Officers got twice that much.

The troops trained and relaxed through June and July. There had been about 100 casualties, and replacements had to be worked into the roster. In August they climbed back aboard an LST for a new adventure.

"They didn't tell us where we were going until we were on board ship. Then they told us we were going to Peleliu, an island about 600 miles east of the Philippines."

The trip took five weeks on the slow boat. "I never got seasick. I'd kind of get headaches and nausea for a few days, and then I was okay."

The officers tried to keep the men fit by conducting exercises, but, with the decks full of equipment and the necessity to stand in line for chow all day, the exercise regimen was a little lax. Men would pass the rest of their time by reading, usually Reader's Digest or some such fare, or by playing cards.

When it was time to hit the beach at Peleliu, the officers told the men that they expected this to be a 72-hour mission. The company was delivered to the beach on an amtrac that drove right up on the sand.

"We jumped over the side and were immediately hit by machine gun fire. My first thought on the island was, I thought I had it. I didn't see how anybody could live through what was happening on that beach. It was indescribable. To this day, I can't find words to describe it."

K Company was one of the first units ashore in the 115-degree heat. "They told us on the ship that the beach was a good place to get killed. We believed that, and we headed inland right away."

Anderson was still gimpy from his leg wound, so the military, in its wisdom, made him a runner. His job was to stay near the company commander and do his bidding. Radio communication was very poor, and messages often were delivered by runners.

By 11 a.m. that morning, the Americans had crossed the airport on the lowland near the beachhead. "Infantrymen usually don't have much fun in combat, but that day we had some fun. We formed up in a straight line and started cutting loose at the jungle at the edge of the strip. We just wanted to keep the

IN CHINA AFTER THE WAR

Anderson is shown with a buddy in China. Their job was to disarm the Japanese soldiers and send them home.

Japs pinned down. I burned up 20 or 30 rounds in a hurry."

That night they dug in. "The island was all coral, so you couldn't dig a hole. You just piled rocks around you."

His most memorable moment on Peleliu came in the early fighting. "We had run up against a pillbox with a machine gun, and the commander told me to go back and get a

Japanese soldiers, then headed back to Peleliu. The outer portions of the island had been taken, but the Japanese were holed up in caves and fortifications throughout the central highlands of the island. Names like Bloody Nose Ridge, the Five Brothers and the Five Sisters became geographic parts of Marine lore.

"At night we would stay in our posi-

sleep was hard on the Marines. "We were extremely tired. I was as low as I could get. I could hardly put one foot in front of the other. Plus, the place was full of dead Japanese. We couldn't smell it ourselves by that time, but the pilots told us they could smell it when they were a mile away from the island."

The worst thing that happened came right before 3-5-K was to be re-

"I didn't see how anybody could live through what was happening on that beach. It was indescribable."

couple of tanks to come up.

I was going down the path, and I turned a corner, and there was a Jap soldier. I had my rifle in my hand and pulled up and fired without getting it to my shoulder."

The shot went wild, and the enemy soldier did bring his rifle to his shoulder and fired. "I can still see the flame coming out of the gun barrel. But the shock of me shooting first must have unnerved him, because he missed. He had a bolt action, and I had a semi-automatic. He was working his bolt when I got my rifle up to my shoulder and fired.

"That was the closest call I ever had."

K Company worked its way down the western part of the island, then jumped aboard some tanks and roared all the way to the northern tip of Peleliu. From there, the men boarded a little fleet of amtracs and were transported across some open water to Ngesebus Island.

They spent two days on the island clearing out a small pocket of

tions. You knew if you moved, you'd probably get shot at by our own troops. But the Japs would move at night. And they'd bring in replacements at night. During the day, we had air power, and they couldn't move."

Anderson said Peleliu was regarded as the shortest bombing run in the war. The Corsairs and other planes would take off from the airstrip, circle out to sea, and then bomb the high ground above the airport. The total distance from airstrip to bomb target was sometimes less than 1,000 yards. The planes wouldn't even retract their landing gear during the runs.

The Marines would be brought their chow every night along with hand grenades and other ammunition. "The hand grenades came in a little box with tape on it, and we'd take the tape off to hold down the safety pin so there would be no accidents." The men would carry two or three grenades on their backpack straps and a few more in the packs.

The constant fighting and lack of

lieved. "We had an outstanding commanding officer, Capt. Andrew Haldane. We were out, looking over an area for K to move into when the captain peeked over a rock. He was shot right through the forehead. It was a terrible, terrible, terrible thing. It really affected our company. Old, tough veterans just broke down and bawled. To go that long, and then finally get killed..."

About two-thirds of K Company had been killed or wounded by the time it was relieved after 44 days on the front lines. The company was transported back to Pavuvu at the end of October 1944 to recuperate and get another infusion of replacements.

In February, 1945, the company again boarded an LST, and, once at sea, was told its destination was Okinawa. "We were told it was a Japanese home island. We knew it would be tough, but it was a bigger island, and we didn't think the fighting would be as tough as on the beach."

That turned out to be true. The Marines landed without a shot being fired. It was the fourth time Anderson landed without getting his feet wet.

The Marines advanced in company formation up the road, and the only bad news was when a grenade fell off somebody's strap and wounded four soldiers. Okinawa was an agricultural island, and the men were able to live off the land, digging up sweet potatoes and onions as they advanced.

The First Marine Division was assigned the center of the island, and the fighting soon became intense. "We'd be on one ridge. At 6 a.m., we'd call in the artillery on the next ridge, and, after about two hours of shelling, they'd stop and we'd move on to take that ridge. Sometimes we couldn't, and we'd have to try again."

During the action, the Marines came up against a pillbox with a machine gun in it. "We had an awful gun battle for about a half an hour. They'd shoot out of the hole and we'd shoot into it. We could hear them talking in there. Finally, Ted Barrow, who was a cousin of Clyde Barrow of Bonnie and Clyde fame, climbed on top of the bunker with his Thompson. We threw hand grenades into the pill box, and they all came out running. Ted stood upright on top and cut them all down."

Anderson got a bayonet and scabbard for souvenirs from the incident, and he still has them.

"Our artillery was coming awfully close to our position one night. We couldn't move back, because you just didn't move at night. You'd get shot. The commander came to me and said, 'Andy, do you think you could get back to that artillery and have them stop?' I said, 'I'll give it a whirl, sir.'

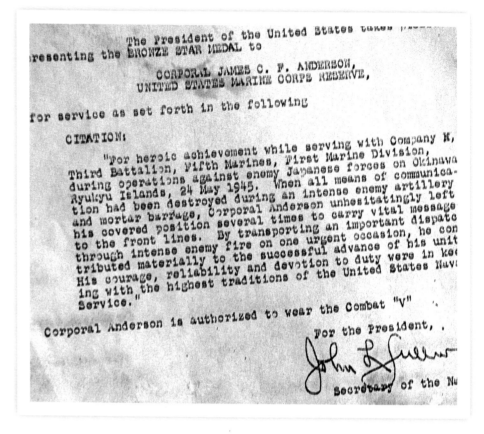

BRONZE STAR

Anderson was presented with a Bronze Star for his work as a runner during the invasion of Okinawa.

"I had a very rough time getting to the rear, getting shot at by our own men and everything else." When he finally got there, he found the officer in charge of the artillery and told him the situation. The officer told him he was full of baloney.

"I had to use strong language. I told him if he kept shooting, somebody was going to get killed. It's not easy for a corporal to talk that way to a lieutenant, but I really laced it to him." The officer finally decided to halt the bombardment.

For this effort, and for other incidents of extraordinary bravery, Anderson was awarded the Bronze Star.

The fighting went on through April, May, June, July and August. The rains came, and the trucks couldn't get through to bring in supplies. The men would put large plastic sheets out to mark their position. Navy dive bombers would come over and strafe on one side of the sheets and drop food and ammo on the other side.

The Marines got to the south side of the island just a week before the atomic bomb was dropped on Hiroshima.

"I was in a tent camp on Okinawa when they announced on the loud speaker that Japan had surrendered. All the guys ran out into the street and were shooting their M-1s into the air. There was screaming, hollering, carrying-on. It was really something, a wild celebration. The next day, they made us turn in all our ammunition."

Okinawa was also tough on K-3-5. By August, the 220 men had been reduced to about 110. Some of the men had enough points by then to go home, but Corporal Anderson, who was one of 19 survivors of the company that landed on New Guinea, did not.

After a short rest, the company was again put on LSTs and this time was shipped to China where its duty was to disarm the Japanese soldiers and send them back to their homeland. It was pleasant duty for the Marines after the past year or so. The men received a huge amount of back pay, and prices were very cheap in China for a time.

In January 1946, Anderson finally built up enough points and took a train to the coast, where he caught a transport to America. He was discharged at Great Lakes Naval Station near Chicago.

He married in 1948, and he and Beverly had three children. Anderson worked as a mechanic for about 20 years, then was the postmaster at Colfax, Wisconsin, for the next 21 years. Beverly and Jim live on the outskirts of Cameron and volunteer during the summer at the nearby Barron County historical complex.

Anderson's story has a bookend. During the 1990s, he became curious about a Japanese battle flag he had taken off a dead Japanese soldier on Okinawa. He found somebody who could translate, and he got the name of the soldier who had died. Through the Japanese welfare agency, he was able to track down the man's son, Isao Kito, who lived in Tokyo.

He wrote Kito a letter about the flag. The son replied and told him he had been conceived while his father was home on leave, and that he had never known his father. He also wrote, "I most humbly request that you return my father's flag."

"I couldn't think of any reason to keep it, and so I mailed it to him. He wrote back and said: 'I came home from work, and there was a package from America on my kitchen table. I broke down and cried because I knew my father had touched that flag.'"

The Andersons and the Kitos still exchange Christmas greetings every year.

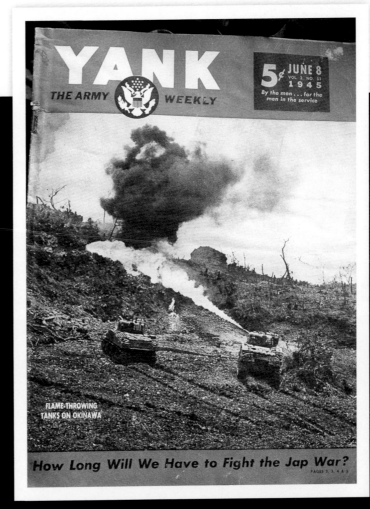

YANK MAGAZINE
Yank, the Army Weekly, carried this front-page story on the fighting on Okinawa. Company K of the Third Battalion, Fifth Marines, lost half its men on the island, killed and wounded. Only 19 men remained of the ones who had first landed at New Guinea.

FAMILY PORTRAIT

As the youngest brother, right, at bottom, Chester grew up getting into fights. It was a skill that stood him well during his time in the Airborne.

Unless indicated otherwise, all photos are from Stewart Chester's personal collection.

members one of his fellow escorts missing a curve, driving into a barn at top speed, crashing against the far wall and killing himself.

During his stint as a military policeman, he worked the more tawdry areas that soldiers would frequent on their time off. One of those places was the red-light district in Tacoma. The GIs would enter the whorehouses through the front doors and exit out the back into the alleys, where they often would get mugged by local hoodlums. Chester's job was to protect the soldiers and get them back to base with their wallets intact. "I'd be involved in about five fights a night."

About this time he joined the boxing team, a sport at which he excelled. The training came in handy one night when he was called outside the barracks because someone

wanted to meet with him. "When I got out there, the guy stuck a gun in my face and told me to leave his girlfriend alone. I grabbed the gun, and he wasn't able to shoot it. I leveled him with one punch."

It turns out that the man had found Chester's raincoat in his car and had put two and two together. The problem was that Chester had loaned the raincoat to a friend and had no idea about the girlfriend. "I told him I'd kill him if he ever came back. But a few minutes later, he drove back and asked for his gun. I dropped the shells out and gave it back to him."

Chester spent time in the Philippines and was involved in a landing in the Aleutians after the war started. The regiment had moved permanently to Fort Ord, and during this time he was urged by his superiors that he should apply for

Officer's Candidate School. It was 1942, the United States was at war, and the Army was desperate for high-quality officers.

"At first I rejected the idea. I didn't want to leave the guys, and I didn't want to leave my company. They were good people."

Eventually, he gave in to the pressure to apply. Despite his tenth-grade education, he passed the tests and the board interview and was sent to Fort Benning, Georgia, for OCS.

"I didn't get off to a really good start. They assigned us to these hutments. I went to headquarters and got my bunk assignment, but, when I got to my hut, there was already gear lying on the bunk. I asked the guy whose stuff it was if he had a bunk assignment, and I asked him to move his gear. He just looked at me and said he'd move it when he got his assignment."

That was not the answer Chester was hoping for. A few seconds later, the other man's foot locker was sailing into the muddy road outside the hutment. A few seconds after that there was a fight.

"Later, the CO called me in. He said, 'Chester, you're off to a roaring start. You've already put a guy in the dispensary.'"

Things settled down after that, and Chester managed to finish third in his class, graduating in December 1942. He had linked up with a fellow candidate who was strong in math. The friend helped Chester with math, and Chester helped him with Army tactics and other information that he knew first-hand.

The course was 90 days, but Chester was extended for further training. He said that, even at that time, he

CHESTER'S MEDALS

A display in the Rice County Historical Museum honors Chester as the most decorated soldier during World War II from that county. The display was created by Chester's nephew, Newell Chester.

wanted to get into the newly formed Airborne training, but instead he took an assignment with the 4th Motorized Infantry Division in Augusta, Georgia, as a second lieutenant. The division was trained to travel quickly in halftracks, and Chester was assigned to the motor office. He said part of his job was to figure out how to get the halftracks on the railroad flatcars.

His next assignment was at Fort Dix in New Jersey, where he trained soldiers on how to take fixed fortifications and work through minefields. The Army was already planning how to crash through Ger-

the United States at war both in the Pacific and in Europe. Was Chester anxious about getting into the fighting? "No, I wasn't antsy at all. I had the world by the ass. I was enjoying myself."

That enjoyment was over in June 1944 when the Allies landed at Normandy and the Airborne units took a pounding. They were in need of qualified officers.

"I'd always wanted to be in the Airborne because they did their fighting and got out. They weren't kept on the line constantly like other units. I'll take my chances. Plus they got

the 507th was kept in reserve. In December 1944, though, as the Germans launched a major attack through the Ardennes, the 507th went into action. "It was the Battle of the Bulge, and that's where I started getting serious about war."

The first step, though, was to get the 507th into the action from where it was in France. A convoy heading for Belgium was strung out along a road, and it was attacked by a group of German Me 109s. Chester got his men off of the trucks and into the ditch. As they were about to get back in the trucks, they could hear the air attack coming around again.

"We were getting hit hard. Everybody was wounded. Even the medic was hit."

many's vaunted Siegfried Line.

In Washington and Colorado, he had done quite a bit of mountain training, both as part of his Army training and because he liked it. After Fort Dix, he was sent to West Virginia to help set up the Seneca School for training special units in mountain warfare. By this time, he was a first lieutenant. "I had to set up the railhead for the troops coming in to train. A lot of those troops eventually became the 10th Mountain Division. My best friend was another instructor who had been a guide on the Matterhorn."

During this time, he also graduated from Pack Mule School, another necessity in mountain fighting. He also met his future wife, Rosella, while in West Virginia. They eventually had four children.

Meanwhile, the years went by with

an extra $100 a month for jumping."

Chester was sent to England in July 1944 for training. Besides the regular training, he had to do five additional jumps because every officer had to be a jump master. "I had a wonderful time in England," he remembers wistfully.

That time was over when he got his orders to become a part of the 507th Parachute Infantry Regiment. During the war, the 507th was assigned to the 82nd, 101st and 17th Airbornes. The regiment spent most of its time with the 17th Airborne. Chester has all three patches among his memorabilia.

"They had a tough time at Normandy. They landed in swamps and completely out of the drop zones. They were isolated. Their officers were all wiped out."

During Operation Market Garden,

"One of my superior officers told me to get my men back on the trucks, but I told him I wouldn't until the attack was over. He said he was going to report me to the colonel, and I told him to go ahead, but my people were not getting back in those trucks."

The officer stomped off to the front of the convoy and was killed when the planes attacked again. When it was over, Chester ordered his troops back into what remained of the trucks, and off they went to battle.

Their first assignment was to guard a bridge over the Meuse River. "I was pretty good at demolition, and we had the bridge mined with picric acid."

Later, Chester's unit closed in on Bastogne to help break the German siege around that critical city. At one point, part of the 507th was pinned down by enemy fire. A Jeep arrived with the shortest officer Chester had ever seen. He was a forward artillery spotter.

"He was a little major, and I mean little. Even his helmet looked too big for him. He stood up in the Jeep and called in the artillery. Just then, a couple of rounds of German 88s came in and missed us by about 20 feet. The driver and I were both under the Jeep, but the major just stood up there coordinating the artillery on the radio. I yelled up at him, 'If you weren't so short, you wouldn't be doing that.' "

For his actions on December 26, 1944, Stewart was awarded a Bronze Star. The ceremony wasn't held until four years later. Chester declined to comment on how he won the medal.

A few days later, Chester was leading an engineering officer through some contested country. "There were snipers all over the place. We came to a bridge, and I headed below to walk through the creek. The engineer asked me what I was doing, and I said if he was smart, he'd take the low road, too. But he didn't, he decided to walk over the bridge and keep his feet dry, and splat, he was dead. I had to crawl on that bridge to get him off, but he was already dead. There are some things you just don't do in combat."

Near Houffalize on January 19, 1945, the United States had the Germans in retreat, but the fighting was tough, and Chester's men were running out of ammunition. They were up against a German position and were outmanned and outgunned. "The Germans were so close, we couldn't use artillery support. We were getting hit hard. Everybody was wounded. Even the medic was hit."

Chester didn't want to go into detail about his actions in the next few minutes as he carried his wounded to safety. "I was all over the place. Somebody had to do it." Reports

OFFICER IN CHARGE

At Fort Bragg, Chester, lower right, leads a group of young paratroopers across the parade field.

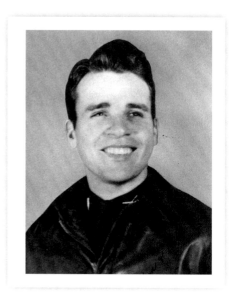

NEW JACKET

Chester was happy to be in England in 1944, sporting his new Airborne jacket.

said he went out five times in the face of automatic-weapons fire to bring back his wounded men. On the fifth trip out, he was hit in both the shoulder and the leg.

The write-up for his Silver Star put it this way: "First Lt. Chester showed superior leadership and sound tactical skill as he checked the position and fire of his men and encouraged them to high achievement. Without regard for his personal safety, he repeatedly exposed himself to enemy fire to help his wounded and to supervise with the withdrawal of his men in the face of superior enemy fire power. His actions were in accordance with the highest standards of military conduct."

During one foray to get wounded, a German bullet hit Chester's helmet, ripping it up but leaving Chester unscathed. Chester was angry, though, because the bullet had also destroyed the spare pair of socks that he kept dry in his helmet.

"War really gets down to serious sometimes."

Chester knew he had to get his beleaguered force out of the area, but that meant exposing them to more enemy fire. "I figured, 'The heck with it, Chester, I might as well go. If I get killed, I get killed.' So I stood up. The men were all yelling, 'Get down, Lieutenant.' But I said, 'Let's get the heck out of here.' And they followed me over a ridge. That's what war is all about. You take your shots."

Chester's specialty was in taking out combat patrols. "We knew we had to deplete these people. We knew they had better weapons than we did."

One of those weapons was the panzerfaust, an anti-tank weapon. "Our bazookas didn't work that well. The Germans kept getting bigger and bigger tanks. But that panzerfaust was the best anti-tank weapon ever invented. It was something we could carry along and feel a little bit better about our chances."

The unit walked to Luxembourg before being taken off the line and was able to get some rest and hot food for the first time in weeks.

The next stop was Clervaux, near the Siegfried Line. As they neared their destination, they came to a crossroads where the signs had been destroyed.

"There was a soldier at the crossroads, sitting like he was on guard. I went up to him and asked him which way to go. When he didn't answer, I noticed he was frozen, stiff as a board. I just said, 'I guess I don't need directions, I'm going the right way anyway.' "

While guarding the outpost near the German border, Chester managed to get into a firefight with American troops. "One of our sentries noticed there were people down in the valley where they shouldn't be. They were in a position where we just couldn't let them go by, so I went down there. I gave them the challenge with the dealies of the day, but there was no response. All of a sudden, we were in a firefight."

Chester took two hand grenades, pulled the pins, and was about to toss them over a ridge when he saw the silhouette of an American helmet in the snow alongside the road. "I yelled out, 'Who the heck are you people?' "

He was suddenly confronted by an American soldier with his rifle leveled a few feet away. "I told him if he shot me, we were both going to die. It was at this point everybody figured out it was Americans against Americans, and there were orders of 'cease-fire' all over the place."

Chester had a little problem, though. He was still holding two live grenades with the pins pulled. The soldiers began to scramble around in the dark for something to replace the pins, and finally one of the men came up with a length of telephone cable that they snipped into the right size pieces.

It turned out to be an American patrol that had wandered about three miles from where it was supposed to be. The final irony of the story was that when Chester got back to his command post and tried to telephone the report into the company headquarters, he couldn't — the communications wire had been clipped to use in his hand grenades.

As spring came to Europe in 1945, the Germans and the 507th took up positions on either side of a river. Each morning, the Germans, just out of rifle range of the Americans, would do calisthenics. "There was this one officer, he must have thought he was pretty nervy. He'd stand with his back to us and lead his men in morning exercises. It turns out, though, that we had captured this German anti-tank gun that shot armor-piercing bullets. It had an unbelievable range, and one of our guys lined up that officer. Poof, he was gone. It was the last time they did calisthenics in front of us."

Chester got to participate in a real jump when the 507th moved to the other side of the Rhine. "It was a day jump into open terrain. It was brutal. We lost over 300 men that day. But we did our job and cleared out those little towns over there. We didn't come to play, we came to be bad."

Somewhere in this battle, Chester earned additional medals for his exploits, but, again, he is loathe to talk about them.

When the war ended, he served in the occupation in Belgium and Germany, and he worked with people who had been in the labor and concentration camps. "We had to be careful how we would feed them. They hadn't had real food for so long. Even our rations were too rich for them. We had these drums of soup, but we'd have to cut it by about five to one so they could eat it."

Another part of the duty was to keep these released prisoners from taking revenge. "We had to disarm them to stop them from taking revenge on the German people." Eventually, the Americans gathered the camp survivors into groups of similar nationality so they could be repatriated.

About this time, Chester came down with hepatitis. "I was as yellow as a canary." He was sent first to Paris and then to England, where he was hospitalized for a month.

When he got out in November 1945, Chester bought a farm in West Virginia, where his wife was from, but he found that he was no better a farmer than when he had lived in Minnesota. He rejoined the Army in 1947, but he had resigned his commission. He went back in as a first sergeant.

In April 1950, after spending too much time away from his family, he quit the Army again. His timing was fairly remarkable, because, two months later, the North Koreans flooded over the border and the Korean War began.

The challenges in his life, however, were not over. He contracted polio in 1952 and still finds it a challenge to walk, partly because of the beating his feet and ankles took from jumping out of airplanes and from mountain training.

He returned to Minnesota. In his working career, Chester was employed by Sheldahl, a materials company in Northfield, and spent much of his time working on projects for NASA, including atmospheric balloons.

He now lives in Dundas.

With his Silver Star and other decorations, Chester is eligible to be buried at Arlington National Cemetery in Washington, D.C., but he says he won't be. "With my luck, they'd bury me next to Bill Clinton."

GETTING BRONZED

The caption for the original picture says that Chester was receiving his third Bronze Star in Pennsylvania in 1949. Chester had rejoined the Army in 1947 as a first sergeant. This medal was for duty during World War II, but was four years late.

JAPANESE CALLING CARD
On one mission, a five-inch Japanese shell passed completely through Dinah Might!, and then passed through the propeller without damaging it.

Unless indicated otherwise, all photos are from Jack Christopher's personal collection.

THE MARTIN
PBM MARINER

Not as celebrated as its cousin, the PBY Catalina, the Martin PBM Mariner earned its wings in some tough action in the Pacific in World War II. Jack Christopher flew 49 missions on the "Dinah Might!." Christopher wants you to know that the PBM was bigger, faster and had a longer range than its older brother, the PBY.

There were two major Navy patrol bombers in World War II. One of them, the PBY Catalina, might be regarded as the celebrity of the two.

It was a PBY that spotted the Japanese fleet at the Battle of Midway. It was a Royal Air Force PBY that spotted the German Battleship Bismarck and led to the sinking of the famous warship. And it was a PBY that was featured so prominently in the movie South Pacific.

The other patrol bomber, the Martin PBM Mariner, never quite got the notoriety of its older brother. In fact, only the most dedicated of World War II history buffs know much about the airplane.

It's a situation Jack Christopher would like to correct. Christopher knows all about PBMs. He knows that they were bigger, faster, better armed, better protected and had a longer range than the PBY. He knows the PBM played a critical role in the war, particularly in the Pacific as the U.S. slowly dismantled the Japanese empire.

He knows all these things because

he flew on PBMs during World War II.

Jack Alfred Christopher grew up in south Minneapolis, not too far from the Navy base at Wold-Chamberlain. "In those days, there were no fences and you could climb right up on the airplanes and look in the cockpit. They were all bi-planes in those days. From an early age I wanted to be a Navy pilot."

His childhood dream almost came true. As he graduated from Roosevelt High School in January of 1943, he headed off to be a pilot. He had taken extra math and science in high school, and had passed the Navy tests for pilot training.

His last obstacle was his flight physical, which he thought would be routine. It was except for one small problem. He failed the blue-green colorblind test. The Navy sent him home."I can't even tell you how I felt. My dreams were crushed. I didn't know what to do."

Uncle Sam had an idea about what he could do, and three months later, in the spring of 1943, he got his draft

notice. This time, he had no problem passing the physical, and he was offered the opportunity to enter the Navy rather than the Army.

After boot camp at Camp Farragut, Idaho, his high test scores again enabled him to get some choices, and he picked aviation ordinance, hoping again that he would be able to fly. "I figured I'd be in an airplane somehow."

Ordinance school was at Norman, Okla., and after graduation in December of 1943, he volunteered for

aerial gunners school. Again, he had to take a flight physical, but this time he passed the blue-green test. In fact, he passed it three times.

"Either God didn't want me to be a pilot, or the balanced diet I got in the Navy corrected my deficiency." He had graduated in the top 10 percent of his ordinance class and so he showed up at Purcell, Okla., for gunnery school as a third class (E-4). The next stop was Banana River, Fla., where he met the first love of his life, the PBM.

But it wasn't love at first sight. The first Martin PBM Mariner Christopher encountered was an anti-submarine warfare version, and it contained very little firepower, not a happy situation for an ordinance expert.

Soon thereafter, though, he met the real PBM, the one he had in mind. This version contained twin .50 cal-iber machine guns in the nose, tail and top turrets, and two more in waist gunner positions. It was also capable of carrying bombs and torpedoes of all kinds.

Christopher's job was to take charge of all the ordinance on the plane. His place on the aircraft was in the bow of the aircraft, below the nose gunner, where he could run a bomb site if necessary. It was also his job to secure the PBM to a buoy when it had completed its flight. This was accomplished by slipping a rope through a ring on the bouy, not an easy task when one minute the buoy is down at your feet and the next minute it's at chest level.

Other members of the crew of eleven included three pilots – a chief pilot who flew the plane, and two co-pilots who took turns acting as navigator – a radar operator, a radio operator, a flight engineer, a bow turret gunner, a top turret gunner, a tail turret gunner, and a waist gunner. The radio and radar men also took turns at being a waist gunner.

At the beginning of June, 1944, exactly a year since he had "volunteered" for the Navy, his squadron, VPB 27, was formed up in North Carolina. It consisted of 15 PBMs and 15 crews. Later, three more crews were added.

The squadron did torpedo training in Key West, Fla., and then headed off to San Francisco via Jacksonville, Eagle Mountain Lake in Texas, and San Diego.

One of the PBMs had to make a forced landing in the desert. "They attached beaching gear (wheels) to the floats, but to this day I don't know how that worked. It's only for getting the airplanes up a ramp. It's not very strong. I'm glad I wasn't that pilot or crew that tried to do

«

JACK CHRISTOPHER

At home in Bloomington

»

DURING THE WAR

Christopher had high hopes of being a pilot, but ended up as a crewman aboard the seaplane.

that. But somehow they made it."

By October, they were at Alameda Naval Air Station, but at that point they had to take a break. The Navy needed their aircraft more than it needed them, and so the planes were taken away and sent overseas while the squadron waited for new planes.

Was he afraid the war was going to be over before he got a chance to participate? Christopher only laughs. "No, I didn't worry about that very much. I wasn't that gung ho to go off to war."

The good news was that when the new planes arrived, they were latest models. The crew gave up their PBM-3Ds for brand new PBM-5s. The major improvement in the new model was going from a 1,900 horsepower engine to a 2,100 horse-power engine.

"The planes didn't necessarily go any faster because they were heavier. But then PBMs were never very fast to begin with. We would normally fly at about 110 knots, which was about 10 knots faster than the PBY."

The squadron made its way to Oahu, Hawaii, and lost its first aircraft with six crew members killed on Christmas day 1944. "I didn't know those guys very well, and I didn't see it happen, so it didn't seem to affect me too much."

The crew practiced using sonobuoys, small detectors that could be dropped into the ocean to pinpoint the location of an enemy submarine, and FIDOs, an acoustic torpedo that had just been developed. They also trained on dropping depth bombs, which similar to depth charges except they have aerodynamic fins.

The squadron island-hopped its way to Saipan and arrived on Feb. 13, 1945. The crew was stationed aboard the USS Onslow, a converted destroyer escort that had been converted into a seaplane tender.

"Mainly we flew anti-submarine patrols, and we just made sure the Japanese weren't doing anything in the area."

The PBMs would also fly "Dumbo" missions to rescue pilots and aircrew that had crashed into the sea. The missions were named after the popular Disney cartoon featuring a flying baby elephant. "Mainly we used radar to find them, but there were times were everyone on board the airplane would be looking. It's

TAXIING TO TAKE OFF

The PBM Mariner, fully loaded, sometimes had difficulty leaving the water and becoming airborne. One of the jokes in the fleet was that "the Mariner never actually takes off, it just goes over the horizon."

PBM-5
Mariner Statistics

PBM-5 Data

Manufacturer
Glenn L. Martin Company

Engines
Two 2,100 horsepower Pratt and Whitney R-2600-34 Double Wasp, 18 cylinder

Crew
Eleven

Armament
Eight .50-caliber Browning machine guns; weapons bay with 5,200 lb. capacity; two externally-mounted 21-inch torpedoes

Maximum Speed (clean)
205 miles per hour

Ceiling
18,500 feet

Range, Loaded
3,275 miles

awfully hard to spot a life raft in the sea."

Sometimes, the PBMs would land and pick up the downed airmen, but often the seas were too rough.

decided to swim out."

The squadron's missions varied from day to day. Sometimes, they would fly up and down the Chinese, Formosa or Korean coastlines

a convoy of Japanese ships had been spotted. Volunteers were requested, and Christopher's pilot agreed to go. Three PBMs were chosen from one squadron and three

---

"The Navy way of referring to a PBM is Peter-Baker-Mike, but we got fired on so often, they began calling us Peter-Bogey-Mike."

"We'd fly over them and waggle our wings to let them know we saw them. We'd drop them a float light if they needed one, or a raft. Usually we'd just circle until a ship would come to pick them up."

The circling often went on for hours, but that was one of the PBMs strengths. It could fly for 14 hours or more. If a rescue ship still hadn't come before the gas ran out, another PBM would be called to take up the vigil.

Christopher's PBM, designated E-2 in the squadron and named "Dinah Might" by the crew, never was able to land to pick up survivors, and so the crew never met any of the airmen they rescued. At one point, though, they rescued a group of high ranking officers who had been along for the ride in a B-29 on a bombing mission. The PBM crew was invited to a party on Tinian to celebrate the rescue, but they had to leave for Okinawa.

With the battle still going on at Okinawa in March, 1945, the PBMs settled into a small group of islands nearby called Kerama Retto.

"The Japanese had been cleared out – somewhat," Christopher said. "But they were still up in the hills. We'd have to sit on the wings all night with our tommy guns in case they

searching for Japanese ships that might try to sneak across to the homeland.

They also did ASW work, flew Dumbo missions, and flew picket duty around Okinawa to make sure the Japanese didn't try to sneak in reinforcements.

"One time we thought we'd made a sub contact. The pilot called us to battle stations, and we were all ready to go. It turned out to be a whale. We didn't shoot at it."

On a day the Dinah Might was not schedule to fly, a report came in that

from another because the mission was considered so dangerous the Navy didn't want to decimate one squadron.

"We went out to the airplane in the arming boat, and they had already loaded in the bombs and torpedoes. And they told us they'd laid in new ammunition for the .50 calibers. We knew this was going to be interesting."

Christopher only had one problem with the mission. He was sick. "I had a terrible headache and I was nauseous. I unhooked the cable and got

DINAH MIGHT!'S CREW
Eleven sailors crewed the aircraft. Christopher is in back, second from the left.

PBM MARINER IN FLIGHT

The Mariner, once aloft, could fly over 3,000 miles. It had a gull wing design in order to keep the engines high and out of the ocean spray.

us off the buoy and singled up the line, and then I just laid down in the bow with a bucket beside me.

The enemy convoy was in the mouth of the Yangtze River. "We were still about 50 miles from the target when the pilot said, 'Look at all that anti-aircraft fire.' Both groups were supposed to go in at the same time, but the other group had arrived first and went in ahead. They woke up the Japanese pretty good."

Christopher answered the call to battle stations, but he was still very ill. "I prayed to God to make me well, and I was well, just like that."

The PBMs made their attack, and all survived the defenses of the convoy, but not without some souvenirs. Christopher's airplane was hit with a 5-inch shell that passed completely through the fuselage.

"We must have been too close for the shell to arm itself. It came in one side of the airplane and went out the other. One of the crewmen was sitting on the back of his seat rather than in it, and the shell went right where he should have been sitting. After it exited, it went right through the arc of the propeller." Amazingly, the prop was not damaged. "It was just like it had been synchronized."

One of the planes in the group had so many holes in it that it taxied right up to the seaplane tender and was hoisted aboard before it sank.

The Dinah Might had a confirmed report that one of her 500 lb. bombs had landed on the fantail of a tanker. "We didn't see it. We were taking evasive action and heading into the clouds."

What if the propeller had been shot off? "We practiced quite a bit flying

the PBM with one engine. You'd have to get rid of a lot of stuff, like all the extra gas and the ammo. You'd have to throw a lot of stuff over the side."

When the crew got back to the seadrome and had tied up, the crew was given little bottles of brandy for the boat ride to the tender. Christopher, who didn't drink, gave his to a crewmate.

On another mission, Christopher's aircraft attacked a formation of twelve Japanese transports and two destroyers. "The weather was clear when we left, but it got soupy and misty and rainy as we got closer. We were able to pick up the targets on the radar. The anti-aircraft fire was bursting around us, but we got closer and closer and we dropped our torpedoes."

Well, all but one. The last torpedo,

ROCKET BOOST

This 1949 photo of a Mariner taking off shows the added boost from the rockets attached on either side. *Wikipedia Commons photo.*

which was hanging from the wing of the Mariner, got hung up and re-fused to drop.

The plane could have called it a day, but the pilot quickly informed the crew that they were going back in to drop the final torpedo. "You don't even react to something like that, you just do it. Heck, we're all 19 years old. You don't get scared at that age."

But how to drop the recalcitrant torpedo? The only way to do it was for somebody to crawl up into the wing and drop it manually with a screwdriver in the manual release mechanism. The problem with that was how to let the volunteer out in the wing know when to release.

"We formed a human chain. I was out in the wing with the screwdriver. Another guy was stretched out behind me, and the waist gunner, with head phones on, was stretched out behind him. When the pilot gave the word, the waist gunner tapped the other guy on the leg, and he tapped me on the leg. I jammed the screw-

REFUELING

PBMs could be refueled from the stern of a seaplane tender. *U.S. Navy photo.*

driver into the torpedo release and the torpedo dropped. We heard that it was running hot and true before we got back up into the soup."

The mission wasn't over yet, though. On the way back, the crew spotted a group of "sugar dogs," small Japanese trawlers. "We strafed them and got in a lot of hits with our .50 calibers. It was like a shooting gallery. You know there are people down there, but you don't think of that. You are taught to hate them anyway. It's part of the training."

Sometimes the threat to the PBMs didn't come from the Japanese. "We got fired on one time by the 5th Fleet. We have a device on board called an IFF that tells our guys that we're a friendly. But the IFFs always seemed to get knocked out by the rough water. The Navy way of referring to a PBM is Peter-Baker-Mike, but we got fired on so often they began calling us Peter-Bogey-Mike."

In the end, the crew of the Dinah Might flew 49 missions. Was there a top end for PBM crews? "If there was, we didn't know anything about it." The Navy rewarded the crew by giving every one of them a Distinguished Flying Cross. Christopher also received an air medal and Combat Aircrew Wings with three Gold Stars. He had advanced from E-2 to E-6 in two years.

As the war wound down, the squadron was moved up to Buckner Bay seaplane base on the island of Okinawa. "One day we were standing the normal buoy watch. The radioman had a speaker rigged up so we could listen to the radio, and one of the guys came running up. He said the Japanese had surrendered and were seeking a cease fire. We were all so happy. We were hugging

and jumping up and down. We prayed."

At the end of September, the crew was moved to Sasebo, Japan, as part of the occupation force. In October, the Dinah Might was lost when it ran into a reef while taking off. "We were barely able to save Dinah Might from sinking."

The crew got a new, all black PBM-5. Their last flight together was a journey around the southern Japanese island of Kyushu, including a low level view of the destruction at Nagasaki.

They were sent home in a ship. Christopher went back to LaMaur Inc., a manufacturer of shampoos and other hair products, where he had worked part-time before the war. He worked his way up to production supervisor. He also did a stint in the Naval Reserve, but got

out just before the start of the Korean War.

He retired from LaMaur in 1987 at age 63. "I retired because of the computers. I used to do all the production planning myself, and now the computer was telling me what to do. I didn't like that."

He married in 1949, and he and his wife, Irene, had two children, a boy and a girl.

One room in the Christopher household is called the PBM room, and it contains a score of photos of Jack and his aircraft and several scale models of the Mariner. He is happy to show off his memorabilia, the stories he wrote for various veterans publications, and even his wartime logbook.

"I've got to keep telling the story of the PBM. Not enough people know about it."

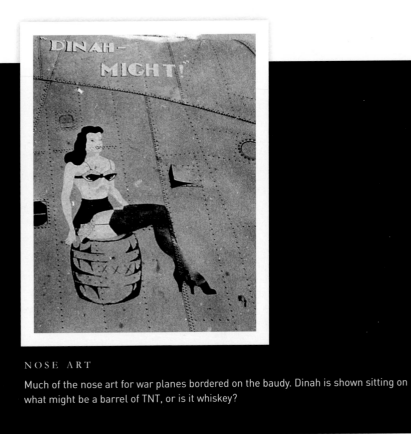

NOSE ART

Much of the nose art for war planes bordered on the baudy. Dinah is shown sitting on what might be a barrel of TNT, or is it whiskey?

Vera Peters spent two months at Dachau after the death camp was liberated in 1945. This pass allowed her to go to work each day.

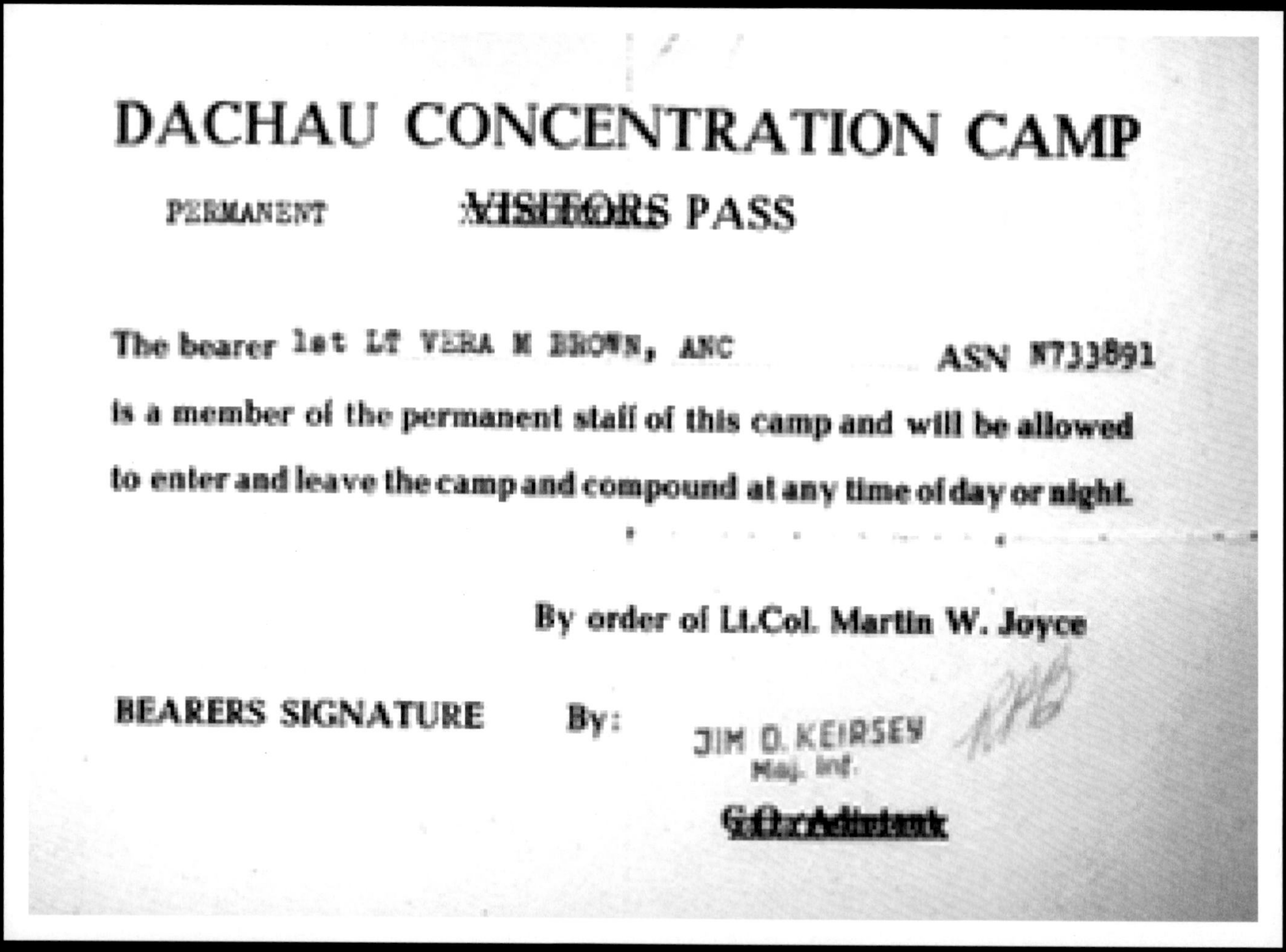

DACHAU CONCENTRATION CAMP

PERMANENT ~~VISITORS~~ PASS

The bearer 1st LT VERA M BROWN, ANC   ASN N733891

is a member of the permanent staff of this camp and will be allowed

to enter and leave the camp and compound at any time of day or night.

By order of Lt.Col. Martin W. Joyce

BEARERS SIGNATURE   By: JIM D. KEIRSEY
                                        Maj. Inf.

~~G. Orchelnbank~~

Unless indicated otherwise, all photos are from Vera Peter's personal collection.

ARMY NURSE AT DACHAU

Growing up in Minnesota, Vera Peters looked forward to the day she could be a nurse. During World War II she got to live her dream as an Army nurse stationed stateside and then in Europe. The dream turned into a nightmare, though, when she was assigned to a newly-liberated concencentration camp called Dachau.

Vera (Brown) Peters wanted to be a nurse from the time she was a little girl.

"Ever since I was knee-high to a grasshopper, I was putting a uniform on and taking care of other kids." Growing up on Maryland Avenue in St. Paul, Peters never gave up on her dream.

There were five children in the family, including Vera's twin sister, Veda. "No, we weren't identical. She was small and slight, and I was big and clumsy. And she always had a tough time in school, poor kid. She had dyslexia, and in those days, nobody understood it. Later she became a good businesswoman, but she took so many hard knocks in school."

Her father Tom Brown retired from the St. Paul Police Department in 1937, and the family moved to Morris where he bought a liquor store.

With the family moving, Peters transferred from St. Joseph's Academy in St. Paul to St. Mary's Academy in Morris, where she graduated in 1939.

She was determined to become a nurse, a decision that didn't sit well with her parents. "They thought it was such hard work. My dad said all I'd do was empty bedpans all the time. But in the end, he said, 'If that's what you want to do, you'd better do it.' "

Peters returned to St. Paul and began her training at St. Joseph's Hospital. "I loved every minute of it." She was still in training, working in the nursery at St. Joseph's, when the United States entered World War II in December 1941. "My aunt came over to visit me and she told me about Pearl Harbor, and that we were at war."

After Peters graduated in 1942, St. Joseph's offered her a job and promised her supervisory RN wages, about $70 a month. She took the job. "The first check came, and what they'd promised wasn't there. The second check came, and it still wasn't there. Here I was, graduated from school, and I'm supposed to be out there and independent, and I'm still asking my dad for money.

"I decided to join the Army. At least there I could make $70 a month and get board and room."

She enlisted at Fort Snelling and in one day went from being a civilian to a second lieutenant in the U.S. Army. There was no training, no lectures, no marching, and no orientation. "They just put us to work right there at the Fort Snelling hospital. They just put us out on the floor and we began doing our job.

"We still had those old blue uniforms, and when my mom came to see me I wanted to look so good in that uniform. I was so proud of that uniform, but I didn't even know how to tie the tie. I asked my mother to do it."

In March 1943, Peters was transferred to Fort Warren near Cheyenne, Wyoming. It was routine hospital work, with no casualties from the war. Only the usual accidents and illnesses filled the beds of the base hospital.

After a time, the Army paired Peters and another nurse with a nurse anesthetist so they could learn that skill. "After nine months, they hauled her out and sent her overseas and left us holding the bag. We weren't ready, but it didn't make any difference."

Peters said that mainly sodium pentothal and a relaxant were used for anesthesia. Nitrous oxide was another option. Some of the better and newer gases were not allowed because they were explosive.

Not long after that, Peters was shipped overseas and was assigned to a "station" hospital at Perham Downs, England, about an hour outside of London. The unit was the 103rd General Hospital. It was just before D-Day. The movement of troops south and the rush to get the hospital operational were big clues that the invasion of France was near.

"We were told we had two weeks to get the hospital up and running. We worked like the devil getting it ready."

The army had different levels of care for wounded soldiers. Normally, they would first be taken from the front lines to an aid station or field hospital, then to an evacuation hospital near the front lines, and finally to a station hospital, often in England at that point in the war.

Two days after D-Day, the first casualty arrived. And then it was a flood of wounded young men.

It was at the station hospital that much of the surgery was done for combat-wounded GIs. "We would do several surgeries and then take a break for a few hours while people cleaned up the operating room, and then do some more. There were a lot of guys who had had their arms or legs shot off. A lot of them who were shot in the stomach died. We just worked around the clock. The casualties were far more than we had expected, but we had a job to do. The hardest part of my job was seeing those boys have to go back after being wounded."

There was no penicillin, and infection was a constant danger at the hospital.

Conditions for the nurses were not terrific. They slept four to a room, and the rooms were cold and damp. Peters said she sent home for flannel pajamas. Several of the nurses contracted tuberculosis while in England.

«

VERA BROWN PETERS

Photographed at her home in White Bear Lake in 2004, a year before her death.

»

DURING THE WAR

Peters served both stateside and in Europe during her time as an Army Nurse.

In April 1945, Peters was assigned to the 27th Evacuation Hospital. "I just happened to be in Paris on VE Day on my way to my new assignment. What a celebration that was. They were up all night, swinging from the chandeliers. I remember the French people dragged the prisoners of war down the street. They were just unmerciful to those prisoners.

"The people were swinging from the upper floors of the Opera House. They were so happy the war was over, they didn't know what to do with themselves. Nobody slept a wink that night, or for the next two nights."

Her next destination was Sternberg in Austria. Although the war was over, the hospital still had quite a few casualties at the beginning of Peters' time there. In a few weeks, the number of patients had been reduced drastically.

The Army had another assignment for Peters. It was at a place called Dachau, just across the border in Germany. Peters was among the first group of 15 nurses to be sent to the camp.

The massive concentration camp had been one of the cruelest in Europe. It was where prisoners of war, Jews, political prisoners, and others who had caused trouble at other camps were sent. When it was liberated, there were still 32,000 prisoners there.

"These prisoners were reduced to something less than human. When I got there, they were still dying at a rate of 150 to 200 a day.

"These men had just lost their sense of decency. They couldn't even talk. We'd put clothes on them, and they'd take them off and go wandering off down the street. They had lost all sense of what it was to be a human being. We'd hand them a plate with food on it, and they'd go over to the corner and eat it like a dog.

"They were so undernourished and underfed that they'd just lie on those slabs in the barracks. They would die right in front of you. We couldn't begin to take care of them."

Every day when Peters and the other nurses would go to work, they'd be doused in DDT to protect them from disease. "And you know how dangerous DDT turned out to be. But it seemed like it didn't hurt any of the nurses."

There were few doctors. "The ones who helped the most were the priests and the rabbis. I don't know what we would have done without them. I don't know where they came from. I suppose some of them were from around there; but they were the ones who did the most." Many of them had been prisoners themselves.

The goal was to get the prisoners out of the camp, and there were

CHRISTMAS, 1944 IN ENGLAND

The nurses were told not to cut down any local trees, but Vera Brown was not to be denied. Despite the pretty tree, Vera looks a little homesick.

agencies set up from the various countries — Germany, Poland, France, and others — to arrange to bring the inmates home. It was a difficult business, because many of

Even where the nurses were sleeping, a converted SS barracks at the camp, the smell was awful. "Finally, they found a body in the basement that had been dead a long time. That

little joke, or something. We did what we could."

From there, in July 1945, Peters was sent to a women's hospital near Wiesbaden. "I was glad to get out.

'I was young. I just had to will it out of my mind. I knew I couldn't think about it. When I first got there, I would cry all the time. "

---

the prisoners were near death or insane.

There was also a problem with supplies. "They would only let us use German supplies for the prisoners. So many of them had open wounds, and you'd put one of the German dressings on them, but they were only made of paper and they didn't work. I don't know why they wouldn't let us use American supplies."

And what supplies they had seemed to vanish regularly. "The people who were there from the different countries had nothing, and so they'd steal our supplies."

The nurses tried to feed the prisoners, make them drink water, and keep them dressed in clean clothes, but for many it was a difficult task.

"There just didn't seem to be much we could do for them."

When Peters arrived, the Army took the nurses on a tour of the huge camp. "We saw where they still had the bodies stacked up. The stench was unbelievable. The smell got to me — it got to all of us.

"A lot of the girls went up to see the crematoriums, but I couldn't do it. I just couldn't stand it. I couldn't stand to see where these people were tortured."

was what was causing the smell. "Peters spent three months at Dachau, and while she'll never forget, she said it didn't give her nightmares later. "I was young. I just had to will it out of my mind. I knew I couldn't think about it. When I first got there, I would cry all the time. You'd try to help, but so many were just beyond help. So many of them had just stopped thinking. It was horrible, horrible."

The nurses would try to keep each others' spirits up the best they could. "We try to cheer each other up. Maybe somebody would make a

We had a job to do at Dachau and we did it. But I was glad to get out.

"Now it just seems like a bad dream to me that I was there. I have so much respect for the Jewish people, to have endured that and to have survived. So many came to America and made good lives after that.

"Why people do that to other people, I don't know."

Because she didn't have enough points to qualify for going home, Capt. Peters remained in Europe after the war until December when she was finally given orders to travel

DACHAU COMPLEX

A handful of American nurses tried to help thousands of near-death prisoners at Dachau in 1945.

to LeHavre for a ship home. It was another experience she won't forget.

"It was an Italian freighter, and it was packed. We had to sleep in shifts. As we went across the North Atlantic, a storm came up that was so bad we all thought we were going to drown. The ship was pitching so violently that the propellers would come right out of the water. At one point, the portholes burst and we all got soaked. Everybody was sick."

The cruise took 14 days, but the ship finally did land in New York. From there it was a train ride to Fort Dodge, Iowa, where Peters was given terminal leave as her final paperwork was being done.

"I had gotten the flu on the train ride, and I was so sick. But my sister and brother came down in a car from Morris to get me, and we set off in this awful snowstorm. We drove through that snow all day and when we got near to Morris, we finally couldn't go any further. We had to walk the last three and a half miles into Morris, and I didn't have any boots.

"They had planned this big celebration, but by the time we got there it was three in the morning and everybody had gone home."

The family moved to Ely for a time, and Peters worked part time in a hospital there, but she eventually ended up back at St. Joseph's in St. Paul. She took a course at the University of Minnesota to become a nurse anesthestist, and that was what she did for the rest of her career.

She married Alfred Peters in 1949, and they had five children together. "Every time I got pregnant, I'd have to leave my job, and so I worked at a lot of different hospitals. But I loved it so."

Alfred died at age 59, and Peters has never remarried. She retired in 1984, and lived in a retirement community in White Bear Lake. In addition to her five children, she had 10 grandchildren and two great grandchildren.

Peters served as commander of American Legion Post 521 in Mendota Heights. She was one of 11 veterans who represented the Minnesota American Legion in 2004 at the dedication of the World War II Memorial in Washington, D.C.

Part of this story came from a story Vera Peters wrote for the Military Vehicles and Arms Museum publication. Peters died February 14, 2005.

TENT HOSPITAL

The 27th Evacuation Hospital was a complex of tents that could be moved quickly.

ARMY NURSE

Vera Brown, shown in this wartime photograph, later represented the American Legion from Minnesota at the dedication of the World War II Memorial in Washington, D.C. in 2004.

Unless indicated otherwise, all photos are from Kurt Wilhelm's personal collection. This photo, and one other in this story, is from famed combat photographer David Douglas Duncan's book This is War!

'LOOK AT THOSE MAGNIFICENT BASTARDS'

At the beginning of the Korean War, the North Koreans almost pushed the South Koreans and their American allies off the Korean peninsula. Kurt Wilhelm and the rest of the Provisional Marine Brigade helped stave off the attack and began fighting back. In time, Wilhelm also fought at Inchon and the Chosin Reservoir.

When Kurt Wilhelm served in the Marine Corps in Korea, he managed to be involved in:
1. The landing at Pusan and the battle of the Pusan perimeter.
2. The landing at Inchon and the capture of Seoul.
3. The landing on the east coast of Korea and the battle at the Chosin Reservoir.
4. Taking two bullets to the face from the enemy.
5. Rehabilitating in Japan.
6. Getting sent back to his company on the front line.
7. Getting rotated home.
And all that happened in eight months.

Kermit "Kurt" Wilhelm grew up in south Minneapolis, attended Roosevelt High School, and found himself without a full-time job after graduation in 1948. He and three buddies decided to join the military together and flipped a coin to pick the branch of service.

The coin toss was for the Navy, and the young men went to the recruiter the next day. The Navy representative told them there were no openings, but there would be in a week, and they would all be called in then.

A couple of days went by, and while Wilhelm was working his part-time job, he missed a phone call from the Navy. By the time he showed up at the recruiting station, his two friends were gone.

"Heck, the whole idea was that we were going to join together. So, I just walked across the hallway and joined the Marines."

After recruit training, Wilhelm ended up in Guam, where he spent the next two years.

"We trained and we trained and we trained. We chased each other around the jungle. It was a real challenge to try and outdo each other. It never got boring, there was always something going on.

"I think we were the best-trained Marines ever. Nobody ever had that much training."

In early 1950, the men were sent back to the United States, not be-cause of any big military plan but because their base disappeared. "A typhoon came along and blew our base away. All that was left were the foundations. There was green corrugated metal all over the place."

Back at Camp Pendleton, the men did more training. The unit also took

30 days' leave, one-third of the group at a time. When North Korea attacked South Korea and the U.S. troops stationed there in June 1950, Wilhelm's unit was sent overseas again.

"We were supposed to go to Korea and form a division, but we were told that Korea was going to go down the toilet if we didn't get there fast." The transport went directly to Pusan. The perimeter around the town, at that point in early August, had shrunk to about 50 to 75 miles. It was the Allies' last foothold in the country.

"We were a pretty gung-ho group of guys. We could hardly wait until we got into battle. That lasted until the first firefight."

Sgt. Wilhelm was a machine gunner in charge of a small group that included one assistant gunner and six ammo carriers. The machine gun itself weighed 30 pounds, and the men would take turns carrying it on a long march. "After a while, your arm and fingers would just be numb. Someone would have to take the gun from you, because you couldn't put it down."

The Provisional Marine Brigade's job was to take the hills around the perimeter and begin to push the North Koreans back. Looking back, Wilhelm can see that the Army personnel were in a difficult situation, lacking proper wartime training and having been sent there only as peacetime occupation troops.

At the time, though, there was some animosity between the Marines and the Army. "Sometimes we'd take a hill, turn it over to the Army, and then a few days later we'd have to go back and take it again. I remember once when we were turning over a hill to the Army, and one of them asked where the escape route was. We asked him what the hell an escape route was."

The going was very tough at first. The men only carried ammunition and C-rations, and there was little transportation. "I think we only had hot food once or twice the first 30 days. We got pretty beat up, and we lost some people. When they finally pulled us back, we set up in a soybean field. Our clothes were just rags by then. It was 95 or 100 degrees every day, with humidity about the same, and the clothes just rotted off our backs. We just threw them in a pile and burned them."

Wilhelm only carried one canteen at first, but soon acquired another. "Guys were getting dizzy and passing out from the heat. You didn't dare drink out of the rice paddies, because they fertilized with human excrement. If you did have to drink

«

KURT WILHELM

At home in Burnsville

»

DURING THE WAR

Wilhelm practiced his quick draw for a buddy with a camera during training on Guam prior to the Korean War.

MACHINE GUNNERS SCHOOL

Wilhelm is crouching, third from the right, at machine gunners school in California.

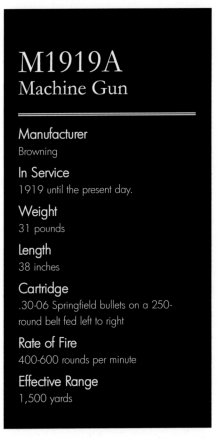

M1919A
Machine Gun

Manufacturer
Browning

In Service
1919 until the present day.

Weight
31 pounds

Length
38 inches

Cartridge
.30-06 Springfield bullets on a 250-round belt fed left to right

Rate of Fire
400-600 rounds per minute

Effective Range
1,500 yards

the local water, you immediately went to sick bay to get some paregoric to plug up your butt."

The basic operation was for the Marines to head down a road until they encountered enemy fire from a surrounding hill. Then they could go and take the hill. Wilhelm usually set up his .30 caliber, Model 1919A1 machine gun in a position where he could cover the attack, often by firing directly over the charging Marines' heads. The gun could fire 250 rounds per minute, with every fifth round a tracer, so the gunner could adjust his aim.

"I loved being a machine gunner. We had practiced so much. It was great when you set up and gauged the distance and fired off a burst and you saw the hat flying off the enemy. You knew you'd done it just right. We were supposed to fire off about five bullets in a burst, but I figured if five was good, then six or seven was even better."

The long training on Guam had allowed Wilhelm to become more than familiar with his weapon. "I probably cleaned that thing a thousand times. I think I still could take it apart today with my eyes closed."

Wilhelm has seen movies where the machine gun is fired while somebody is holding it, but he said he only did that once. "We had some bad ammo sometimes. Most of it was from World War II, and it had been packed back in 1942 or 1943. I was firing up a hill one day when the gun jammed. It had baked an empty brass shell casing. I was busy prying it out, and we were coming under pretty heavy fire. The Marine next to me was the assistant gunner. He was an Indian and a very brave man. He was firing his .45 to keep the enemy off both us, and he got hit in the neck, and it came out his armpit. The Chief never even knew he had died.

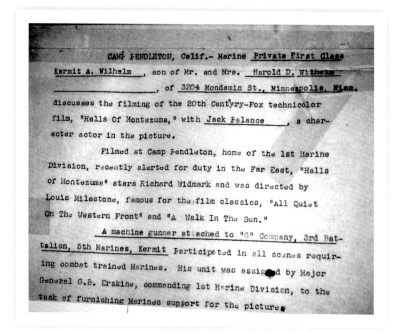

ALMOST A MOVIE STAR

During the making of "Halls of Montezuma," Wilhelm posed with future star Jack Palance. The press release explains Wilhelm's role in the movie.

"Well, I just got the gun cleared out when the officer said, 'Let's go.' I didn't have time to put it on the tripod, I just held it with my asbestos glove and sprayed the hillside, and

Wilhelm said his unit probably took 15 or 20 hills in 30 days, and each one was a challenge. "Guys would get to the top of the hill when it was over, and they'd just be babbling.

senger. The truck just rolled into a ditch, but it wasn't damaged. For a while, G Company had a truck. Our supply sergeant had a truck."

"I wanted to put my hand there and touch it to see how bad it was, but I couldn't. I didn't have the courage to touch my own face."

up we went. That was the only time I did the John Wayne thing."

The success of the Marines in pushing back the North Koreans was due in part, Wilhelm said, because most of the Marine officers and NCOs were World War II veterans with a lot of combat experience. "One of them was Gunnery Sergeant Perez. He had eyes like an eagle, and he saved my life more than once."

The adrenaline was going so fast. It just took a while to slow down and to realize that we're on top of the hill and we're alive."

While the Marines were taking the high ground one day, a North Korean truck came within range of Wilhelm's machine gun. "I had one lucky burst. One bullet hit the rearview mirror, one bullet took out the windshield, one bullet killed the driver, and one bullet killed the pas-

With the perimeter secure around Pusan, the regiment was pulled out and was put on a ship heading for Inchon for the major landing there on September 15, 1950. The landing was the plan of Gen. Douglas MacArthur, who was in command of the UN forces in Korea.

Wilhelm's unit was assigned the task of taking Wolmi-do, an island that strategically controlled the port at Inchon. The island had been soft-

ON THE STREETS OF SEOUL

Wilhelm (center) and his crew from G Company take a position on a Seoul street as an American tank rumbles by. *Photo by David Douglas Duncan*

ened up by American shelling for several days before the landing.

Most of the North Koreans who had survived the shelling were in bunkers and caves and had to be coaxed out. "I remember one of our flamethrower guys came up and asked us for cover. He got up there pretty close and hit the trigger for his flamethrower and nothing happened. He had forgotten to turn his tanks on. He turned about as white as a piece of paper. It wasn't funny, I suppose, but he had that look on his face, and we had to laugh. There are times in combat when there's real humor.

"We took the island in two or three hours, and then we were done. There was kind of a dome shape on the island, and we sat there and watched the landing at Inchon. It was like watching a movie. It was too far for us to fire, so we just sat and watched. It was a great show."

The fighting moved through Inchon and up into Seoul. "At one point, they dumped us off in a field, and the North Koreans were all around us, running in all directions. We felt like Custer at his last stand. It was a hell of a wild firefight that lasted maybe three or four minutes. That was one of the wildest times I remember in Korea."

In Seoul, Wilhelm's unit happened to be the one that captured the national capitol, and the men were able to raise the American flag at the capitol building. The area was soon host to Allied dignitaries.

"Yeah, we saw MacArthur and all those other officers with the chrome (helmets). Dugout Doug, I saw him in Seoul. He had an ego as big as a truck. He had an opportunity there to back off, but he didn't. Once the Chinese intervened, it was three or four more years of war."

Not long after, Wilhelm and the Third Battalion, Fifth Marines, were brought back to Inchon, loaded on transports again, and brought up around the other coast of Korea. They headed up to Hagaru-ri on the southern edge of the Chosin Reservoir area, then took a position on the east side of the reservoir for a couple of days before being relieved by an Army unit.

Wilhelm and his comrades then marched up the west side of the Reservoir to a spot near Yudam-ni, about 14 miles from Hagaru. It was about 15 degrees below zero at night. The Third Battalion, Fifth Marine Regiment, First Marine Division was the northernmost force on that day, November 27.

"It got kind of wild and wooly. I was sleeping on a frozen rice paddy, and I just had time to get my boots on when a whole bunch of Chinamen came around a hillside. We were kind of lined up along a road, and the Chinese were on the other side of the road."

The Marines beat off the Chinese attack and recaptured a hill that overlooked the valley they were in.

As the fighting continued, Wilhelm was at his machine gun, and the bullets were whizzing by. "The assistant gunner was bringing up more ammo, but he got wounded. I got up to get the ammo. I had just picked up the other can, and I was asking a guy named Palmer how he was when the lights went out. The next thing I knew, I was on my hands and knees and there was a singing in my ears. It was like a siren going off. And there was blood everywhere."

One bullet had passed through Wil-

MACHINE GUN PLATOON

As a young Marine, Wilhelm posed at his barracks.

helm's parka and cut a pack of cigarettes in half. Another severed the chin strap of his helmet. A third hit him in the cheek, slicing through the bottom of his nose. A fourth bullet glanced off the middle of his forehead. "It just sort of bounced off this thick head of mine. I'll never know for sure what hit me, but I'm almost positive it was a Russian-made burp gun."

"We called for a corpsman, and I was helping Palmer, and he looked at me and said, 'Christ, Kurt, they shot your nose off.' I wanted to put my hand there and touch it to see how bad it was, but I couldn't. I didn't have the courage to touch my own face."

The corpsman gave Wilhelm a shot of morphine and wrapped bandages all around his head, leaving only a narrow slit to see through.

Wilhelm walked down the hill with three or four other wounded men. "It was just about dark, and we were hanging on to one another as we were going down that hill. The walking didn't bother me, but I had a really bad headache.

"The aid station was in a farmhouse or a barn, and the doctor rebandaged me with some smaller stuff. I wanted a cigarette, and that was when I saw that my pack had been shot in half. A corpsman took me over to a corner and gave me a little pill and one of his cigarettes. I took three or four drags, and that was the last thing I remember until the next morning."

Wilhelm was placed on the hood of a jeep in a sleeping bag, and the Marines began their slow withdrawal from the Yudam-ni area. "The heat from the engine kept me warm. They gave me a Browning Automatic Rifle to hold in my lap, and that made me feel better. But after a couple of days there was some guy who was shot up really bad. I told them I could walk, and this other guy got my spot on the jeep. I walked, and I rode on a trailer full of dead Marines and some wounded for a while.

"It took us four days to go 16 miles. We weren't moving too damn fast."

As the column neared Hagaru, an officer began gathering up all the walking wounded into a temporary unit. "He got us organized, and we marched into Hagaru. I heard someone say as we marched by, 'Look at those magnificent bastards.' "

The temperature was still sub-zero, and Wilhelm was taken into a hospital tent with a heater. "I hadn't eaten in three or four days, and I was just so damned tired. But, there was a big bowl of Tootsie Rolls there, and we helped ourselves. Within minutes, the whole group of us were asleep. Half the guys fell asleep with the Tootsie Rolls in their mouths."

The next morning, Wilhelm was flown out on a C-47 to the Korean coast. "I went up to a corpsman and asked if I could have something for my headache. He said he couldn't give me anything, but then he went in his own pocket and pulled out a bottle of Anacin. A couple of those did the trick."

He was then flown to Japan. "It was just so nice to be warm again. We were in an Army hospital, and guys were still wearing their parkas and ammunition belts. Sometimes a grenade would go rolling across the floor."

Wilhelm spent January and February in Japan, then rejoined his com-

pany. But this time, his unit was in central Korea, not far from the line that was later drawn to separate North and South Korea. He was back for three weeks when a rotation schedule was announced. Because of his Purple Heart, Wilhelm was near the top of the list.

"The last day in Korea, we were involved in a firefight. We had been sent out to rescue a patrol. As it turned out, the enemy was on one side of the hill, and we were on the other. We were lobbing hand grenades back and forth at each other. All of a sudden, a runner came up and said Gunny Perez and I were to report to headquarters to be sent home.

"I took my last grenade and threw it over the hill, and then I walked down. That was the end of my career at war."

Wilhelm finished his duty at NAS Memphis and was honorably discharged from the Marines in August 1952. "I signed up for three years, and they gave me four."

Wilhelm became a surveyor in civilian life, and was a chief surveyor in a nine-state region for the U.S. Department of Fish and Wildlife. He retired in 1986, and he lives in Burnsville. He and his wife, Fern, have two daughters and a grandchild.

It has taken four operations over the years to allow Wilhelm to breathe through his nose correctly.

LAST MAN'S CLUB

In his basement, which contains much of Wilhelm's war memorabilia, is the bottle of whiskey for the Last Man's Club, Upper Midwest Chapter, of the Chosin Few organization.

When Wayne Pickett was released from the POW camp after two-and-one-half years, he and others were given a booklet to catch them up on what had transpired in the world during that time.

Unless indicated otherwise, all photos are from Wayne Pickett's personal collection.

A PRISONER OF THE CHINESE, 999 DAYS

Wayne Pickett of Duluth was captured when Chinese Communist forces attacked his Marine company at Fox Hill near the Chosin Reservoir during the Korean War. For the next two-and-one-half years, Pickett survived brainwashing, bad food and the awful tedium of life in a prisoner-of-war camp.

Wayne Pickett was never bitter about his 999 days as a prisoner of war.

"I volunteered for the Marines. I volunteered for the Active Reserve. It's an occupational hazard of the job, and you just deal with it."

Pickett was a guest of the Chinese Army at Prisoner of War Camp 1 in North Korea from late 1950 until the Korean War ended in 1953. He endured bad food, endless tedium and constant attempts at brainwashing by the enemy. He lost 60 pounds. He watched many of his comrades die from sickness or simply a lack of resolve to survive.

In the end, he was treated to a hero's welcome in his native Duluth, complete with limousine, color guard, a large crowd at city hall, and a jubilant group of supporters waving "Welcome Home Wayne" signs.

None of that was even the faintest blip on Pickett's radar when he enlisted in the Marine Corps right out of high school in 1946.

It had not been an easy childhood for Pickett. He was born in a township north of Pequot Lakes, and when he was five years old, his mother died while giving birth to twins. They were the eighth and ninth children in the family.

His father tried to keep the family together, but when Pickett was six he was sent to an orphanage, the Owatonna State Public School. He later spent two years on a farm in western Minnesota, then more time at the orphanage.

At nine, he was adopted by Allan and Clara Pickett of Duluth. He grew up on Duluth's West End and graduated from Central High School in 1946.

"My dad had been in the Marines in World War I, and he always told me how tough Marine boot camp was, but I didn't believe him." He did survive boot camp in San Diego, and was sent to Sea School to learn the ways of the Navy before being assigned to the USS St. Paul, a heavy cruiser, as a seagoing Marine.

The cruiser's overseas base was in Tsing Tao, China. On one occasion, "Our officer wanted us to have plenty of experience with landings, and, so, he was leading us ashore all the time. Once, when we were bivouacked on a point leading out into the ocean, the Communists came by and told us to move or we'd be flooded when the tide came in. They were right. The Chinese communists were just like anybody else — sometimes they were friendly and sometimes they were not."

Pickett took an early out from the Marines in 1948 and went home to Duluth.

"First, I signed up with the Inactive Reserve, when I was getting my paperwork done at Great Lakes Naval Base, but, when I got back to Duluth, some of my friends talked me into going into the Active Reserve.

"And even that wasn't so bad. My enlistment was up in 1950, and my big mistake was in re-enlisting."

Pickett and his fellow Marines in B Company, Fourth Infantry Battalion of the Reserves, began to hear rumors in 1950 that they might be called up.

The North Koreans invaded South Korea on June 25, 1950, and the rumors became facts. On August 1, Pickett's unit was called up. His recollection is that the announcement didn't make that much of an impression on him. "I don't know. I really didn't think a whole lot about it."

He and his fiancee, Helyn, decided to postpone their marriage until Pickett returned.

On Aug. 21, the men of B Company marched down Superior Street to the Duluth Depot to board a train for San Diego.

The North Koreans had pushed the South Korean Army and the American forces into a small perimeter on the tip of the Korean Peninsula before the U.S. and Republic of Korea forces began pushing back.

Gen. Douglas MacArthur planned a massive landing at Inchon, south of the South Korean capital at Seoul.

The Marines landed at Inchon on September 21, exactly one month since their festive march down Superior Street in Duluth.

What were Pickett's thoughts heading into battle? "Well, there's always that possibility of being shot. And there's a smaller possibility of being killed. Becoming a prisoner of war never entered my mind. Mostly you just take things as they come."

Pickett had been assigned to Fox Company, Second Battalion, Seventh Marine Regiment, First Marine Division.

After the landing, the unit first got into the battle about 20 miles north of Seoul. "We heard fighting coming from the area held by Dog Company, and then we came under fire later that same day.

"The first time you hear a bullet go by, you really don't know what to think. You just make yourself as small as possible."

The company helped the U.N. forces free Seoul from the North Koreans on September 29, then continued in action around the capital until the middle of March 1950. The unit was

«

WAYNE PICKETT

At home in Blaine

»

DURING THE WAR

Pickett had served a tour in the Marines before going on active reserve. He was called up when the Korean War broke out.

put back on a ship and sent on a second landing, this time near Wonson on the east coast.

Fox Company did some patrols out of Wonsan and then headed north toward the Chosin Reservoir. On November 2, the Seventh Marine Regiment relieved ROK troops west of the Chosin, and almost immediately encountered Chinese troops.

Fox Company eventually got to Hagaru-ri, on the southern tip of the Reservoir, in mid-November. Marine units were advancing up the west side of the reservoir, and, despite the encounters with the Chinese, optimism was still high that the war would soon be over.

"There was some betting among the troops on whether we'd be home by Christmas."

Thanksgiving dinner was at Hagaru-ri, and it was a treat for the troops. "We had turkey and sweet potatoes and mashed potatoes and stuffing and everything else. When they handed it to me, it was hot, but, by the time I found a place to sit down and eat it, it was cold."

Fox Company got orders to occupy the Toktong Pass, a critical part of the road between Yudam-ni and Hagaru-ri. If the enemy occupied the pass, it would have been easy for it to cut off the Marines to the north. There was only one road.

The company was able to hitch a ride with an artillery unit heading north, and took up positions on November 27. "Captain (William E.) Barber (who later won the Medal of Honor) had driven up the day before and scouted the position, so he knew where he wanted his people. The ground was completely frozen, so it was hard to dig in. Our foxhole was mostly a big rock right behind us."

Because they arrived late in the day, the Marines were unable to do some of the things they would have liked, such as putting trip wires around the perimeter with tin cans attached to warn of an enemy attack.

Pickett was the leader of a four-man fire team, and they were joined by another Marine, Daniel Yesko, who had been given hardship discharge orders and was to depart Korea the next morning. "He said it was his last night here, and he wanted to spend it with his friends."

"The platoon leader was pretty nervous, and he kept coming around to see how we were doing. First we just had one person staying awake, and then they called for two of us to be awake at any time."

The temperature that night, by some accounts, dropped to 30 below zero. "I have no way of knowing. I just know it was cold."

About one or two in the morning, on November 28, 1950, the Chinese attacked.

"They were on us before we knew what was happening. I heard, years later, that we were on one of the main points where they attacked. They pushed our line back about 15 or 20 yards. They hit us and took us down. I could hear Yesko yelling, 'I've been hit. I've been hit.' "

IN CHINA

Pickett is in the center, bottom, of this photograph of Marines on a river in China in 1947.

Pickett and several others were taken prisoner and were brought down to a company command post. "There was a discussion. They didn't know what they were going to do with us."

In the end, the Chinese soldiers began to bring the handful of Americans back toward the U.S. lines. "I'm not sure what they were going to do. It seemed like they wanted to return us to our lines. But when we got close, an American machine gun opened up on us, and that was the end of that."

The next stop was a battalion command post, where the prisoners spent the rest of the night in a barn. "They got us out in the morning, and we hadn't been out of that barn for ten minutes when a Mustang (fighter plane) came by and blew it to pieces."

The prisoners were marched about four miles to an enclosure surrounding a Korean dwelling. By this time, there were seven or eight Americans. "They put us in the enclosure and pretty much left us alone, except at meal time. We were not allowed to go out, even to go to the bathroom."

Pickett said, at this point the treatment by the Chinese was good. "Most of the front line troops were pretty decent. But the further you got toward the rear echelon, that's where you found the bad ones." Many of the front line troops had once been in the Nationalist

Chinese Army and had little personal hostility toward Americans.

The Americans bided their time and took care of two wounded Marines, including Yesko. He had been shot in the buttocks. Finally, the two wounded Americans were taken away by ambulance.

The prisoners were moved up to Yudam-Ni, which had been evacuated by the Marines as they retreated south through the Toktung Pass, guarded by the remainder of Fox Company. In the end, the company had 26 dead, 89 wounded and three missing — including Pickett.

Next was a long march south to another holding area. "They had five guards for two prisoners. I don't think they were that worried about us escaping, they were just trying to protect us from the North Koreans. The North Koreans would just as soon shoot you as look at you."

All through this time, there was no interrogation. "I think they were still trying to figure out what to do with us."

This early stage in his captivity, Pickett said, might have been the best. The prisoners ate the same food as the guards, and the security,

> ## "Most of the front line troops were pretty decent, but the further you got toward the rear echelon, that's where you found the bad ones."

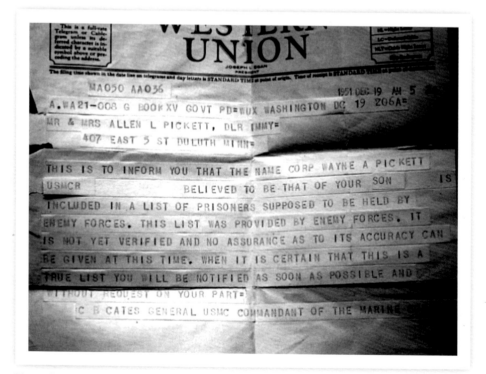

THE LATE NEWS

A telegram informing his parents that he was a prisoner of war arrived a year after his capture.

DEBRIEFING
After his release, Pickett talked with Gen. Joseph Burger at Freedom Village in South Korea.

while not lax, was not overly cruel or unusual.

The next walk was more difficult. The Chinese wanted to move the prisoners all the way across the Korean Peninsula to permanent camps that were being set up.

"On the first day of the hike, a Corsair buzzed the column. I dove and hit the ground, but the ground was frozen and it hit back a lot harder than I hit it. My knee swelled up three or four times its normal size. Every day of the march, everybody would start out at the same time, but I would arrive three or four hours later than everybody else. My guards would stay with me, and now and then they'd help me carry my rice supply."

Pickett arrived at Chang Song, in what was first called POW Camp 3 and later renamed POW Camp 1. It

was in northwestern Korea, about seven miles south of the Yalu River, the Chinese border.

Back home, his family was still in doubt as to what had happened to him. Helyn recalls that they assumed he had been captured because they heard from other Marines in Fox Company that there were no bodies where Pickett's foxhole had been.

It was over a year before the U.S. Government officially notified the Pickett Family that their son was a prisoner of war.

The prisoners were fed twice daily, at about 8:30 a.m. and about 4 p.m., but rice became a luxury. Instead, the food was usually something made from barley, sorghum or millet. Now and then there would be a little rice or even some noodles or something that looked like

dumplings.

In late 1952, a bakery was set up, and the prisoners started getting a barley bread once a day instead of their bowl of whatever. "It was almost a beet color. Most people, when they first tried it, got sick."

There were quite a few deaths in the camp early on as people adjusted or didn't adjust to prison life. "A lot of guys got sick and died because they wouldn't eat the food. Other guys got dysentery or some other sickness. I remember 10 or 12 funerals early on."

The officers were put into one group, sergeants into another, and the rest of the men into a third group. Likewise, prisoners were separated by nationality.

The brainwashing began sometime during the summer of 1951. "They were trying to convince us that their way of life was better than our way of life. It was a technique that had worked on the Nationalist troops, but it didn't work too well on us."

Pickett described the technique: "We would sit out in a big field and listen to someone who couldn't speak English tell us how great life was in a communist country. They would do it for two or three hours in the morning and then two or three hours in the afternoon.

"Now and then, they would hand out Russian books written in English, or copies of the London Daily Worker or the New York Daily Worker. There were a few guys who fell for it. I think there were about 19 turncoats (out of 11,000 U.N. prisoners).

There were also a few who tried to escape, even knowing how futile it was.

"Where could you go? And of course

WELCOME HOME

Pickett, his parents, and his wife-to-be Helyn, were greeted by hundreds outside the Duluth City Hall. Pickett teases Helyn that she looks "stuck up" in this photo, but she says she was only trying to keep a teardrop from falling.

you'd stick out like a sore thumb. The Koreans wouldn't dare help you. A couple of guys took off when we were harvesting wood, and they were caught in just a few hours. They got six months hard labor. I never have heard of a successful escape from those camps."

Pickett said one of the greatest hardships of the camp was the tedium, and he partially overcame it by having long and deep discussions with a couple of friends he made from Texas, Mickey Scott and Bob Arias. "We had discussion groups. We'd do anything to keep our minds going."

The men were issued dark blue clothing in the summer and light blue, padded clothing in the winter. They slept on the floor on top of a bamboo and straw mat. Lice were a problem early on in the camp, but

that was mostly solved when the prisoners were sprayed with DDT. The Americans had no toothpaste, toothbrushes or soap.

Mail delivery was haphazard. "We got to send four letters a month, and I'm not sure how many of those got through. I think about ten percent of the mail that was sent to us got through."

"Flies were always a problem, especially at certain times of the year.

"They would award people who killed the most flies two or three cigarettes. So we'd take turns and give all our flies to one guy every day. The next day it would be somebody else's turn."

The main break in the routine each year was when the men would be sent up into the surrounding hills to bring firewood back to the camp.

"We would carry these logs, six to ten feet long and five to ten inches in diameter, on our shoulders back to camp. The best part about the firewood detail was that you were fed three times a day. That was really a big deal."

The men were kept informed of the progress, or lack of progress, in the peace talks. "Of course, everything that went wrong was America's fault."

As time went on, though, and prospects for peace became more evident, conditions improved slightly at the camp. A barber was allowed to cut hair. "We were all pretty shaggy with long beards, but our food was so poor that our hair didn't really grow that fast."

Later, there would be a tobacco ration, with two packs of cigarettes on one's birthday. In early 1953, the Chinese allowed all the sick and wounded prisoners to go home.

Finally, on July 27, 1953, the United States, North Korea and China signed an armistice. "It was mainly a great sigh of relief. We knew we were going home, even if we didn't know exactly how long it would take. Before that, it had seemed like it was never going to end."

For the prisoners, it meant a definite improvement in life. Red Cross packages were finally allowed in, and the men could clean up. The food got better, but Pickett still had lost more than 60 pounds by the time he was released.

Most Americans who were captured made it home. Many did not. Pickett said that early in his captivity, he heard a voice that told him he was going to make it. "After that I never doubted it. I got dysentery and diarrhea, but I had just decided that I was going to make it back. I ate my food like a good little kid."

On August 21, 1953, the prisoners were loaded on trucks and brought to Panmunjom, where a little bridge to freedom awaited them. "You stood there until they called your name, and then you went across. When you got to the other side, they put you in an ambulance and took you to a field hospital to check you over."

A few days later, Pickett was on a ship, and, on September 9, he was in San Francisco, where he was greeted by his parents. On September 11, he was back in Duluth, where he was greeted by a delegation, color guard and limousine that took him, Helyn, and his parents downtown for a major celebration. He was given a watch. "At first they said they were going to give me a car, but then they found out there

were three other guys in the Duluth area that were also POWs. So we all got watches."

After six weeks of recuperation leave, he was given his discharge at Great Lakes. His official Marine records showed that he had been held prisoner for 999 days, and he was paid quarters and rations for that time. He had earned only about $2,500 in back pay, since most of his pay had gone home in an allotment.

Helyn laughs at the 999 days. "I told him he couldn't even make a thousand."

Wayne replies, "That's because the Chinese couldn't take me any longer."

The couple used the money to marry. Jobs were scarce in Duluth at that time. The Picketts moved to California for a time before returning to Minnesota where Wayne took a job with 3M as an engineering designer. He worked there for 33 years

before retiring in 1994.

The Picketts have six children and eight grandchildren. Wayne uses some of his free time as a member of the Fort Snelling Rifle Squad and as a volunteer bus driver for a senior center.

He said he harbors little resentment about the lost time in his life, due in part to the support he received when he arrived home.

Helyn agrees. "The community was there when he needed them. I think there were times when he wished people would leave him alone, but they didn't. Plus, he had no bitterness. That's why he's adjusted so well."

STILL TOGETHER
Helyn waited three years for Wayne to come home to get married. "He was worth it," she said.

Tim Kirk crouches in a field in northern Laos in 1967. The recon team has just been inserted into the country, but, in the process, their helicopter has been shot down.

Unless indicated otherwise, all photos are from Tim Kirk's personal collection.

SPECIAL
FORCES

Tim Kirk wanted to be with the best of the best, and so after Airborne training, he volunteered for the Special Forces. Soon he was on his way to South Vietnam, Laos, Cambodia and North Vietnam, where his missions required that he go into combat with absolutely no identification. Even the number on his weapon was removed.

Doing Special Operations in Vietnam meant losing your identity.

Soldiers would go on missions, often behind enemy lines or actually into North Vietnam, with absolutely no identification. Their uniforms bore no markings. The numbers on their weapons had been removed.

If they were captured, they had no hope of survival. Among the hundreds of POWs in North Vietnamese hands by the end of the war, not one Special Forces soldier was released by North Vietnam.

It was a tough job, often a terrifying job, and it was one that Tim Kirk volunteered for.

Kirk grew up in Dayton, Minnesota, and was, by his own admission, "a rebellious youth."

He quit school during his senior year at Elk River High School, and his father gave him a couple of options. "My dad said, 'Well, you're not going to hang around here. You can either find a job or join the Army.'"

And so, in March 1965, at age 17, Stephen Timothy Kirk joined the Army for a three-year enlistment.

Boot camp was at Fort Leonard Wood, Missouri, and during the training, the young men were given a talk on the possibility of going to parachute jump school and joining the Airborne.

"Our company commander knew exactly how to play me. He said, 'Kirk, don't even think of signing up for jump school. You'll never make it.' I said, 'Where do I sign?'"

Jump school was at Fort Benning, Georgia, and Kirk went on from there to parachute rigger school at Fort Lee, Virginia. He finished both schools and was assigned to the legendary 101st Airborne Division as a parachute rigger.

As a member of the 101st at Fort Campbell, Kentucky, Kirk still wasn't a happy camper. "I've got something in me that wants to be the best of the best. I wanted to be the elite. I got this desire to go into Special Forces."

At 18 years of age, though, he was too young to volunteer for Special Forces. Some bargaining with the U.S. Army allowed him go into Special Forces if he agreed to extend his enlistment for a year. In January 1967 at Fort Bragg, North Carolina, he became Special Forces-qualified

and was assigned to the Third Special Forces Group as a parachute rigger with a specialty in light weapons.

"The training was very intense, and it went into a lot more detail. I learned about every weapon from a .45 pistol to a howitzer. We learned tactics. We learned hand-to-hand fighting."

Kirk's goal was to be assigned to Vietnam. "I had no idea what I was getting myself into. Now that I look back, I really wonder what I was thinking."

He telephoned a woman who handled all the personnel requests for Special Forces, and asked for transfer to Vietnam. In about three weeks, he had orders and was on his way.

"We landed at Cam Ranh Bay, and I remember getting off the plane and walking behind the jet wash from the engines, and it was so hot. I walked another 100 feet or so, and then I realized: It wasn't just the jet blast, it really was that hot everywhere in that country."

Cam Ranh Bay was a fairly secure area, but it was still pockmarked with shell holes and other reminders that the newcomers had entered a war zone. Kirk was assigned to the Fifth Special Forces Group, Command and Control North at Forward Operation Base 1. His first stop was at Nha Trang, just north of Cam Ranh Bay, where the Special Forces were headquartered.

"I was unsure what Command and Control North meant, but everyone I talked to said, 'Be afraid.' I was starting to get a sense that maybe this Vietnam thing wasn't such a good idea."

In May 1967, Kirk left Nha Trang with Staff Sgt. Sam Robison of San Angelo, Texas, for Phu Bai, a base about 75 miles south of North Vietnam and the location of FOB-1.

"Everything started to be really clandestine at that point. They brought us in a room and had us sign a lot of documents stating we would not disclose any information about the top-secret operations we were involved in."

The Special Forces at that point of the war were doing secret missions into Laos, Cambodia and even North Vietnam. The missions were for reconnaissance, to extract downed flyers (called Bright Lights missions) and to take out "targets of opportunity."

The American soldiers on these missions carried no identification on their person or on their equipment. The teams got their choice of wearing the black pajamas, tiger stripes, or regular Army olive drab. If they

«

TIM KIRK

At home in Elk River

»

DURING THE WAR

Kirk is shown at the airport as he departed on his second tour in Asia.

THAILAND, 1968

Spike Team Idaho was photographed at Nakhon Phanom Air Base, Thailand in January 1968. After Kirk, kneeling in center, front, and Steve Perry, far left, came home from Vietnam, the team disappeared while on a mission. Glen Lane, standing at the back, is still listed as missing in action.

were captured or killed, the United States would not even acknowledge they existed.

In fact, it was well known among the SOG (Studies and Observation Group) personnel that being captured was not an option.

While in-country, the Special Forces did carry an identification card that said they were allowed to go where they wanted. There was a telephone number on the card that a suspicious gate guard could call.

"We called it our 'get out of jail free card.' It explained that we were working for an agency of the U.S.

government. We were allowed to carry concealed weapons anywhere we went. The card indicated we were not to be questioned on our actions or what we were doing. It was pretty serious stuff. Of course, there were a few who used that card to get out of trouble."

Kirk arrived just after a large operation in the A Shau Valley, in the northern part of South Vietnam, had gone amok and 26 Americans had been killed.

He was assigned to work with a team of "indigenous Vietnamese." These soldiers had been recruited

into the Special Forces and were mainly made up of the Montagnard people from the highlands and the Nung, or Vietnamese of Chinese ancestry. They joined mainly because the pay was astronomically better than their other choice, being drafted into the Army of the Republic of Vietnam.

Kirk's team was made up mainly of Nung volunteers. "They were very good soldiers, excellent soldiers. The only thing they required was that they trusted you. Once they were okay with you, they would do anything for you. But once they sensed fear on your part, they got scared, too."

Kirk carried a modified M-16 with a shortened stock and barrel, and he was assigned to Spike Team Idaho, a

signed to check out the highland area atop a limestone bluff on the Laos-Vietnam border called Co Roc Mountain, a few miles from the U.S. base at Khe Sanh. It was about a

us our coordinates and left. We didn't find out until the next day that they were the wrong coordinates."

The team knew the direction it wanted to go, and it moved stealthily

---

"At that point they didn't know who, if anybody, was still alive. They just knew it was ugly."

---

reconnaissance team. Once again he went through a training period with his men. "The whole purpose of the training was so that out in the field, a group of six to 12 men know exactly what everyone else is doing.

"The men learned hand signals and tactics and how to respond to any situation. They also had to learn to move quietly through the countryside."

When a reconnaissance team was brought in via helicopter, the goal was to melt into the jungle without a trace. The last thing it wanted was to engage the enemy. "If you end up in a firefight, you'll start out facing just a few North Vietnamese who were guarding that area. Within 15 minutes, you'll be facing a platoon. Fifteen minutes after that, you'll be facing a company.

"Fifteen minutes after that, you'll be facing two companies."

If contact with the enemy was made during an insertion, the plan was to use maximum fire for about two minutes, then hightail it to another location and disappear. "You wanted to break contact as quickly as possible and evade."

Kirk recalls one recon mission that got interesting. His team was as-

month before the siege of that base would occur, and the North Vietnamese were marshalling artillery for the attack.

The team originally went in as part of a larger operation. After the other troops left, the recon team tried to cross a river to get to Co Roc Mountain, the site of the bluff. "The river was too high, though, and we almost lost our point man."

The next day, the team was again inserted, this time behind the bluff. "They tried a couple of false inserts, and they kept going until they found a spot they could get in. They gave

through the country for the next couple of days, checking in by radio now and then.

"On top of Co Roc Mountain, we found a lot of troubling issues," Kirk said.

"There were very well-used trails, and we found track marks from heavy equipment. And the spider holes (used by the North Vietnamese to duck into during an air attack) were not handmade, but were done by an auger. That was very unusual. We started getting pretty nervous."

They called in their coordinates and

SECOND BRONZE STAR

Kirk was part of an awards ceremony at Phu Bai, Vietnam, in April 1968. At his left is his good friend Robbie Robison.

PARTY TIME

Kirk, along with members of the unit, enjoyed some R&R at Phu Bai, Forward Operations Base. Kirk is at right, and his commanding officer "Bulldog" Smith is at center.

were told by the "covey rider," the expert flying in the air to direct traffic and support in the area, that there was no way they could be there. They checked their instruments again and radioed that position again. A discussion ensued between the team and the covey rider about where they were, but it was interrupted when the Nung team sergeant hollered loudly, "Dung li," or "Stop."

"After three days of quiet and never talking above a whisper, the loud command was pretty shocking." The men turned and found that a North Vietnamese force was advancing on them.

"We began to fire on them, and we saw several of them go down. It all happened so fast. There's screaming and shooting. It gets chaotic, real chaotic in a hurry, and that's where all the training comes in. We bailed over the side of the cliff and beat feet down the side of the mountain. I had the radio, and I'm trying to call in an air strike. I got pretty excited, and I quit using code. I was just giving the coordinates straight out.

"The covey rider decided he needed to remind me to use code. I told him, 'Every son of a bitch in the world knows where we are except you. Give us some cover on top of that mountain.'"

Gunships were soon on the way, and the team was able to break contact with the enemy. The mission was not over, however. "Because there were heavy equipment tracks, they wanted to know more. They wanted us to go back up the mountain and see if we could capture any of the wounded North Vietnamese."

Another recon team was brought in to double the strength of the unit. There was only one problem. During the escape, the men had laid anti-personnel mines, called "toe poppers," along the paths to cover their withdrawal.

Darkness was falling, and they had to dig in for the night. "That's kind of super-scary, because you know that they know you're there.

"But no one came in that night." In the morning, the combined team carefully made its way up the mountain, through its own minefield, to the top of the cliff. "We found plenty of blood trails, but no wounded and

WITH HIS DAD

Kirk and his father, Leon, had their picture taken at their home in Dayton in 1967.

WITH HIS BUDDIES

Kirk was able to reunite with his comrades at a reunion in 2002. From left are Steve Perry, Robert "Spider" Parks and Kirk. At another reunion, he was able to get together with other friends, including Sam Robison and Kahn Van Doan, a Nung mercenary who escaped from Vietnam after the communists took over.

no bodies. They had been removed."

There was sporadic fire as the North Vietnamese Army tried to locate the team, and the American force finally sought shelter in some eight-foot-high elephant grass. It wasn't long, though, before they could smell smoke. The enemy had set the grass on fire.

There was only one clearing in the elephant grass where a helicopter could land, but smack in the middle of the clearing was a large tree. The team radioed for an extraction, but first had to deal with the tree.

"We tried to blow it away with our M-79s (grenade launchers), but we were too close and they wouldn't detonate. And so we started hacking at the tree with our knives. The trunk was about 16 inches thick."

In the meantime, the group was assaulted on one side of their perimeter. "We had enough people and a tremendous amount of firepower." The first attack was beaten back, but by now the fire was only about

GEARED UP

Kirk is shown at Forward Operations Base 1 in Phu Bai, Vietnam, in 1967.

100 feet away, and the second enemy assault came from two directions. The Americans could hear the choppers coming in.

Most of the men were protecting the perimeter, but Kirk and three others were chopping frantically at the tree. Just as a new assault came in, the tree went down. The helicopters were able to land.

"It took three choppers to get all of us out, but we got out. We didn't lose one person. We figured it took about 10 minutes to chop through that tree with knives. It's amazing what you can do."

Three weeks later, the assault on Khe Sanh began. The Special Forces had a small base at Lang Vei, about six miles southwest of Khe Sanh, that was overrun by a large enemy force on February 6, 1968.

Kirk had gone back to his base at Phu Bai after the previous recon mission, but he was now assigned to a "hatchet force" that was going to Khe Sanh to help defend the besieged base. Khe Sanh was mostly a Marine operation, but the Special Forces had a Studies and Observation Group compound there.

"When we got there, everybody else had already dug in, and we had to start from scratch to create our defensive position. And the whole time we were under some pretty intense fire. But it got a lot worse."

Kirk's unit was composed of one lieutenant, three sergeants and 80 indigenous soldiers.

On that night, the men could hear the attack on the Lang Vei compound, but there was nothing they could do about it. At dawn they were informed that Lang Vei had been overrun. "At that point they didn't know who, if anybody, was still alive.

They just knew it was ugly."

Word finally came in that there were Americans still alive, but that they were just barely holding out. A disagreement ensued between the Special Forces and Marine officers about rescuing the Lang Vei troops, further slowing down a relief party. "We didn't know about any of that political crap going on. All we knew was that our buddies were out there, and the Marines were not going to get them."

The Special Forces command asked for volunteers, and every man in the compound stepped forward. Not everyone could go, but a hatchet force of about 40 men was formed and put aboard helicopters.

"Just by coincidence, I had received a telegram that day that my first

daughter was born."

The choppers headed for Lang Vei. Two large Chinooks held most of the troops, while several of the smaller Hueys flew shotgun. Kirk's squad was put aboard one of the Hueys.

"When we got over the compound, we looked down and it was totally decimated. There was nothing left of the camp, no bunkers, no buildings; it was just flat. We found out that the survivors were in a bunker a little ways away in an old camp that had been abandoned."

Looking down, Kirk could see the bunker, and he could see troops all over the old camp. He believed that the troops were Americans. He tapped the shoulder of the Huey pilot and told him to go down.

"The pilot looked at me like I was

WITH ONE OF HIS MEN

The Nung were indigenous Vietnamese of Chinese ancestry who fought against the communists.

crazy, but I signaled I wanted him to go down." With the other choppers circling and providing support, the Huey landed about 50 or 60 feet from the bunker. The troops in the compound Kirk had hoped were friendlies — were not.

"There was so much fire coming in, it was unbelievable. Mortar fire. Automatic weapons fire. We could see the Americans in the bunker, and we ran for them. They started coming out. Some were wounded badly, some were walking wounded. They were all banged up. They all looked really bad. Only about half of them had weapons."

Kirk helped carry some of the soldiers to the medevac helicopter, then was ordered to take his squad and protect the southwest perimeter of the landing zone.

"We headed for our position, and at one point I ducked down behind some cover. I realized after a moment that I was behind a stack of bodies. There were bodies everywhere, hundreds and hundreds of them. There were weapons and bodies everywhere you looked.

"We were taking heavy fire from a machine gun and a mortar team. I grabbed the M-79 from one of my guys and started firing as fast as I could at that machine gun. I bet I fired 20 rounds, but we knocked it out." An M-79 fires 40-millimeter exploding rounds, something like grenades.

Kirk turned his attention to the mortar.

When the enemy tried to flee its position, he caught two of them with an M-79 round. "After that, there wasn't much firing from the area in front of us."

The call was given to pull back, and

Kirk and his team were on the last helicopter to leave Lang Vei. They had rescued 14 Americans. The mission had taken about 45 minutes.

 For his efforts, Kirk received a Bronze Star for heroism. A few weeks later, he would earn one of South Vietnam's highest awards for another daring act.

Back at Khe Sanh, the siege was continuing. "There were times where we were taking 1,200 to 1,500 rounds of artillery every day. It was so bad that guys wanted to go on patrol. They felt safer outside the compound than in it. If an artillery shell hits within 20 feet of you, you're dead. That can make you nervous after a while.

"After a while, though, you adapt somewhat. I can't say you get used to it, because you never get used to it. But you can hear when they fire the artillery, and you know you've got the count of seven to find some shelter. Like if you're taking a break to go to the can, you know you've the count of seven to get back in a trench."

Kirk led his team as part of a larger force that set up an ambush position near Khe Sanh village, a couple of miles from the base. They were hoping to catch the North Vietnamese coming down a ravine.

While they were waiting, Kirk noticed a few enemy soldiers go into a hut in the village. "I felt we could make a capture, get a prisoner, if we did it right. I took my point man and team sergeant with me, and we got to what probably was a burial mound not far from the hut."

Kirk's plan was to stand up and throw a grenade into the hut, and for his two men to fire at whomever came out – and to take a prisoner if

possible.

 "I pulled the pin on the grenade, and I stood up. Just as I stood up, an NVA soldier stood up five feet in front of me on the other side of the mound. I don't think either one of us knew the other was there. The team sergeant took him out, but in the meantime I had been pretty startled, and when I threw the grenade, it landed 20 feet in front of the hootch. So the whole thing turned into a disaster. The grenade went off, the guys came out of the hut, and we ran back to our positions about 75 meters away.

 "I got there and jumped behind some cover, and it was at that point I realized my point man wasn't there. Our whole platoon was putting down a hellacious fire, but I could hear him calling me. 'Trung-Si Tim, Trung-Si Tim.' ("Sergeant Tim.")

"I was scared shitless. Part of me wanted to just leave him out there. I didn't know what I was going to do."

 One of Kirk's fellow non-coms and a close friend, Sam Robison, came over and said, "You know you've got to go get him."

"So I did what I had to do. I bolted out there; it was about 40 meters, and I put him on my shoulder. There was lots of fire. I could hear them going by. But I was kind of on autopilot by that time. I made it back to the perimeter."

The action had two outcomes. The first was regarding his relationship with his squad. "They would do anything for me after that." The other outcome was the awarding of the Cross of Gallantry with Palm by the South Vietnamese government.

Kirk earned a second bronze star for his overall performance during his time in Vietnam, and he was also awarded the Army Commendation Medal for his leadership in defending the perimeter at Khe Sanh.

After 77 days at Khe San, he and his unit were relieved. "Most of that time was in the same uniform, with no showers."

He recalled one other incident at Khe Sanh that spoke to the mysteries of war. A group of GIs were gathered in a trench when a mortar shell hit a few feet away. "It just knocked us all down. It just knocked the wind out of us, and we went, 'Wow.' The amazing thing is that not one of us was hurt."

Looking down the trench, though, the men could see a piece of plywood fall away and an arm flop down from a sleeping hole built to the side of the trench. A piece of shrapnel had traveled 100 feet down the trench, had ricocheted off something to make a left turn, had gone through the three-quarter-inch plywood, and had hit a sleeping soldier. The shrapnel went right into his heart and killed him instantly.

The men who had been a few feet from the blast didn't get a scratch. "I've often wondered through the years, 'Lord, what was the purpose of keeping me alive during those times?'"

By the end of the siege of Khe Sanh, Kirk was near the end of his tour in Vietnam, and he was shipped home in May 1968. In January 1969, he was back for a second tour. "I don't know why I went back. I still don't know."

He was there about a week when he got wounded. "I was at Na Trang, which is a relatively safe place, when I got hit by a mortar round."

He was hit by shrapnel, and his hand and arm were broken. Despite his injuries, he was sent to a base at Ban Me Thuot, but wasn't able to participate in any missions because of his wound.

"By the end of March, my enlistment was up. It just wasn't the same. I'd been home and seen my daughter. It just was different. I decided to get out."

He said his reception in his small hometown was good. He found a job and "lived a pretty crazy life." He worked for Control Data, went to forestry school, and eventually ended up doing construction work for over 20 years. He fought and licked an alcohol and drug problem, but in the process, he was divorced.

After a major heart problem, Kirk was told he could never do physical labor again, and so he returned to school, eventually earning his degree in organizational administration from Northwestern College in Roseville, finishing at the top of his class. He now serves as a building inspector for the city of Richfield.

He has four children from his first marriage, and he and his second wife, Sheila, have two children. She also has two children from a prior marriage.

Kirk and his wife live in Elk River. He has served as chaplain for Chapter 470 of the Vietnam Veterans of America, and he is active in the Special Forces Association.

In 2001, Kirk attended a Special Operations Association reunion in Las Vegas. While there, he met several friends he had not seen in over 30 years, including Sam Robison and Kahn Van Doan, one of the Nung mercenaries who escaped from Vietnam after the communists took over.

WITH HIS DAUGHTER

Kirk got to meet his daughter for the first time when he returned from his first tour in Vietnam.

Unless indicated otherwise, all photos are from Clark Dyrud's personal collection.

THE POINT MAN

Clark Dyrud, a native of Thief River Falls, volunteered for the draft, volunteered to go to Vietnam, and volunteered to drive armored personnel carriers. He often was a point man for night ambush patrols in Vietnam. Now, he's a point man for making sure Minnesota veterans have access to care for their war injuries, including PTSD.

DURING THE WAR WITH Iraq, the American press and the American people seemed shocked by the numbers of U.S. troops killed by friendly fire.

"I'm amazed that people don't realize how many are killed and wounded in any war by friendly fire," Clark Dyrud said. "The number is very high, and it always has been."

Dyrud should know. He faced the enemy for a year in Vietnam, often as night patrol point man or as a armored-personnel-carrier squad leader.

But his only wound came when an American 105-millimeter shell exploded 10 yards from where he was standing.

Clark Kenmer Dyrud grew up on a farm near Thief River Falls. His early education was at a one-room schoolhouse. The farm work was long and hard. "You know, you can never wash that smell of manure out completely."

After graduating from Thief River

Falls High School in 1964, he received a scholarship and attended the University of Minnesota. He survived his first year, but after returning in the fall of 1965, he dropped out. "I didn't know what I wanted to do, but I knew I didn't want to be in school.

"In 1965, the war in Vietnam was just cranking up. There was no anti-war movement at that time. I wanted to see what war was like. I wanted to see what was going on there."

Dyrud volunteered for the draft at Warren. "The Selective Service person just said, 'Sign quick before you change your mind.'"

He left for Fort Leonard Wood, Missouri, for basic training on Jan. 21, 1966, and after a few days of Army life he decided that he wanted to be a helicopter pilot. He was put through a battery of tests and physicals, and his application was forwarded to the Fifth Army.
In the meantime, he was sent to Fort Riley, Kansas, where he awaited the word on his application.

The only Army training school there was for truck drivers, and Dyrud was assigned.

The Fifth Army eventually approved his application to be a pilot and sent on to the Pentagon. "One day, I was walking guard duty, when it came to me that I'd already been in the army 12 or 13 months, and that I had less than a year to go. If I went to flight school, it would have been a five-year commitment. It was like I came

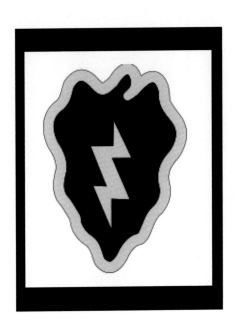

to my senses. I canceled my application for helicopter pilot and filled out a 1049 form requesting duty in Vietnam."

After a long leave at home, Dyrud got his wish. He was sent out of the Oakland Army Terminal and Travis Air Force Base to Ton Son Nhut Airbase in South Vietnam. "It was like a 24-hour flight. We had to stop to refuel twice. I spent the whole time on a seat facing backwards, looking at a pallet loaded with our duffel bags. They served us Swanson TV dinners."

He arrived on April 1, 1967. Dyrud was sent to a truck battalion in the 25th Division at Cu Chi, but after standing a few "truck and boots" inspections, he decided this wasn't why he had come to Vietnam. "I did a walking tour of the base, and I stumbled across a mechanized infantry unit in the corner of the base.

I had driven Caterpillars on the farm, and so I was pretty sure I could drive an APC (armored personnel carrier)."

Inside the company's HQ, Dyrud told the first sergeant that he wanted to transfer in as a driver. "He looked at me just like that Selective Service lady had looked at me. He just stared."

The sergeant did sign the paperwork, though, and Dyrud was soon a member of Company A, Fourth Battalion, 23rd Infantry Regiment (Mechanized). His first job was to actually drive the APCs, or "tracks," large, box-like, treaded, armored vehicles used for protecting troops on the move.

"Most of the guys would ride on top if possible. There were a couple of problems with riding inside."

The first problem was a Russian-made recoilless rifle that was used

by the Viet Cong to fire what were called RPGs at the tracks. "The armor-piercing shell would usually go in one side of the APC and go out the other side. While it was going through, though, it would really mess up what was inside. I always rode with my legs up. If you dangled a leg down in there, you might lose it."

A second danger was hitting a mine. "Often, when the APC hits a mine, it will burst the eardrums of anybody inside."

Dyrud recalled one instance in which he and another soldier had been on night patrol and were dead tired. When the APC left for a new assignment the next day, both soldiers were sound asleep inside the vehicle. They were awakened by a violent explosion.

"When it hit the mine, it only caught the edge of it, and so most of the

«

CLARK DYRUD

At work for the Minnesota Department of Veterans Affairs

»

IN THE ARMY

Dyrud served in Vietnam during his two-year stint in the U.S. Army.

SQUAD LEADER

Dyrud, in the center holding a Lucky Strike, waves at his buddy, Jon Hovde, who was on top of another APC close by. Hovde, also from northwestern Minnesota, took this picture. Not long after, the track that Hovde was riding hit a mine, and he was severely injured.

right in front of us, right where we would have been if we hadn't slowed down. The VC had timed us out. We got out of there lickety-split."

As the APC headed out of the paddy at full tilt, it took a corner, and one of the guys took a header from the top. "I remember this guy catching up to us. He was covered in mud from head to foot. He didn't think it was very funny."

One of Dyrud's goals was to be the point man in a night ambush. The maneuver was done frequently when the APCs were gathered into a circle for the night. A group of 12

blast went up the side of the APC instead of under it. The other guy and I were fine, but some of the guys riding on top had their eardrums burst."

As Dyrud stayed with the outfit, he became the machine gunner and then a squad leader.

"When people would ask how I became a squad leader so fast, I tell them it was because of my outstanding leadership abilities, my coolness under fire, and because of the fact that other guys got bumped off."

He became the senior sergeant in the unit, and he was awarded the

privilege of driving the lead "track" on any mission. "I always liked to go first. It was kind of a macho thing, I guess."

At one point, Dyrud's track was heading through a rice paddy when an RPG round shot past. "I saw the burst from the tree line, and I saw the shell hit just short of us. Usually what we do is to turn and head right for where it came from while opening fire with everything we've got. But we were at the end of the day, and so we just headed off at full speed. The driver was really clipping along, but he had to slow down so we could go over a berm. Just as we slowed, the RPG landed

M113
Armored Personnel Carrier Statistics

M113

Manufacturer
FMC

Engine
Detroit Diesel 6V53T, six-cylinder diesel engine. 275 horsepower.

Crew
Two, plus eleven passengers

Armament
M2 Browning machine gun

Maximum Speed
42 miles per hour

Number Built
80,000

Range, loaded
300 miles

soldiers were sent out about 1,500 to 3,000 meters to set up an ambush for any enemy that might be around. They took with them a machine gun. "They would send us to what they thought was a logical point where the enemy might come stumbling along. But the whole time I was there, I never heard of a night ambush patrol that actually ambushed anybody. The enemy usually knew where we were."

The point man had to read the compass and take the squad through the pitch dark to the assigned ambush point without losing his way. If the men set up at the wrong point, the group was liable to be shelled by its own artillery.

Dyrud had no qualms about being in front. "The most afraid I was in Vietnam was in the hospital. I always felt the safest when I was in the field. At least there, you had a sense of efficacy; you've got weapons, and you can use them. You can go hunting. You can be proactive."

On his first try at being point man, Dyrud, however, did get that sinking feeling. "It was during the monsoons, and it was gushing rain, so, of course, it was pitch black. They cut a gap in the concertina wire to let us through. I had the compass, and I was intent on staying on course when all of a sudden I realized there was no ground beneath my feet anymore."

Dyrud had stepped into a farmer's well, and the only thing that saved him was an automatic reflex to throw his arms out. His comrades helped him from the well.

That was a learning experience. "After that, I would go into a different state of being when I was on point. It was like my feet had antennas. I could see better in the dark.

All my senses became stronger. And I lost all track of time."

In order to keep its bearings, the patrol had to follow a straight line no matter what kind of terrain it encountered. And when it got to its position (one of the squad's men counted the paces), the soldiers never knew what it would be like.

"One night we set up on a nest of squirming bugs of some sort. We had repellent with us, but these things were very large. Another time, we set up in the middle of a rice paddy that the farmers had just prepared for planting.

"It was just like back on the farm, except that on the farm I don't ever remember actually sleeping on the manure pile.

"Another time we had to sleep in standing water. You end up with dishpan bodies, you know, where you're white and wrinkly all over. And talk about cold. Oh, that's so cold."

The jungle fatigues provided some

protection against the mosquitoes and other pests. "I used to sleep with my helmet on, using the liner as kind of a pillow. Then I'd wrap a towel around my head, leaving enough room to breath. Then I'd put my hands in my pockets. You'd be so exhausted, the moment you laid down, you'd be zonked out."

Being tired and exhausted was part of the routine. "We were always short of men, and so you never got enough sleep. You were always doing guard duty or were up at night for some reason, and it would go on for weeks."

"Wars are mainly days and weeks of boredom and exhaustion, followed by moments of sheer terror. You never enjoy your rest. There are just not enough troops to do what has to be done. You never get a good night's sleep."

Dyrud laughed about the colorful language used by the soldiers and servicepeople in general. "There's a reason for that. In any given unit, people come together from all walks

END OF TOUR

As the months wore on, the strain of the duty began to show in Dyrud's face.

"They say you never hear the one that gets you. I was flying through the air in slow motion..."

of life. Some are college grads and some are borderline. Some are from the city, and some are from the farm. They're all different. The first thing the army does is cut off your hair and put you in the same clothes so that everybody looks alike. It's the same with the communication. It sinks to some kind of common denominator.

"A lot of what people say has to do with the tone of the voice. You can call somebody a blankety-blank, and that's the highest praise. Or you say it in another tone of voice, and those are fighting words.

"A camaraderie develops. Nobody fights a war for country or flag or anything like that. Once you get there, you're fighting for survival. You quickly learn to depend on the other guys, because their number one goal is to stay alive also. You have that unified goal, and these people can help you achieve that goal."

In the end, Dyrud said, the combat experience leads to "total acceptance of people." He acknowledged that as the war wore on and morale slipped, there were racial incidents and other signs of deterioration.

"But, when we were there, it was different. We still thought we were going to win. We had pride in the Army, pride in our outfit."

There were a couple of things, however, that Dyrud said he wasn't proud of during his 10 months overseas. One such incident was when his unit was ordered to exhume Vietnamese graves. "They wanted to know who was in it, whether it was a soldier, and how they died. So there we were, digging, and I was the lucky one whose shovel broke through to where the body was. This incredible stench came out. We all looked at each other, and somebody said, 'This is B.S.' We covered it back up and told them that the body was not recognizable. It was all because the government had this incessant need to report body counts. In the future, when we found a grave, we never dug it up."

A second regrettable experience came when his squad was ordered to go into an area along the Saigon River where there were several small dwellings. With the roar of the APCs, it was not surprising that the dwellings were empty when the Americans arrived.

"An order came down from somewhere that we were to destroy the contents of the homes. Well, these people had so little. Finally I brought my boot down on a low table and broke it in half. One of the guys knocked a picture off the wall, and the third guy backhanded some stuff off a table. We all kind of looked at each other and shook our heads. This had nothing to do with war. We didn't obey that order. But I did break that table, and I'm ashamed of that."

The APCs would head out either on search-and-destroy missions or to guard the Rome plows that would knock down large portions of the jungle. "That really didn't work very well because the jungle would grow back so quickly, and then it was really impenetrable."

One day, while out on a mission, Dyrud had only four men on his track. The Army flew out a hot meal of chicken and mashed potatoes.

"I wolfed down my share, and then I grabbed a handful of trip flares to put in the concertina wire we had set up around us. I didn't even bother to put on my helmet or flak jacket. I just headed on out there."

The next thing Dyrud knew, a pillar appeared about 10 meters away. "It was black and gray and orange and green, and it had some purple in it. It was about three or four feet wide and taller than I was. I picked up my leg as if to run from it, but I just went up in the air." A 105-millimeter American howitzer shell, not quite on target, had landed and exploded.

"They say you never hear the one that gets you. I was flying through the air in slow motion — at least it seemed that way to me — when I heard the ka-boom of the shell exploding. I was flying, just like you see those guys in the war movies, and finally I came face down in some brush.

"I felt like I was sweating, and I ran my hand over my face and I looked at it and it was all covered with blood. I had this vague sense of being wounded, but as I laid on the ground, I just sort of drifted. It was the most peaceful feeling I've ever had in my life, before or since. It was just this intense feeling of well-being. The thought of dying was not frightening."

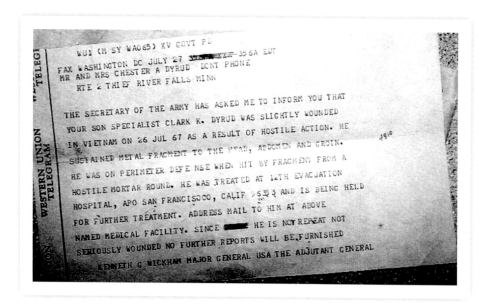

TELEGRAM HOME

After Dyrud was wounded, his parents received this telegram from the Army. It misstates both the cause of the wound and the severity.

Dyrud said his first thought was, "Now I can get out of the mud. And then I thought, now I can get some rest. After that, I thought of death, but that didn't seem real. I could hear people calling my name, and I tried to yell but nothing came out."

He had been hit by at least four pieces of shrapnel. Two in the upper leg and one in the head were not serious wounds, although the head wound bled profusely. The fourth piece had blown a hole in his gut and had lodged somewhere in his abdomen. He couldn't yell because his diaphragm was paralyzed.

One of his comrades found him. "A look of horror came over his face. His eyes got as big as dinner plates. He couldn't even yell." The soldier was too shocked by the amount of blood the head wound was producing.

A medic arrived and rolled Dyrud over. "That was the first time I felt any pain, and then it was intense.

When you're gut-shot, all you want to do is curl up, and all they want you to do is lie flat on the stretcher. Every breath is an agony."

It was something of a miracle that Dyrud was even in one piece. "The killing radius of a 105 is 35 meters. I was 10 meters away. The only thing I can figure out is that it was monsoon season, and the ground was very soft. I think that's what might have happened. The ground took up much of the explosion."

He was put in a helicopter and evacuated to a hospital. "I was really having trouble breathing, but when they put me into the helo, my head was sticking out a little bit. I could turn my head into the jet stream and force air down into me, and then turn my head the other way. When I needed my next breath, I'd turn into the jet stream again."

At the hospital, Dyrud heard the doctors talking about how he had probably lost his spleen. An anes-

thesiologist was trying to insert a tube down his nose, but Dyrud would gag and prevent it from going down. Finally the man said, "If I don't get this down, you're going to die," and he gave one large push on the tube. This time, the gag reflex caused Dyrud to throw up. The tube was finally inserted, though, and Dyrud was knocked out for the surgery.

Three days later, he woke up in intensive care. It was only then that the doctors told him of the operation he had undergone. As standard procedure for shrapnel wounds to the gut, all of Dyrud's insides had been taken out and meticulously examined to see where the shrapnel had ripped or torn any membranes. Then they were all put back in. "Probably not in the same way they were originally. It was very painful for a few days."

The doctors also told him that they were mystified because they could not find the piece of shrapnel. As it turned out, the shrapnel had been lodged in Dyrud's lunch that day. When Dyrud had thrown up, he had also brought up the shrapnel. The fact that it had lodged in the contents of his stomach had probably saved him from additional injury to interior parts.

"I've been partial to chicken and mashed potatoes ever since then."

Dyrud was in intensive care for two weeks, an experience he will never forget. Shortly after he got there, the man in the next bed died. Not long after that, a group of wounded soldiers was brought in. "There was such a high rate of infection in Vietnam that the wounds were packed but left open for five days to make sure there wasn't any infection. And so, I got to watch them change the dressings with all the ooze and muscles twitching. One guy was blind and had lost both arms. It's scenes like that, that stay in your mind."

Eventually he was moved to another hospital at Vung Tau. One day he returned from being away from his ward and found his Purple Heart certificate and medal lying on his bed. "That was all the ceremony I got."

He recuperated at his base camp for another month before rejoining his outfit in September 1967. "It was too soon. I had fixed up my chair with padding, but the bouncing of the track was too much. I was doubled over in pain, and the medic sent me back on the next helicopter. As I left, I could look down and see another guy sitting in my place. I found out later that the track hit a mine, and he broke his back."

Dyrud was sent to a leadership school, and when he finished first in his class, he received an automatic promotion.

As Dyrud's year came to an end, he began to see some major changes occur in troops sent there to fight the war against communism. "When I got there, nobody smoked dope. By the time I left, half the people there were smoking dope."

Another change was in the aggressiveness of the enemy. "It was almost eerie how quiet it got toward the end of the year. Nobody knew why. We found out later, of course, that they were getting ready for the Tet Offensive."

The casualty rates at the end of 1967 were much lower. "The only thing we did that was really dangerous was called 'road running.' We'd run the tracks up and down the roads at

high speed at night to make sure the roads weren't being mined by the enemy."

With three weeks left in his tour, Dyrud was called into the headquarters office at Cu Chi to do "charge of quarters" work. His duty was to man the office at night. He also was called over on occasion to identify the bodies of men in his company who had been killed in action.

Finally, on Jan. 10, 1968, Dyrud got on a plane headed back to the United States. With the help of the international dateline, Dyrud also arrived in California on Jan. 10, and he was mustered out that day. By the next morning, he was back in Minneapolis.

"I thought I'd hang around and draw unemployment for a while, but I was too wired up for that. Three days later I took a job as a bread delivery guy."

That started a long odyssey for Dyrud that included time in San Francisco, a cruise on a halibut fishing boat in Alaska, two years in Europe, working on a Norwegian freighter, and time in Albuquerque, New Mexico.

Back in Thief River Falls, he took a job and was later laid off from the Arctic Cat company. He took a job as the county veterans service officer, half time. He worked there for three years, and he did a stint working in the psychiatric unit at the local hospital. Later, he took a job as a claims representative at the Fargo federal office. In 1985, he became supervisor of the claims division of the Department of Veterans Affairs at the Whipple Federal Building in Minneapolis.

He is presently the commissioner of the Minnesota Department of Veter-

ans Affairs.

Through the years, he has helped hundreds of veterans with claims, many of whom developed post-traumatic stress disorder. "I had PTSD before it was invented," Dyrud said. "That description only came around in the late 70s, but so many veterans had it through the years."

Dyrud notes that he did little to address his own situation until recent years. "It's just like the plumber who never fixes his own leaky faucets."

Through his years of working with veterans, he has found that one way for combat veterans to deal with PTSD is for them to talk about their experiences. "It's just not a good idea to let it fester, because later in life it will start burbling up. For some veterans, the more it burbles, the more they clamp down.

"Once they start dealing with it, they get a tremendous sense of relief. And then the healing process can begin."

IN COMBAT

Clark Dyrud has spent much of his life helping others deal with the personal cost of war.

PART OF THE SECRET WAR
Khao Insixiengmay and his American-made M-16 rifle were part of a guerilla force that fought the communists in Laos.

Unless indicated otherwise, all photos are from Khao Insixiengmay's personal collection.

FREEDOM FIGHTER

Khao Insixiengmay fought against the communists in his native Laos for 13 years, and he spent another dozen years in a prisoner of war camp. He was part of what is now called the "Secret War" in Laos, part of the larger war to the east in Vietnam. Insixiengmay is now a U.S. citizen and helps other Lao people to adjust to a new culture.

His experience in fighting the war against the communists began in 1962 when he was 18 years old.

He was wounded for the first time when he was captured. The enemy tied telephone wire around his arms so tight that he still bears the scars 44 years later.

He escaped and rejoined his nation's army.

He was wounded the second time by a grenade that almost blew his legs off. He recovered, and rejoined his nation's army.

He trained in France and the United States, and worked his way up to the rank of major.

After 13 years of fighting, the war ended. He was put in a prison camp where he stayed for 12 years. When he was finally released, he moved to America.

For Khao Insixiengmay, the war in Southeast Asia was an experience that involved a quarter century of his life. The first 13 years were spent in fighting a variety of enemies of his homeland of Laos: the Chinese, the

Vietnamese, and the Pathet Lao. The last 12 years were spent serving time in a prisoner of war camp and being called a traitor to his country.

Insixiengmay was born and raised in the city of Savannakhet along the Mekong River in southern Laos. Across the river was Thailand.

His father had been a soldier, fighting for the colonial French. Insixiengmay initially had dreams of being an English teacher, but he gravitated toward the military.

He enlisted to be a pilot, but when it came time to take his physical, he found out he was too short. Instead he was sent to a military school in Vientiane, the capital of Laos. The nation needed officers, and so after only one year's training he was made a warrant officer and sent to duty in January, 1962.

Insixiengmay was made a platoon leader in the 15th Airborne regiment of the Royal Lao armed forces. The regiment was soon sent to the very northern tip of Laos to take on both the North Vietnamese and the Chinese troops who had occupied that

part of Laos. The Pathet Lao, or the native Lao communists, was also part of the mix.

The fighting near Louang Namtha provided a quick education for Insixiengmay. "They asked me to go out to the rear of the North Vietnamese forces and disrupt their line of com-

munications. They chased us out. We had been taught in school that we were the bravest and the strongest, and this was the first time I learned that they were stronger than we were. This was real, and they chased us away.

"We had to hide in the bushes for a day with no food. It was raining, and we were surrounded by the enemy." In the end, Insixiengmay was able to get away.

As the year wore on, he was commissioned and became the executive officer of his company. His company went in to reinforce another company and they were engaged in a battle that went on for three days and three nights.

"In the morning, I went to see the company commander. He was sharing a foxhole with the other company commander, and it was hit by a shell. They were both dead." Insix-

iengmay was 18 years old and in charge of both companies.

The strength of the companies had been reduced by 50-percent casualties in that action, and so they were combined into one company. Insixiengmay was ordered to take his men north and engage the Chinese. There were reports that 7,000 Chinese troops had crossed the border.

"We tried to make an ambush on the Chinese, but our forward position fired too early. Instead of following the road, the Chinese circled behind us and ambushed us." Insixiengmay moved his forces into a new position, but once again the Chinese attacked from the rear.

"They did it differently than any military tactics we knew. We weren't prepared for this kind of warfare. This was a different strategy. They were too smart."

Later that night, in the dark, Insixiengmay was grabbed by a Chinese soldier. "I just gave him my carbine and took off running. They chased us. I could see the tracer bullets going by me, and I think I ran faster than the bullets. I ran for four hours." In the end, Insixiengmay's force was reduced from 135 soldiers to 75.

The Royal Lao army was in full retreat and disarray. Insixiengmay was told to provide a rear guard while the army escaped into Thailand. "They said we had the strongest company, and we were to stay behind. We walked west for five days and five nights."

Insixiengmay was only about 30 miles from the Thai border, and he and his companion were already dreaming about getting a good meal in a Thai restaurant when they were captured. "We were talking about

«

KHAO INSIXIENGMAY

At work at the Lao Cultural Center in Minneapolis

»

DURING THE WAR

Khao was a graduate of the Fort Benning Advanced Officer's Course in 1971.

how much money we had and how good the food was going to be.

"We were looking backward and not forward, and there were about 25 of the enemy in front of us, waiting for us." Five of the enemy aimed their AK-47s at Insixiengmay from close range, and Insixiengmay was shot

through his left arm during the struggle. "They tried to kill me. I was very lucky. I felt something hot go through my arm."

It was May 17, 1962, at 4:25 in the afternoon. Insixiengmay had been in the army for about four months.

"For 15 days I was tied up." Insix-

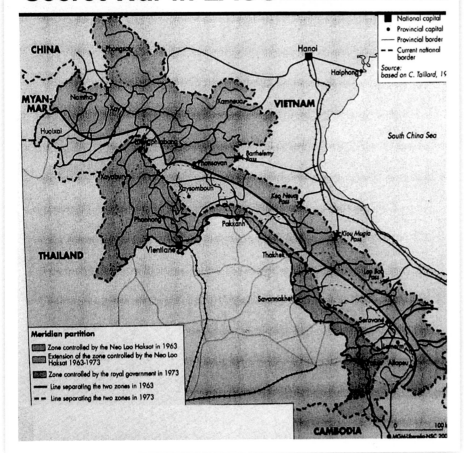

Forces Deployed During the Secret War in LAOS

US Air Force	40,000
Thai Troops	20,000
South Vietnam Troops	20,000
Royal Lao Army	87,000
= (80,000 Lao Lowland +7,000 Lao Hmong)	

LAOS AS A BATTLEGROUND

The secret war and civil war in Laos went on for over a dozen years, with the United States backing the Royal Lao government. When Vietnam fell in 1975, Laos also was taken over by the communists. The U.S. now recognizes Laos as a full trading partner.

The Secret War in Laos

Laos is a landlocked nation bordered by China and Burma (Myanmar) on the northwest, Vietnam on the east, Thailand on the west and Cambodia on the south.

In the 20th century, Laos became part of the French empire and remained a colony through World War II. Laos became independent when France was defeated in Vietnam in 1954.

The country was racked by civil war for the next two decades, and the communist forces in Vietnam were part of the nation's struggle.

The United States' presence in Laos never amounted to more than about 2,000 personnel, but the Royal Lao government was the beneficiary of millions in foreign and military aid. The CIA was heavily involved in Laos.

The civil war intensified in the 1960s, and there were several coups in the capital at Vientiane. The Royal Lao army crumbled under attack from North Vietnam, and the U.S. began a guerrilla army in Laos.

While Laos was officially neutral in those years, the guerrilas fought for a non-communist government and tried to sabotage the Ho Chi Minh trail, the main supply line to the south.

The Vietnam War ended in 1975, and the communists took over in Laos.

iengmay was bound with telephone wire around his upper arms. "They tied it too tight. My hands were swollen up and black. I cried out to them, 'Please, I feel very bad.'"

ment, Insixiengmay underwent a great deal of military training, first in France and then several times in the United States. He came to the U.S. in 1966 to Lackland Air Force

tried to push him back onto the aircraft because of the heavy fire in the area. It was too late; though, as McNaulty took a bullet in the forehead. He was the first American officer

---

"I became a very strong commander. Now it was I who could do something that the enemy did not expect."

Finally, his captors relented and Insixiengmay was released from the bondage. He and others were ordered to stay in a house with a family. There was no medicine for his wounded arm, but it healed anyway. He could tell their presence wasn't appreciated. "They didn't like people from the south. We had strange accents, and they said we were crazy."

After three months, including many sessions of learning communist doctrine, Insixiengmay discovered that his and other prisoners' lives were in jeopardy. It was time to leave. Insixiengmay led an escape with eight other prisoners. They were supposed to be foraging for food.

For seven days they walked through the rugged countryside, using the sun to get their direction since they had no compass. They finally got to the Mekong River where they called for help. The forces on the other side were suspicious. "We put our hands up and said, 'Don't shoot.'" Finally a boat was sent to pick them up.

"The first thing I did was to wash my shirt. It was full of blood and it smelled very bad."

Over the next few years, with the financing of the American govern-

Base to learn military terminology, map reading, and more English, "so we could work with the Americans."

He went to Ft. Knox and was introduced to tank warfare. He also went through officer advanced training at Fort Benning. "We had to learn to fight the American way."

Back in Laos, he was assigned to a Special Guerilla Unit, or SGU. The Royal Lao traditional army forces were being demobilized and the guerilla units were taking their place as the war in Vietnam was heating up. The U.S.

wanted to use the SGUs to harass the Ho Chi Minh Trail, running in a 50-mile corridor down the middle of Laos. The trail was used to bring supplies to the communist forces in South Vietnam.

"It was not a single trail, but a whole series of roads. If you bombed one road, they would switch to another road while they repaired the first road. There was no way to block it."

It was during this time that Insixiengmay was present for a sad historical moment. He was clearing an area of the enemy, when an American helicopter landed to bring rice to the battalion. An American officer named McNaulty got off the chopper, and Insixiengmay immediately

killed by the communists in Laos. Insixiengmay is mentioned, because of that fact, in at least one history book of the era.

Insixiengmay had been married in 1964, and he and wife had six children as the war continued on for the next 11 years.

In August, 1969, while fighting on the Plain of Jars, Insixiengmay was serving as the battalion executive officer. He was sent behind enemy lines on a mission, and a grenade went off right next to him. He was severely wounded, with five shrapnel holes in each of his legs, a lacerated arm, and pieces of metal in his eye and mouth.

A telegram was sent to his wife that he was severely wounded, and using his American connections, he was evacuated to a hospital near his home for a week. He was finally hospitalized at a U.S. Air Force hospital in Thailand for two months.

"When I was in the hospital, they needed interpreters so the American doctors could talk to the patients. So they used me. They'd push me along in my wheelchair, with my arm all bandaged up and my head in a big bandage, and I'd do interpreting."

He asked to be sent home so he

GUERRILLA OFFICERS

Khao Insixiengmay is in the front row, left, in this photo of officers of the Regimental Special Guerrilla #33 in 1973. The unit was controlled by the Royal Lao forces and by the Central Intelligence Agency.

could see his children. At that time he was still encumbered with a cast, but at his home Insixiengmay put his leg in water and, as the cast dissolved, he was eventually able to unwind the bandages.

Insixiengmay was on crutches for a long time, but he found work in the headquarters of the chief of operations in his military region. He would fly out twice a day in a small plane to gather information from the military sites on the ground and then do operational reports.

"They paid me $5 an hour, and that was great. I'd get cash at the end of the month for a thousand dollars. I thought I was a rich man."

In 1971, Insixiengmay was back in the United States at Ft. Benning for another officer's advanced course. In early 1972, he was back at duty, and his rank had risen to major.

For several years, the Lao government was involved in a battle in the highlands of Laos. The government would take over territory in the dry season when they could maneuver and use U.S. air support, and the communists would recapture the territory in the wet season. Insixiengmay said his training made a great difference in his ability to lead his troops. "Now I knew how to maneuver a unit, how to organize our forces, how to prepare for an action, how to do reconnaissance, how

WORKING WITH THE CIA

A CIA case worker meets with Guerrilla leaders in Laos. Insixiengmay, at right, was the interpreter for the session.

to patrol, how to attack.

"With what I learned, I knew I'd never be overrun again. I'd simply move my forces. I became a very strong commander. Now it was I who could do something that the enemy did not expect. I knew I could win."

Not that life was easy. Insixiengmay can't remember how many times an enemy mortar exploded only a few feet from him. Plus, because he could speak English, it was his job to call in the U.S. 104s for a bombing run, and in his advanced position, the task was very dangerous. "Sometimes I'd only be 200 meters from the target. I'd watch the air strike and almost get killed by the fragments."

One time he was observing from a building when fragments hit the frame of the window he was looking out of. He jumped for the ground, and a mortar exploded a few feet away. He was unscathed, but shaken. "I said, 'This is too much for me today.'"

After the 1973 pull-out of American forces in Vietnam, the war went downhill for the Lao forces. Insixiengmay's forces moved westward and southward to get away.

In one action, he needed to stop a column of enemy tanks, but he only had two anti-tank shells left. "I asked the gunner where the rest of the shells were, and he said they got wet and he threw them away." Insixiengmay got his men into position. "Two rounds came very close, and I was very scared. But we fired our two rounds, and the tanks turned around. I had learned at Ft. Knox that tank drivers can see very little, and if they don't know where something is coming from, they will turn around."

Over time, Khao's unit knocked out five and damaged three North Vietnamese tanks.

"I would tell our people that tank drivers are scared people. We needed to build up our confidence. This was our country, and we have a right to defend our country. I would tell our troops that the enemy has low morale, not us."

Also during this time, Insixiengmay led rescue missions that brought back nine American fliers, five from a helicopter crash and four from a supply plane crash in the jungle. "We had to move very fast to get to them before the enemy did. I didn't even wait for orders, I just went."

In 1975, as Vietnam fell, so did Laos. "The communists took over Laos not by war but by words. They were very tricky." The Royal Lao troops were told they were being gathered so they could join the new country, but instead over 30,000 were put in prison camps.

Major Insixiengmay was a prize prisoner because of his war record. He was sent to an area on the eastern side of Laos on the Vietnam border where there was little chance for escape. For several years, he was joined by his family in captivity, but when his wife got sick, she and four of their children went back home.

"Even after I was in camp for 10 years, I'd still hear my name on the radio. They were still using me as an example of a traitor to the country. But I never killed any Pathet Lao, only North Vietnamese." The prisoners did subsistence farming, and were allowed a small amount of rice most days. They often survived on potato leaves.

In 1987, after 12 years of captivity, Insixiengmay was in bad shape. "They told me I had no hope; that I would stay there forever. They said I had done crimes to the people and to the country. They said I had sided with the enemy and called in air strikes.

"I became very sick. I had diarrhea and I was almost dead. I was mentally dead too. I was almost blind.

"They still had almost 200 officers in prison camps then, and I was one of the last ones to be released."

Insixiengmay went home. He was sick, and he was broke. He had no money and little chance of making a living. Fortunately, a friend who had been released earlier and immi-

grated to the United States sent him a ticket.

For a time Insixiengmay worked in a church, and he had other jobs. He eventually became the executive director of Lao-America, an agency that helps Lao people through the problems of life in a new country, including gaining citizenship. He was able to earn money and send for his family.

Insixiengmay himself is now a U.S. citizen, but he is not entitled to any government benefits. None of the native Southeast Asian people who fought for the United States during the Vietnam War are eligible for benefits. He is not considered a veteran despite 12 years of service under U.S. command.

Insixiengmay is still struggling to bring his family to America. He was able to bring his wife and three children to America, but not three other children. One of them has since died, and he has run into a stone wall trying to bring his grandchildren over.

Overall, though, he has loved his experience in America. He is one of 300 Lao veterans in Minnesota. "I have been treated quite well."

Insixiengmay said he would like to see more recognition for the Lao veterans in the United States, and the role they played in the war. In Minnesota, because of its large Hmong population, there is some understanding of the role that group played in Vietnam and Laos, but not the other Lao. "Since the Lao people are very quiet and peaceful, we keep ourselves calm, and so it is hard to put issues that concern us out to the public."

One issue is the number of Lao veterans, particularly those who were made invalids by the war, who still live in Laos. He would like to see the American government do something to help those veterans.

And he would like to see more comradeship between the Lao veterans and the American veterans they fought alongside for so many years.

END OF THE WAR

Khao Insixiengmay, as the commander of a guerrilla unit, was present at a ceremony near the end of the war.

SEEING THINGS IN BLACK AND WHITE

Richard Bergling was at the Dong Tam combined forces base on the Mekong River when the Tet Offensive began in 1968. Years later, Bergling dealt with post-war stress by getting involved with dozens of veterans projects. His experiences caused him to see the world in black and white, with fewer shades of gray.

Dick Bergling says he tends to see things in black and white.

And one of the clearest of those clear opinions is that Vietnam veterans were not treated well by their nation when they came home.

When Bergling began to experience some dramatic psychological aftershocks, many years after the war, it led him to get involved in veterans activities, particularly in the Vietnam Veterans of America. He has held state and national offices in the VVA, and he is a member of the Anoka VVA honor guard, one of the most respected in the state.

"The VVA for me was a way to channel my anger," Bergling said at his Anoka home. "It was a constructive way, through activism. If you cut me, I bleed red, white and blue. There were issues that needed to be addressed."

Those issues included Agent Orange, POWs and MIAs and getting Vietnam veterans active in their community. Along the way, his activism led to a close friendship with U.S. Sen. Paul Wellstone, who

earned a reputation as a champion of veterans' rights before his death in 2002.

Bergling was born in Minneapolis and is a 1965 graduate of Anoka High School. "The high school years were the best years of my life. I loved high school. You don't have the responsibilities like you do later in life. It's a free period in your life."

As Bergling's high school career wound to a close, his career in the United States Navy took over. Just one week after graduation, Bergling was in boot camp at San Diego.

By the end of the year, he was in Virginia going through fire fighting, boat coxswain, cargo handling and other schools. In November 1965, he was assigned to the USS Okinawa, part of Uncle Sam's amphibious Navy. The ship was a landing platform for helicopters, and it contained a large contingent of Marines.

Bergling's goal was to get into engineering, a job in the Navy often referred to as a "snipe." He wanted to work on the engines that drove the ships. Instead he was assigned to

the boiler room.

"I was not a happy camper, but it was my first duty station. I didn't make a big stink. I did my job."

He learned his boiler technician duties as the ship finished a drydock rehabilitation, then set to sea. The first long voyage showed Bergling how good the Navy could be. "We were all over the place – Panama, Venezuela, Trinidad, Barbados, Guantanamo, St. John's, Martinique, Aruba.

"It was a beautiful cruise, and the

weather was perfect."

In mid-January 1966, the USS Okinawa set sail for the western Pacific, passing through the Panama Canal. When the ship got to Okinawa, it was cause for a major celebration as the island and its namesake were reunited.

"It was one of the most beautiful places I've ever seen in my life. It was hard to believe that 20 years earlier it was the scene of a lot of dying."

The ship was deployed to Yankee Station, off the coast of Vietnam, and spent most of its time cruising between Da Nang and the DMZ. The ship was part of PHIBRON 5, a group of ships designed to bring the Marines quickly to where they were needed.

"I was doing maintenance on the boilers and working in the fire room as a fireman. It was so hot down

there that they'd send sailors down there for punishment. I asked the chief one time, 'What did we do wrong to get sent here?' He just laughed and said, 'I hear you.' "

Sometimes the Marines would all fly in on the choppers and be gone, and then they would reappear. "We'd have no idea where they went. They just went where all Marines go."

By July, Bergling had had enough of the boiler room. "I volunteered for in-country service. I really don't think I knew what I was asking for, but I knew I wanted to do something different. I thought it might be an opportunity to get into engineering."

He was flown into Da Nang, but only long enough to catch a plane back to the United States for 30 days' leave. "My parents were surprised to see me. I hesitated to tell them what I'd volunteered for. I wasn't so sure myself."

Bergling reported back to California for survival training and Marine Corps boot camp, including small-arms training. Was he apprehensive about his new duty? "I wasn't terrified. I didn't feel that."

After training, he got another short leave in Minnesota before heading west. "I came downstairs on Thanksgiving morning, and the turkey was already in the oven. I put my sea bag by the door. My mother took one look at me in uniform and started crying.

"Twenty-two hours later, I stepped off a plane in Saigon in 120-degree heat. I could still smell that turkey cooking in the oven.

"It was the beginning of a journey I'm glad I lived. It made me the person I am today."

He went through Navy processing at Ton Son Nhut airbase, but was told not to even unpack his seabag. "I

«

DICK BERGLING

At home in Anoka

»

DURING THE WAR

Bergling was tired of the boiler room at sea and volunteered for in-country duty in Vietnam.

was just glad to get out of my blues and into some fatigues. I got some chow, and they issued me a helmet, rifle and flak jacket."

Bergling was lying in his rack, trying to sleep, when he saw something quickly run over the chest of the man in the next bed. "I said, 'Ye gods, what the heck was that?' The man didn't move a muscle, but he said, 'Don't worry about it. They keep them fed.' "

It was a rat. At three in the morning, there was a mortar attack on the base. Again, his bunkmate, without moving, said, "Don't worry, they're walking away from us."

Welcome to Vietnam. "I said to myself, 'Well, Bergling, you did it this time. Maybe this wasn't such a great idea after all.' "

He flew in a Caribou, a cargo transport, over the treetops to Dong Tam, an Army and Navy base on the Mekong River, south of Saigon. "We banged down on the tarmac, got to the end of the runway, they threw my sea bag off, and I jumped off, and they were gone. I was standing in the middle of the runway, all by myself."

After about five minutes, a Jeep picked him up and took him to the Navy side of the base, where he was assigned to a hooch. The Navy had converted a rice paddy into a harbor at the base, and it was full of boats that patrolled the river. His unit was part of the Riverine Force.

Much to his dismay, Bergling was again assigned to a boiler on the base. "I never complained in the Navy. I just did what I was supposed to do."

The boiler job, however, had only lasted a month when the Navy hired a Korean civilian contractor to run the boiler. This freed Bergling for other duties, including base security, bunker duty, working at the repair facility for the river boats, and going out with the boats. "We didn't travel far, maybe two or three miles. We'd bring the patrols out, and we'd bring them back."
And he got to do engineering on the boats, finally doing the work he had been chasing for half a world.

Bergling was at the base during the Communists' Tet Offensive in 1968.

"Tet changed my life. It didn't change my political beliefs, but it changed the way I looked at the world. Everything became more black and white, with fewer shades of gray. I wouldn't want to live through it again, but I wouldn't give it up for anything. I remember praying at the time, 'Lord, don't make me a coward.' "

The base was surrounded by an earth berm. "They were silt embankments. For six months a year, they were powdery, and for the other six months they were like wet cement. At night, they glowed incandescent. You could see a gnat crawling over it."

MAN'S BEST FRIEND

The sailors at the base were allowed to keep dogs, and Bergling posed with two of the pets.

On that night of January 30, 1968, it was the Viet Cong coming over the embankment. "That was the first time in my life that I ever fired a rifle at a human being. You come to the

Bergling's tour ended in January 1969, and he headed home. If he expected a welcome, he was wrong. "We were fighting a war for those people. I wondered 'what in the

"It was what started my internal anger at my own country. As I saw more vets treated with open hostility when they came home, over time I became more and more angry."

"Tet changed my life. It didn't change my political beliefs, but it changed the way I looked at the world."

realization that it's the right thing to do. You either live or die by the decision you make.

"You find that life is all about taking care of your buddies. You find that you're involved in something bigger than yourself. It changed my perspective on what it's all about. Are you willing to die for that issue?"

In the morning, there were 200 enemy bodies at the foot of the embankment. "And that was just the beginning of Tet. I later came to have great respect for the Viet Cong and the North Vietnamese Army. They were also willing to die for what they believed in."

Bergling's tour of duty after Tet was less intense, and not one man in his unit was killed. The boats were shot at many times, but not in a concerted way. Occasionally, the patrols would lose a soldier to a booby trap or ambush.

"Once, a patrol came back with some Viet Cong suspects. They brought back one of their own wrapped in a poncho. The people were very quiet. We went about doing our work. Nobody inquired. It was none of our business.

"Everybody looked at that body lying there, and knew it could be them. It raises that specter of mortality."

world's going on with my country?' " Bergling said he knew comrades who changed into civilian clothes at airports on their way home because they felt safer that way.

Bergling said he went into the VFW club in Anoka and was told to leave. "We don't serve your kind," someone said.

THEY WERE SAILORS ONCE, AND YOUNG

Bergling, in the center, enjoys a cold one with his Navy comrades on their day off.

MEKONG RIVER BOAT

Artist Tom Nielsen depicted the type of boat that Bergling and many others in the Mobile Riverine Task Force used as part of the "Brown Water Navy."

"I tried getting on with my life, yet it was hard. There was something inside me eating away at me. I had a tough time living in this multi-colored world when I saw everything in black and white."

As the years went by, Bergling's interior battles did not subside. It all culminated one day when he had a major blowout with his in-laws. "My marriage was on shaky ground anyway. All this stuff came pouring out of me. I couldn't stop. I had held it back all those years.

"My wife told me to get help, or we were all done."

Bergling found his way to the Vet Center on University Avenue in St. Paul, where free counseling to veterans was offered. "They identified some things for me, but they also opened a can of worms. I had more issues coming out than I did going in."

What was helpful for Bergling was his exposure to other Vietnam veterans. "I hadn't been around that many veterans. I was surprised to find that other people felt the same way I did. I wasn't as distorted as I thought I was."

That connection with fellow veterans led him to the Vietnam Veterans of America. "Most guys are too independent, and there's no way they'd trust an organization. But I needed to channel some of the anger. I needed a constructive outlet. It's no slam on the big three veterans' organizations, but in 1986, the VVA was the only one addressing Vietnam veterans' issues."

Bergling got involved in a big way, forming a chapter of the organization in Anoka. "We had to get 35 guys to sign up to get our charter in 1989. It wasn't easy, but we did it."

By 1990, he was president of the state council for the VVA, serving two terms. The organization ex-

panded from eight to 14 chapters during his terms. By 1997, he was serving on the National Board of Directors of the VVA.

In the first meeting of his new Anoka chapter, he told his comrades, "This chapter is yours. Do what you want."

"But I wanted the chapter to be a force in the north metro area. I thought it was time the Vietnam vets got off their rear-ends and started doing something positive."

The chapter worked on food shelves and other community projects. The chapter did Adopt a Highway and worked on MIA/POW awareness. It did symbolic walks to bring attention to missing children. Soon the chapter grew to 80 members. "It's a looser organization, not as structured as the Legion or VFW. It's part of the rebellious side of us."

Bergling eventually also joined the VFW, and when he helped his post move equipment one time, he was

FORMER RICE PADDY

The Navy and Army carved a harbor out of a former rice paddy along the Mekong River. The boats are tied up at left.

rewarded with a lifetime membership. "It's funny. They wouldn't serve
me in 1969, but in 1989, they bought
me a life membership."

As head of the VVA, Bergling served
on the Commander's Task Force
with other state veterans group
commanders, including Dan Ludwig
of the American Legion. He got to
know many in the veterans community. Bergling said he learned softer
ways to get Vietnam veterans' issues
discussed. "It worked a lot better
than just telling somebody they were
full of crap."

Along the way, he arranged a short
meeting with Sen. Paul Wellstone to
discuss veterans' needs. The meeting lasted two hours, and he and
Wellstone became friends.

DONG TAM

The base consisted mainly of Quonset huts and other metal buildings. The berm, where much of
the fighting was done during the Tet Offensive, can be seen in the background.

When Wellstone stood in front of the Vietnam Veterans Memorial in Washington, D.C., to make a political statement at the beginning of his term, Bergling called him. "I told him, 'I might make a political statement, but I wouldn't do it in front of your Wailing Wall. The vets fought for your right to express yourself, but don't do it on our sacred ground.'"

Wellstone apologized and vowed to make it right with veterans. "We held his feet to the fire and made sure he did."

In recent years, Bergling turned his attention to his church, serving as chairman of the elder's board and chairman of the church council. "During those bad years, I was mad at God, too. I've since repented for that sin."

One of his proudest accomplishments was in 1997 when the chapter formed an honor guard to work at funerals, and he became a member.

The color unit started slowly, but has become a sought-after honor team at funerals in the Twin Cities. The team will often do over 200 funerals a year.

"We started out in blue jeans, but we changed to fatigues and ball caps. We have special hats for wintertime."

His work in the VVA has changed Bergling's life. "It was more than I ever envisioned. I'm very proud of it, even though pride is a sin. It's beyond my wildest dreams."

His black-and-white world still doesn't understand some of the finer distinctions other people might find. "I see Vietnam as the price we are willing to pay for our way of life. America lives in a bubble, and the government does a good job of keeping us in the bubble. Two-thirds of the world wants what we have. They want that bubble."

America, he said, must be willing to fight for its survival. "When it comes time to step up to the plate, we'd better have people who are willing to step up to the plate. Or it's all gone."

Bergling is a toolmaker at Tooling Science in Anoka. He and his wife, Mary, have two children, Johanna and Erik.

This past year, he organized a special veterans' ceremony at his 40th high school reunion. Each Vietnam veteran came up and was presented with honors by the school principal.

Bergling said he hoped the ceremony helped to heal the differences between those who served and those who protested the war from his class.

"Never again should we have troops come home and have to sneak into our country. I hope that's a lesson we learned well from Vietnam."

BUNKER POSE

An unfortunate aspect of preserving the soldier's and sailor's history of the Vietnam War was the proliferation of Kodak Instamatic cameras that produced fuzzy pictures almost every time. Bergling is shown at Dong Tam on top of sand bags.

Unless indicated otherwise, all photos are from Mike Clark's personal collection.

HOPING THE CHOPPER WASN'T FOR HIM

Mike Clark was an easy-going guy. He let the Army pick his school, and it made him a medic. For nine months, he was there whenever somebody yelled for a medic, no matter what the conditions. He hoped that the Medevac would never come for him, but one day on patrol a grenade showered shrapnel through his legs.

Anybody who's ever watched a war movie has seen the scene where a brave soldier is engaging the enemy and suddenly takes a bullet.

And — as the bullets are whizzing by and the bombs are exploding and the grenades are flying through the air — what's the first thing he and his buddies scream?

"Medic!!!"

Mike Clark knew that call well. During his tour of duty in Vietnam, he served as an Army medic. "It was important that the guys have confidence in their medic. And so if it was at all possible to get there, I would. We didn't run blindly to our deaths, but if it was possible, we got there."

The job was to keep the soldier alive until he could be evacuated to a hospital. Even in the jungles of Vietnam, a wounded man could often be in a hospital setting within 20 minutes of when the medical helicopter touched down.

Growing up in St. Cloud, Clark never suspected that there would come a

day when he would be a medic. And, as a medic, he never knew when that medevac chopper would be coming for him, but it did.

Clark graduated from St. Cloud Tech High School in 1965, and two weeks later he was at basic training at Fort Knox, Kentucky.

"I wanted to join up, and it was just a matter of which one I picked. I got seasick one time on Lake Mille Lacs, so I ruled out the Navy. The Air Force uniforms weren't that neat. They looked like postal uniforms.

"I liked the Marine dress blues, and my dad was a Marine, but they couldn't take me right away. And so it was the Army. There was no delay getting into the Army."

Clark did well on his tests, and was asked what schools he would like to apply for. "I told them, 'You pick it.' They picked medic school. All I knew is that I didn't want to be an Airborne Ranger or anything like that."

Clark was hoping his military career would take him to Germany. "I

wanted to try their strong beer and frolic with the frauleins." In fact, most of his class at Fort Sam Houston did go to Germany, but Clark was kept back to take additional operating room training.

For several months, Clark was stationed at Fort Leavenworth, Kansas, but he found the work tedious. He asked his first sergeant if he could transfer to an infantry outfit. "He said, 'Clark, are you crazy? Well, it's your funeral.' "

In April 1966, Clark was at Fort

Riley, Kansas, where the Ninth Division was being formed up. In fact, Clark was one of the first people there, which meant he got the job of going around the massive camp and painting over all the signs that said, "Big Red One." The First Division had just left Fort Riley for Vietnam.

By October, the division began packing for duty overseas. Many of the men still had dreams that they would be stationed in Europe or some other choice locale. "But then the Junction City newspaper ran a story that the Ninth Division would be heading to the Mekong Delta in Vietnam."

Clark was assigned, as a medic, to the headquarters unit of the Ninth Division, Fourth Battalion, 39th Infantry. He was assigned to Company A.

The men in the division were not officially informed of their destination until they were several days at sea aboard the troop ship General Alexander Patch. "I was lucky because I was already an E-4. We were sharing a room above sea level that had two portholes. I felt guilty, but not guilty enough to want to join those guys down in the hold.

"On December 26th, we pulled into Okinawa, and they put us in a restricted area where we all got drunk. Back on the ship it was awful, with everybody sick, toilets overflowing, the works."

The troops went ashore at Vung Tau, which was an Australian-run port of entry into Vietnam. "The Aussies strung two bodies of VC up in the trees with a big sign that said, 'Welcome, Yanks.' I was wondering what kind of deal is this? I mean we had just stepped on shore."

The bulk of the division got on trucks and was transported inland to Bearcat Base. Along the way, the Australians were guarding the road and yelling encouragement to the new combatants like, "Only a year to go, Yanks."

The division had to build up the base, do sandbagging, and begin to do patrols in the area of the base, mainly to build up its own stamina in the heat.

"I found out pretty quick that the two canteens they wanted us to carry weren't enough for me. When guys would get dehydrated, I'd give them my water, and I'd soon be out. I started carrying six canteens."

The first casualty in Clark's unit was a soldier from Michigan who was shot one night by another American soldier in the dark. It was an honest mistake, Clark said, and the real tragedy was that the soldier who shot him later committed suicide.

The patrols from Bearcat kept going

«

MIKE CLARK

At home in Anoka

»

DURING THE WAR

Clark was a young soldier during the Vietnam War.

further and further into the countryside, and began encountering more booby traps and more quick ambushes. The country itself was a major enemy.

"There were the damn leeches that would fall on you, and the swarms of mosquitoes, and the fire ants. If a fire ant was biting you, it felt like someone pinching you really hard. When a guy got a bunch of fire ants on him, we'd just take his clothes off him and try to beat the ants off of him."

And, from shorter patrols at the beginning, the soldiers were now going out for weeks at a time. "We never knew how big the whole effort was. It might have been a whole battalion, but all we knew was our little platoon and where we were."

Clark said a soldier never knew how he would react to being in a combat situation until it happened, and the same for medics. "What they taught us in medic school and what I learned in the operating room didn't prepare me for Vietnam. The first time out, you didn't know if you'd freeze or not. You're going to see a lot mutilated men. It was the stomach wounds I hated the worst."

When a medic arrived on the scene, he would first ask the wounded man where he was hit, but then not trust that completely. "One wound may hurt more, but it may not be the worst wound. You'd just try to stop the bleeding anyway you could, and do whatever else you could to keep the guy alive. I did two tracheotomies while I was there. That's a pretty scary thing."

The use of morphine was always controversial, and the medics had to do paperwork to show where every dose had gone. "I would always leave the Syrette in the guy's clothing so that they'd know at the hospital that I'd given him morphine."

Clark always carried an M-16. He was offered a .45 pistol when he got to Vietnam, but turned it down because he had never trained on it. "Until I was needed as a medic, I'd fire it. I wasn't anxious to kill people, but I did want us all to get home. I can't say I ever did kill anyone. You're usually firing at muzzle flashes or shadows."

It was important for a medic to earn the confidence of the men, Clark said. And part of that was a quick response to their call. Still, there was some common sense that went with it. "I learned from another

HEADING FOR THE CHOPPERS

At a landing zone, soldiers head for the Hueys that will transport them to a patrol that may take as much as several weeks.

Huey
UH-1 Iroquois

UH-1 Helicopter data

Manufacturer
Bell Helicopter

Engine
One Lycoming T53-L turboshaft, 1,100 horsepower

Crew
One to four

Armament
Two M60 machine guns

Maximum Speed (clean)
135 miles per hour

Ceiling
19,000 feet

Range, loaded
315 miles

Capacity
3,880 pounds including 14 troops or six stretchers

medic that you don't have to run directly at a wounded man. Sometimes it makes sense to come at him from the side or the rear. You try to run where the fire will be the least. It's no good to that guy if you get killed or wounded on your way to him."

Being in the countryside at night could be scary, Clark said. "I remember waking up one night and finding out that every one of the guys in my squad was asleep. To this day, I don't sleep well if there are noises I don't understand."

On one patrol, Clark's unit brushed up against an entire North Vietnamese company. "We just hunkered down and hoped nobody would see us. If they did, we were goners. After they passed, we called in the artillery and got the heck out of there."

The division eventually moved out of Bearcat entirely, and parts of it began operating in the Mekong Delta. "I didn't like the Delta very much. You'd get in mud up to your waist, and it was like moving through a vat of glue. If you came under fire, there wasn't much you could do. You were just stuck in the paddies."

SLOGGING

Clark heads down a path in Vietnam, following his comrades. On his back he carries extra medical supplies and extra canteens of water.

The wet terrain also meant a constant battle with trench foot for the men, and bad feet put more men in the hospital than anything else.

By now, Clark's platoon was not at-

then."

"I didn't like the artillery camps very much. They had bunkers, and so they had rats. You don't get a very good sleep at night with rats run-

"You don't get a very good sleep at night with rats running over you all the time. And then, of course, the snakes would come after the rats."

One time, the unit was heading for high ground to be picked up by the Huey helicopters, but the men were stuck fast in the mud. The helicopters hovered over the men and let them grab onto the skids. "As the chopper lifted off, you could hear these loud sucking sounds."

tached to any base. It would patrol for a few weeks, then come back into the relative shelter of an artillery base, which it would guard. The time at the artillery base was considered rest time. "Your clothing would rot away, and you'd have to get new clothes every now and

ning over you all the time. And then, of course, the snakes would come after the rats."

Clark recalled a time when the platoon bumped into an enemy company and got into a firefight. "We

NEWS BREAK

Clark takes a break at base camp by catching up on the hometown news by reading the St. Cloud Daily Times.

called in the artillery, and they were right on the mark. When they were done, we got out of there. We were there to observe and not to engage. That was a scary night."

The next day, Clark had to be evacuated to a hospital because of the dust in his eyes from the artillery attack. They put gloop in my eyes and covered it with an eye patch. That was the first night I'd slept in a bed since I'd been in 'Nam, and I slept hard. I dreamed that somebody had gone nuts. The next day they told me that a guy a couple beds down had gone nuts and they had to subdue him."

Back at an artillery base, Clark was watching the men at the base launching mortars. "All of a sudden, there was one that didn't have the usual sound. It had kind of a tinny sound. All the guys started yelling. The round had gone straight up, and it was coming straight down."

Clark began to run, but soon stopped and just hit the deck. "I realized I couldn't get away from it, so what the hell? I just lay there." The mortar round landed six feet away from him, but didn't explode. The

firing pin failed to come out. "I had my share of luck with me."

Because of his role as medic, Clark found out that he had other, unusual duties at times. "The men would sometimes come to me with their personal problems. I guess I was as close as they could get to a counselor, or a father confessor. I'd do the best I could with my advice."

The best psychological stance, Clark said, was to take it day by day, and to not ever consider how much time you had left on your tour of duty. He saw one medic refuse to go into combat because of supposed moral objections. That soldier ended up at Leavenworth Prison. Another time, Clark witnessed a fellow soldier calmly put his M-16 up to his shoulder and pull the trigger.

"The sergeant came up and started yelling at the guy, 'You're not going to get out of this war that easy. You'll be back. You'll be back.' But they took him out on medevac, and we never saw him again."

The war was a tough adjustment for anyone, he said. "I grew up a Catholic, but no matter what your religion, you believed in the sanctity of life. Over there, there was no sanctity of life. We were trying to kill people because they were trying to kill us. And pretty soon that just seemed to be the normal way of life."

Clark said he had a few run-ins with officers in his time. On one occasion, his platoon had killed some armed Viet Cong, but then found out that the enemy soldiers had brought their families with them. An injured 10-year-old girl was among them.

"The lieutenant colonel was circling overhead in his helicopter and saw we were trying to evacuate the girl so she could get medical care. He told us to leave her. I got on the radio and told him we weren't leaving her."

It was hard slogging through the jungle carrying the girl on a poncho. "We did slow the platoon down, but after a few hours we got to our objective, and the girl was medevaced out."

The next day, Clark was called over to see the officer. "He really scared me. He had six purple hearts, and he was something of a legend. I didn't know what he was going to say

A COLD ONE

Clark enjoys a beer on his day off at an artillery base.

THE LATEST AMENITIES

Shower stalls at a base camp were strictly utilitarian.

about saving the girl. I was really scared."

The officer fixed Clark with a level gaze, paused, and said, "I've really got a headache. Do you have any APCs?" Clark quickly produced the medicine. "He just said, 'Thank you,' and that was it."

Another time, Clark's unit was crossing a stream when one of his comrades took an AK-47 round in the chest and was killed instantly. "He was a good friend of mine, and he was from Minnesota. He also had a great sense of humor. His name was Larry Welk, and at this time Lawrence Welk was very popular. I used to joke with him about the champagne bubbles, and he'd always laugh."

Back at the base, Clark was asked to take Welk's personnel records to the battalion office. Once there, the lieutenant behind the desk casually cracked a joke about Larry Welk's name. This time Clark didn't think it was very funny, and a shouting match broke out between him and the officer.

The officer called in a sergeant and ordered that Clark be arrested, and the sergeant quickly hustled Clark out the door. As a parting remark, Clark turned and called the lieutenant a "staff weenie."

The next day, as to be expected, Clark was called into the first sergeant's office. Clark expected the worst. The first sergeant looked him up and down and finally said, "Doc, maybe it's time you had a rest. There's openings for the R&R camp up in Taiwan. Why don't you take a few days off?"

"I didn't want to take my R&R right then. I wanted to wait until November. But then I thought, I might not be alive in November. So I said yes. And that's how I got my R&R."

One day, after his return to duty, a replacement came in. "You could tell he was new, because he was husky. All of us were skinny from being in country for so long. After a few weeks, he complained that his feet were bad and he couldn't go on patrol. The captain told me to look at his feet and make a recommendation. I examined him, and I told the captain that the guy's feet weren't any worse than any of ours."

The next day, the replacement not only went on patrol with the platoon, but he was put on the point. Sometime later, as Clark was marching along, he heard gunfire and the call for "medic!!!"

Sure enough, it was the replacement, wounded in the chest and bleeding profusely. Clark did what he could to stop the bleeding, but wasn't having much success. A medevac helicopter tried to land, but was driven off by enemy fire. Clark saw another chopper hovering overhead, the executive officer of the unit.

"I got on the radio and asked that he pick this man up. He didn't want to. He didn't want blood all over his helicopter. I told him, 'If this man dies, you're going to have some blame in it.' He came down, and we loaded the guy into the chopper. I knew I made an enemy, but I didn't care. All I wanted at that point was to do my job and go home."

Not long after that, Clark was accompanying what he now calls the "Buddha Patrol." He and a squad were in a hostile village when they poked their heads into a building that was full of candles and religious pictures.

"The guys thought those pictures were really cool, and they started taking them. I told them not to, it was a religious shrine, but they didn't care."

A week later, that same squad, without Clark, was on patrol and was ambushed. Several were killed, and every man was wounded. "It was sort of a message, karma, or whatever you want to call it. They shouldn't have taken those pictures."

Superstition and ritual were all part of the survival skills of the Americans in Vietnam, Clark said. One of the superstitions had to do with him. "I was considered good luck by some of the guys. I suppose it was because I'd been under fire so much and never been hit. I had bullet holes in my backpack, and bullet holes through the floppy end of my jungle fatigues, but I'd never been hit. Our RTO (radio operator) Lydes Gardner always walked with me on patrol because he thought I was good luck."

One example of his fortune happened when Clark's unit was in a firefight in a rubber plantation. Clark went to treat a wounded soldier, but found the man was dead. "I heard a slight noise and saw a VC pointing what looked like an American .45 at me. I didn't have my rifle, but I reached for a .38 I'd got from an aircrew. As I fell, he fired, and the round cut my jacket at upper stomach. I'd almost lost big time in my only 'Old West' shootout."

Clark described his last patrol. "We were rousted out in the darkness and told to get our stuff together. We had a new medic, and I couldn't find him. He was hiding. When I did find him, I tried to reassure him and get him ready. We went to the assembly area, and the choppers arrived. We got on the Hueys, and it was still dark."

Clark said the mission was fairly routine. On the third day out, the unit was crossing a stream. "As usual, Gardner was right behind me. I stepped out into the stream, but I just had a bad feeling about this branch over us. I turned just in time to see Gardner reaching up for the branch, and then the grenade fell out."

The grenade exploded at waist level, killing Gardner instantly and sending a shower of shrapnel into Clark's legs. "I knew enough as a medic that it wasn't life-threatening unless I went into shock. It might be crippling, but it wasn't life-threatening. I was glad to see the new medic come right up and start to treat me. That meant he was okay."

The medic offered Clark morphine. "I turned it down because I thought he might need it later for someone else. I regretted that later."

The medevac sent for Clark couldn't land in the jungle, so it lowered a cable down and Clark was hoisted upwards. "I was a little nervous about snipers, but they got me inside the chopper okay. That was the end of my war."

Clark was brought to the 24th Evacuation Hospital. The shrapnel had done considerable damage to his legs, and had severed the Achilles' tendon on one leg. "There has been some long-term effect, but at the time I thought it was a million-dollar wound."

An interesting sidelight was when he was in his bed one day and he looked up to see the replacement who had been hit after Clark had told him his feet were okay for duty. Clark was a little apprehensive, but

the soldier simply thanked him for his help on the battlefield and said how happy he was to be going home.

Surgery was done on Clark, and he was eventually evacuated to a hospital in Japan, where the doctors were fighting an infection in one leg. "They put me in the amputee ward. They said it was because they didn't have any room anywhere else, but you have to wonder. It's a very hum-

bling experience to be in an amputee ward as the only guy who didn't have an amputation. Guys had one, two or three limbs gone, but for the most part they were very upbeat. They only worried about how their girlfriends would react to them."

The infection finally cleared up, and Clark was sent back to Fort Riley. He served out his full three years in the Army, although he could never do

PROBABLY NOT HOW IT LOOKED IN MINNESOTA

Clark unwraps a cake sent from home.

physical work or exercise again. The wounds healed slowly and left one of his legs noticeably smaller than the other. "I can walk okay, but it affected my gait, and that seemed to affect everything else — my legs, my hip and my back."

Doctors at the VA Medical Center in Minneapolis still pluck a piece of metal from Clark's legs every few years.

Clark said he drifted around a while after his discharge but eventually earned a degree in teaching from Macalester, and a master's as a media specialist at St. Cloud State University. He taught in several schools, spending most of his career in an elementary school near Princeton.

In 2001, his position was cut by the school because of budget problems. At the same time, Clark's disability rating was raised to 100 percent because of recurring PTSD. He has been retired since.

He said the PTSD is better these days, but for many years, the anniversary of his wound, September 6, 1967, was traumatic for him. He would dwell on the loss of his good friend Gardner as he contemplated his own life.

"I've been very lucky. My wife, Mary, has always been there for me. She is my rock." The couple have two grown sons and four grandchildren and live in Anoka.

Clark feels a deep sense of responsibility to give back to his country. "Retirement for me doesn't mean sitting on my butt watching TV. I like to work with my fellow vets. They're my therapy group. We don't talk about the war very much, but we support each other."

Clark is active with the Vietnam Vet-

erans Color Guard, a unit that serves at funerals throughout the Twin Cities. It is known as one of the best color guards in the state. Clark is also active in the Anoka Post 102 American Legion, the DAV, the VFW, the Purple Heart Association and other service groups. "I'm easy to talk into things."

In the end, he said, he is grateful to have served. "I worked around some very brave people. Those infantry men just go out there into Indian Country. They slogged through it over and over and over again. And then they'd get up and do it again.

"There were so many medics in Vietnam that were killed or wounded. A lot of those medics were just something special. It was a humbling experience just to be around them. I'm awed at what they did. I don't know how I got through it."

ON CRUTCHES

Mike Clark was back home in St. Cloud after his duty in Vietnam, still on crutches after his encounter with a booby trap grenade. He's with his mom, Marion.

HEADING OUT

Lt. John Hobot's platoon rolls out of the gate at Tallil Air Force Base in southern Iraq to protect a convoy heading north.

Unless indicated otherwise, all photos are from John Hobot's personal collection.

PROTECTING THE CONVOYS
IN IRAQ

Whenever an American convoy hit the road in Iraq, it was in grave danger from explosive devices or from a weapons attack. Lt. John Hobot headed a platoon whose job it was to protect the convoys. Before their tour was complete, 22 months later, they had protected 80 convoys.

John Hobot knew he would be joining the military as soon as he heard about the terrorist attacks on September 11, 2001.

He had other reasons, too. His grandfather, Walter S. Hobot, served as a Marine in the Pacific in World War II. "I had always thought about joining the military."

Up to that point, Hobot had done well creating a civilian life for himself.

He was born in Edina, grew up in Brainerd then moved to Chaska when he was 14 years old. At Chaska High School, he played football and hockey and a little golf. He was captain of the football team his senior year as an undersized running back and defensive back. He graduated in 1996.

At St. Thomas University, he majored in political science and minored in business. He considered joining the ROTC, but didn't like the four-year commitment at the end. His decision was to join the National Guard in Minnesota in December, 2002.

"There I was in basic training at 25 years old. I was a little out of shape, but after a couple of months I think I was in the best shape of my life. Basic came pretty easily to me. I was used to having coaches yell at me, and so the mental part was not hard."

As soon as basic was over, Hobot enrolled in the officer candidate program at Camp Ripley and was commissioned in August 2004. Then it was off to the field of his choice – tanks.

"I wanted to be in armor, and, so, in November I was back at Fort Knox for the armor officer basic course. They taught us anything and everything you need to know about tanks to prepare you for war."

And going to war was not just an option. "I knew when I was in the officer basic course that I was going to Iraq or Afghanistan. It was real. I'm going to war. And so everything you studied, everything you learned prepared you for war."

In April 2005, the call came to Hobot's company in the 1-34th

Brigade Combat Team that they would indeed be heading off to Iraq. In October, C Company of the 1-194th AR and several battalions from the 34th headed off to Camp Shelby, Mississippi, for more training.

"It was a very long six months to train, but we had a lot of things to learn as a brigade. It's rare that a

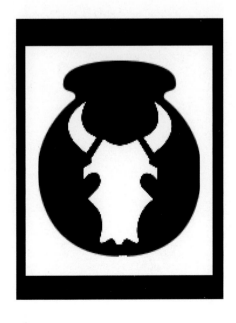

whole brigade combat team gets deployed. There were 5,000 of us to get ready, and we had to learn everything from individual soldier skills to the unit level, battalion level and brigade level."

Still, the process dragged on. "After a while, I was saying, 'Just send me to Iraq. Let's get this deployment going.' "

After a short leave during which he got engaged to his future wife, Amanda, Hobot joined his comrades in the journey over the ocean to Kuwait for, you guessed it, more training.

"For one thing, we just had to get used to the climate. Plus, it just takes a while to get all 5,000 troops there. We had to go to the ranges and re-zero our weapons and get used to going around in full battle rattle."

A soldier in Iraq will carry gear and

wear protective armor that can weigh up to 70 pounds. "Eventually you get used to it, but you do sweat a little bit."

On March 27, 2006, C Company traveled to Iraq. Hobot was a platoon leader.

The possibilities for his unit varied from running checkpoints to doing patrols to "kicking in doors." Their assignment, they found, was going to be in providing security for supply convoys.

"It's one of the most dangerous jobs in Iraq, right up there with patrolling. It's in the top three most dangerous anyway, and I don't think anybody can argue with that."

Charlie Company was assigned to Talill Air Force Base in southern Iraq, about 190 miles south of Baghdad. Supplies would come into the base and would have to be shipped to Baghdad and other points in Iraq. The supplies would be loaded in a 38-truck convoy.

Hobot's job was to make sure those supplies got to where they were headed, and to make sure nobody got hurt along the way. It was a difficult mission with the Iraqi insurgents determined to stop them.

The unit lived in tents for a month, then moved into small trailers.

"It seemed to be hotter in Iraq then it was in Kuwait. Maybe because it's

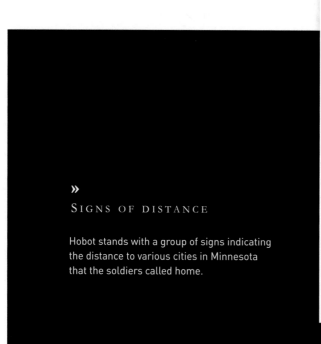

»

SIGNS OF DISTANCE

Hobot stands with a group of signs indicating the distance to various cities in Minnesota that the soldiers called home.

P L A T O O N

Early on in the deployment, the Minnesotans used LMTV vehicles to protect the convoys. Later on, they switched to ASVs, resembling a small tank.

"The ASV is like a little tank on wheels. It was as close as I was going to get to tanks in Iraq."

On May 5, 2006, the Minnesota Guard unit was on its own, and for a month Hobot's platoon lived a charmed existence. "All the other platoons were getting hit left and right, but we had a little bit of luck."

The technique his platoon used was to have two scout vehicles head up the road in front, one on either side. Hobot's command vehicle would be next, and the other vehicles would be interspersed with the convoy, with Hobot's second in command bringing up the rear. There would be six gun trucks in all.

The main danger was the roadside bombs, or IEDs. The trips were often 300 miles one way, so the Iraqi in-

out in the flat desert with no trees or anything. But it wasn't unusual to have days where it would hit 140 or 145 degrees.

"The only thing I can compare that to is when you walk outdoors in Minnesota and it's 30 below and your nostrils instantly freeze. In Iraq, in mid-August, you walk outside and your nostrils burn. It's like running a hair dryer into your nose. It makes you want to breathe through your mouth."

In Iraq, there was more training in cultural awareness and heat awareness. "You just have to drink a lot of water." And there was getting used to the idea that this was going to be your situation for the next year. "You can see what's coming. For the first time, it's real. You might say, 'Holy smokes, this is not a joke.' "

The Minnesotans were replacing the 648th Engineers out of Georgia and

went through a period of "right seat, left seat" on-the-job training. For several convoys, the Minnesotans rode in the right seats, just observing what the Georgians did. The two teams then shifted places with the Georgia soldiers observing and offering advice. In the end, the Georgians went home.

"You have to be careful, because a unit that's been here a while starts to cut corners. They know what they're doing, and they know where they can cut corners, because it helps them do their job better. As new guys, we couldn't afford to cut corners."

Hobot's platoon consisted of 22 soldiers. They drove large, heavily armored and heavily weaponed vehicles to protect the semi-trailer trucks in the convoy. The men had Humvees and LMTVs, a very large truck, to begin with. Later, they got ASVs to go along with the Humvees.

LMTV
Statistics

Light Medium Tactical Vehicle

Engine
Caterpiller 6.6-liter diesel

Crew
Two in cab.

Power
275 horsepower

Maximum Speed
94 km per hour

Fuel
JP8 (jet fuel)

Drive
4x4

surgents had a lot of territory to use in planning an assault.

The attacks might simply consist of one bomb going off. More likely, there would be small-arms fire after

"We felt pretty safe in our vehicles. The Army did everything it could to keep them safe, and they were upgrading all the time. It was about as safe as it could get, but still in the

Baghdad International Airport. There was a loud boom, and a huge fireball came across. I checked on the guys, making sure they all had their fingers and toes and that noth-

"If an insurgent wants to kill you, they'll build a big enough bomb to do it."

the bomb stopped the convoy. And in some cases, there would also be rifle-propelled grenades – called a complex attack because the enemy was using several means to try to kill the Americans.

The main thing, Hobot said, was to get the convoy moving again as quickly as possible and get out of the "kill zone." "They want to confuse you and then attack you."

As officer in charge, Hobot had several options once the convoy was attacked, including fighting back, changing lanes on the highway or moving through the kill zone.

"You just have to make a decision, what you think is right."

On June 6, one of the scout vehicles was hit by a roadside bomb. "I had to quickly assess the damage and check out the guys. They'll be checking each other out too to see if everyone's all right."

In this case, the vehicle had to be transported to Baghdad International Airport for major repairs. Another unit took the convoy to its destination.

"On June 6th, it all sunk in. The reality and the seriousness sunk in. We could have just lost three guys out there. Thank God they were not hurt.

back of your mind, you wonder. If an insurgent wants to kill you, they'll build a big enough bomb to do it."

Again, the platoon had another "lucky" streak, going a month without another incident. But following another IED on the Fourth of July, the pace picked up considerably. Hobot estimated that from that point on, one out of three convoys was attacked. "It was 'game on' after that."

The Independence Day attack was one Hobot won't forget. "It was a 130-millimeter mortar round about 10 meters from my truck, near the

ing inside was hurting."

The bomb shredded three tires on the truck, but the "run-flat" air system kept the tires inflated until the convoy got to a safe point. "There were holes in the truck, and the bullet-proof glass was cracked.

"That was a big wake-up call for me. In the back of my mind it occurred that I might not make it out of here. After that, I was more in a life-or-death mode."

The Minnesotans got better at their job, learning through experience the likely spots for attacks, how to as-

SAND STORM

Sand storms on the desert cast a pallor over the equipment.

FAMOUS LANDMARK

The platoon gathered at the famous Ziggurat of Ur with the Humvees in front and the ASVs in the rear.

sess the damage, and to return fire quickly. The battalion intelligence staff that helped the platoon, Hobot said, did an outstanding job in keeping the team informed about what it might encounter.

The platoon also changed its speed. It had been taught by its forbearers to hustle down the highway at a good speed. As time went by, though, the platoon changed the speed of the convoy to a more moderate rate. "By going slower, we were able to find the IEDs rather than hit them."

Communication was essential. Hobot's vehicle was known as "Bastard 1," and the other trucks were "Bastard 2" and so forth. All the trucks would know instantly where

the attack was coming from.

"We always shot back. Our brigade was known for stopping and fighting the enemy. When we got attacked, we got busy. Later on, I learned from interpreters that the insurgents were learning to avoid attacking the trucks with the big red bull (the 34th Division's logo) on them."

The enemy might be in a building, in a grove of trees, in the tall grass, or on the canals or wadis that are common in the Iraqi countryside.

The Minnesotans would fight back with 50-caliber machine guns and Mark 19s that fired 40-millimeter high explosive rounds. The latter weapon was especially feared by the enemy. The platoon could also call

attack helicopters to the scene.

And on it went for 80 missions. Eighty times the platoon got in its trucks and headed north to protect a convoy, and the reports on the missions fell into a dull and deadly cadence: IED, IED, small-arms fire, complex attack, IED, IED, IED, complex attack, small-arms fire, IED, complex attack.

"You get better and better at it, but at the same time you realize that you could do everything right and still get killed out there." Several in the brigade did get killed. "That was always very tough."

One of the toughest things, though, besides the enemy attacks, was the news near the end of the brigade's

CAPITALISTS

Merchants sold their gear just outside the protective gate of the fort.

year in combat that the tour of duty would be extended for four months.

"We all kind of knew it was coming. We were good at what we were doing, and why would they send us home? They needed us to support the surge."

Still, when the news came, Hobot said morale went into the toilet for a couple of weeks. "The way I told them was that I knew they were all looking forward to spending that tax-free money they were earning. I said they were going to have a lot more of that tax-free money. They just looked at me like, 'Are you kidding me?' "

Hobot said the brigade went through the classic phases of anger, denial and finally acceptance. "All you could do was suck it up and drive on. You had to turn all that anger back into the mission."

The Minnesotans were due to go home in March 2007 and instead stayed in Iraq until July and August.

Hobot's platoon got a new job for a

NIGHT MISSION

Hobot with his friend, Lt. Jon Anderson, get ready for a night mission, the most common type.

time guarding a radio relay station, then did route-clearing assignments on Iraqi roads.

It was during these later months in Iraq that Hobot often worked with an interpreter and was able to hone his Arabic speaking skills that he had learned through a special Army course at Camp Shelby.

"I got to be pretty decent at speaking the language, although I was limited to what I needed for the job. I could say, 'Do you have weapons?' and "Are you lying to me?' and 'I know you're lying to me.'

"It would throw them for a loop to hear an American speaking Arabic. And even though I didn't know that much Arabic, I made them think I did. I would spend an hour each day with my interpreter, improving my Arabic and improving his English."

The last month in Iraq was spent guarding convoys again. It was tense duty. "After 16 months of seeing my guys get attacked, just living in that operating tempo, seeing what we saw, when we did that last mission, it was like having the weight of the world lifted off our shoulders."

Despite the continuous bomb and weapons attacks, not one person in Hobot's platoon was seriously hurt.

The return home was wonderful for the brigade, with warm welcomes in Maine, where they landed, and at Camp McCoy and Volk Field in Wisconsin. There was a police and motorcycle escort to the Sauk Centre armory for the final ceremony.

"The first month back was kind of like a dream world. Am I really out here fishing?"

The hardest adjustment back home for many was simply running their lives again, Hobot said. "In the military, everything is pre-planned for

you. You don't have to do anything except do your job well. Back home, all of sudden you have to make choices about what you want to do with your life."

Another area of adjustment was the fact that 22 months had gone by. "For us who were deployed, it was like 22 months of a dream of how things used to be, but guess what, life moves on. People and things change in 22 months and can be much different than the dream world you left behind."

John and Amanda got married three weeks after the lieutenant got home. "It was good for me. All I had to do is get my tux. Amanda had done everything else for the wedding."

Hobot went back to work at General Electric in Eden Prairie, where he had worked for six years, but the job

wasn't the same. "I didn't feel right. I wasn't enjoying it any more. Plus, I was used to the responsibility of 22 guys."

Hobot did some part-time work with the National Guard, then won the job as public affairs officer in February 2008. "I'm loving it. I know I'm an armor officer, and PA is not the norm for that, but it's something new every day, different things. I enjoy it."

He says that he knows that going back to Iraq or some other overseas duty is likely. "My wife accepts that, too. There's a good possibility that I'll go back in a couple of years. National Guard people often get deployed a couple of times. The Guard used to be a strategic reserve, but now we're an operational force."

SIGHT SEEING

Hobot got a chance to visit one of Saddam Hussein's palaces in Baghdad.

A ROAD IN THE WILDERNESS
In Afghanistan, The 864th Engineering Battalion built the longest paved road the U.S. military has ever built on foreign soil.

Unless indicated otherwise, all photos are from Patrick Sullivan's personal collection.

THE LONG AND WINDING ROAD

Recently graduated from West Point, a Hibbing soldier helped lead an Army engineering battalion that built a major road between two Afghan cities. The road was a tangible demonstration of the goodwill the Americans want to promote in Afghanistan as that nation seeks peace and democracy.

First Lt. Patrick Sullivan was the All-American kid working at one of America's major projects.

The only problem was that hardly anybody in America was paying attention.

With most of this nation's media and energy focused on Iraq in the 2000s, the military presence in Afghanistan received little coverage.

Yet, in 2005, there were 18,000 American soldiers assigned there, doing their best to bring a permanent peace and democracy to a nation that has seen little of either for decades.

Sullivan's project was to build a road, where no road existed, between two of Afghanistan's major cities. It was the longest road ever built by the American military on foreign soil. It enhanced commerce in that nation. It allowed farmers to get their crops to market.

The road was completed under trying circumstances in record time in an area that had been controlled by the extremist Taliban.

Sullivan grew up in Hibbing, the son of Charlie and Shelly Sullivan, and he graduated from Hibbing High School in 1998. His grades and citizenship and potential earned him an appointment to the United States Military Academy at West Point.

He did well in the intensive Army training. Not only did he graduate 43rd in his class of 850, he also managed to complete Airborne training at Fort Benning before his graduation in 2003. After leaving West Point, he was accepted to Ranger School, also at Fort Benning, where he graduated (only about half who enter the school do graduate) in 2004.

His first leadership assignment was to Fort Lewis, Washington, where he became a platoon leader for an earth-moving unit in the 555th Maneuver Enhancement Brigade, 864th Engineering Battalion. Sullivan admits that, despite his college engineering background, bulldozers were not his specialty at that point.

"The NCOs are there, and they can teach you a lot. You just have to learn from them. The platoon sergeant had 18 years experience."

The unit's prior deployment had been to Iraq where it had rebuilt airfields. In March 2005, it began its deployment to Afghanistan.

Sullivan was sent in the advance party to prepare for the arrival of the construction unit. He was the only platoon leader sent ahead. His training as a Ranger helped prepare him for the tactical side of building things in a potentially hostile environment.

WILLING AND ABLE!

The unit brought with it initially 75 pieces of heavy equipment, shipped in huge containers that landed at the Kandahar Airfield in south-central Afghanistan. Along the way the flights had stopped in several places, and then got stuck for five days in Kyrgyzstan when civil war erupted in that country.

Finally in Afghanistan, Sullivan and the others first got a chance to learn from the 538th Engineering Battalion, which was heading home. Eventually, all the men and the equipment arrived, and the battalion set up shop in Kandahar.

The first project was to do an airfield expansion at Kandahar, creating what was called a mobility ramp — a place to park the large transport aircraft. Previously, without parking space, a plane would have to leave before another one could land.

That project was only a warm-up, though, to the main task assigned to the unit. About 80 miles north of Kandahar is another large city called Tarin Kowt. Despite their proximity, the two major centers were connected only by a dirt trail that only hardy vehicles could traverse at a slow pace.

It was a challenge to build the road through the rugged Afghan countryside, one made tougher by the fact that the hilly area had been a stronghold of the Taliban, the radical Islamic group that had ruled Afghanistan after the Russians left.

The Army planners set a deadline of February 2006 to build the road, but the task force commander, Sullivan's boss, proposed that it be done by September 15, 2005 – in time for the provincial elections. "No one thought it could be done in that time."

Sullivan's platoon of earth-moving equipment operators first worked in the south, then moved to the north, back toward Kandahar. The convoy of 60 vehicles took 15 hours to traverse 55 miles.

"There were times when we were just dragging the trailers on their axles. It was all we had left."

Progress on the project at first was slow, only about 200 to 300 feet a day. But the unit learned, and, soon was accomplishing 1,500 feet a day.

The task force commander came up with the idea of putting an operating base in the middle of the project, cutting the commute time for the engineers from more than an hour to about 10 minutes. The unit worked in two shifts, about 15 hours a day, seven days a week, with people rotated out for rest and recuper-

«

PATRICK SULLIVAN

In transit at the airport in Minneapolis

»

IN AFGHANISTAN

Sullivan was a platoon leader and later executive officer of an earth-moving unit in Afghanistan.

RUGGED TERRAIN

First Lt. Patrick Sullivan stands in front of the countryside his earth-moving unit had to cross.

ation.

"The terrain was so difficult at times that our stuff was breaking, we were pushing it so hard," Sullivan said. "We had to schedule a maintenance day or two every week."

The planners created a route that was either right against the mountains or right along the river. The roadway was two lanes with a shoulder, about 35-40 feet wide.

Problems came up when the road had to go through a village or across a farmer's field. It was one of Sullivan's jobs to barter with the local people to keep the road moving forward.

"I would meet with the elder or elders. We'd have tea and some local food. It was an amazing experience." Sullivan used an interpreter, but also learned a few words of the local language, including how to ask somebody's name.

"The kids loved that, when you'd ask them their name. I got along with the children really well." Sullivan said it was critical for the new generation growing up in Afghanistan to not fear and hate Americans. "We need to change that anti-American culture, and that started for us with building that road."

Sullivan said the Russians had spent a decade in Afghanistan and had

never won over the people.

"Afghanistan was Russia's Vietnam. For them it was a political thing. It wasn't for the betterment of the people. The people were never behind them. When you're fighting the entire population, you can't win that battle."

Once the Russians left, an era of warlords took over in Afghanistan, reducing the country almost back to a state of feudalism. The Taliban moved into that situation. "They didn't want anything to be improved."

When the Americans came on the scene, they were regarded with caution by the Afghan people. "We were just another in a line of people who wanted something from them. But we've never taken anything from them."

Working with the translator got in-

other radical group would place an "improvised explosive device," or IED, under the road bed. Often these were old Russian mines or shells. A terrorist would wait in hiding and set

detecting equipment, and the second, called a "buffalo," would be a heavily armored vehicle with a robotic arm to dig up the mine. They would be accompanied by two other

---

"If you let your guard down just a little bit over there, that can happen. Most of the people in Afghanistan like us, but some still don't."

---

teresting sometimes, Sullivan said, and, when it became obvious that the translator was freelancing too much, "I'd have to reel him in." Usually the locals were very agreeable regarding the road, or suggested detours around a town. "The people were all pro-road. The only contention was about where it went."

The Army was careful to find right-of-ways that were satisfactory to everyone. "When we'd talk, we'd joke around. You can share humor between different cultures. We'd go back and forth, and, by the end of the day, we'd have a mile of road laid out. Sometimes they wanted to bargain just because they know that Americans are so wealthy. They want to know what they can get out of the deal."

At one point, though, a farmer brought 50 supporters along to argue about the placement of the road through his field. Sullivan beefed up his platoon with extra equipment and had a rough cut made quickly through the field. The opposition, somewhat hostile at one point, dissolved when the road became a done deal.

Terrorist attacks were always a concern. "They had certain ambush spots, and they had used some of them for years." The Taliban or

off the device as a vehicle passed over it.

Part of the American plan was to respond to such attacks quickly. "If we got attacked, we wanted to be aggressive, we wanted to get these guys, or we'd be facing the same thing tomorrow."

A major help to the construction workers was a mine-detecting unit that would check the area before work every day for IEDs. The "sapper" unit consisted of four vehicles.

One would be a smaller vehicle, called a "meerkat," with mine-

vehicles with fire-power to provide aggressive support. "They were a huge asset for us. They cleared the route for us every day, and that was important because it was very obvious where we were going."

Despite the work of the mine-clearing unit, the road builders still unearthed mines. One time, there were four in one day. Fortunately, none exploded.

As the construction moved on, there were days during which three helicopters would circle the area to make sure no terrorists were

IED RESULT

A Humvee shows the results of an encounter with an improvised explosive device along the road.

PART OF THE JOB

Part of Sullivan's role was in working with the local people who would some day benefit from the road.

in the surrounding hills ready to detonate a bomb.

Just before the completion of the
road, tragedy struck. Lt. Laura
Walker, one of Sullivan's closest
friends and a classmate at West
Point, was killed by an IED.

Walker had been a platoon leader,
but had been assigned as the battalion's public affairs officer. She was
traveling with the task force commander on the new road when the
bomb exploded.

"Most of the road was paved, but not
in the low areas where the water
crosses the road," Sullivan said.
"Eventually that will be covered with
concrete, but not yet. They were able
to bury the IED in the road bed."

Setting off an IED by remote control
needs perfect timing. Too soon, and
the bomb will only strike the heavily

armored front end of the Humvee.
Too late, and the vehicle will be past
the danger. The unit had been hit
four times by IEDs, but, every time,
the bomb had been timed wrong and
the passengers had survived.

In this case, the bomb exploded
right under the driver, killing him instantly and ejecting him from the vehicle. Walker was sitting directly
behind the driver, and her legs were
severely injured. The task force
commander and the gunner were
only slightly injured. Tourniquets
were applied to Walker's legs, but
she died of blood loss before she
made it to a hospital.

"It was definitely the worst experience I ever had," Sullivan said. "It
makes me respect those World War
II guys even more. That kind of stuff
happened to them every day, but
they carried on."

"If you let your guard down just a little bit over there, that can happen.
Most of the people in Afghanistan
like us, but some still don't."

Work continued at a furious pace,
and the road was completed on September 1, two weeks before the
self-imposed deadline set by the engineers and six months ahead of the
deadline set by the Army.

Sullivan said the rapid progress was
monitored closely by the Pentagon,
and the construction scene drew
high-ranking officers frequently.

With the road completed, the task
was getting the equipment back to
Kandahar for the next mission. The
forward operating base also had to
be torn down. By the end of September 2005, everything was out.

It was time to refit the equipment,

ARMY LEADERSHIP

Sullivan, left, poses with a fellow officer while standing on a rocky hilltop.

TALKING IT OVER

The progress of the road often led to discussions with the local Afghan leadership. Everyone was in favor of the road, but not necessarily its course.

which had been used to the extreme. "We were down to bubble gum and duct tape at times. It was tough to get parts. You fixed it when you could, or just ran it till it died."

As the unit got ready to move to a new location, near the Pakistani border, Sullivan had been promoted to executive officer.

At its new location, the construction battalion immediately began constructing a base of operations, including a barracks, laundry, barber shop, chapel, first aid station, internet building for the soldiers, mess hall and 64 buildings similar to World War II's Quonset huts.

Again, Sullivan had little experience in what the Army calls "vertical construction."

"It's the NCOs that know how to do it. It's the officer's job to make sure that everything is ready for the next day, the building materials, the plans."

Down the road, so to speak, Sullivan hopes to earn a master's degree in engineering management and continue his career in the Army.

At some point, he would like to teach at West Point, and he also wants to work with the Corps of Engineers on projects in the United States, perhaps in Minnesota.

He is proud of his service overseas. "So many good things are going on in Afghanistan. It's too bad the media only focuses on the negative side."

His fondest memory of Afghanistan is the children. "They'd learn my name, and when they'd see me coming they'd yell out 'Sull-ee-vun!' The kids were great. They could just sit and watch those big vehicles all day long. I think personal relations make all the difference over there."

THE BOSS

Sullivan got a chance to shake hands with Lt. Gen. Carl Strock, commanding general of the Army Corps of Engineers, while in Afghanistan.

LOCAL CHILD

An Afghani girl clutches her Fig Newtons, a gift from the American soldiers.

About the Author

Al Zdon was born and raised in Northeast Minneapolis. He served in the U.S. Navy and is a bluewater Vietnam Veteran. He has a bachelor's degree in journalism and a master's degree in liberal studies, both from the University of Minnesota.

Zdon has been a newspaper editor for his entire professional life, and he is presently the editor of the *Minnesota Legionnaire* newspaper where these stories first appeared.

He served on the Minnesota State Board of Education, the University of Minnesota School of Journalism Alumni Board, and the Minnesota News Council. He is a member in good standing of the Greater Mesabi Mens Book Club.

He enjoys basketball, golf, reading, crossword puzzles and his two banjos.